Challenging Subjects

Challenging Subjects

Critical Psychology for a New Millennium

Edited by
Valerie Walkerdine

palgrave

Selection, editorial matter and Introduction
© Valerie Walkerdine 2002

Individual chapters (in order) © Anthony Elliott; Mary Walsh and
Mark Bahnisch; Ute Osterkamp; Couze Venn; Erika Apfelbaum; John Cash;
Stephen Frosh; Swatija Manorama; Lisa Blackman; Helen Lee and
Harriette Marshall; Benjamin Sylvester; Kathleen McPhillips 2002

All rights reserved. No reproduction, copy or transmission of
this publication may be made without written permission.

No paragraph of this publication may be reproduced, copied or
transmitted save with written permission or in accordance with
the provisions of the Copyright, Designs and Patents Act 1988,
or under the terms of any licence permitting limited copying
issued by the Copyright Licensing Agency, 90 Tottenham Court
Road, London W1T 4LP.

Any person who does any unauthorised act in relation to this
publication may be liable to criminal prosecution and civil
claims for damages.

The authors have asserted their rights to be identified as the
authors of this work in accordance with the Copyright, Designs
and Patents Act 1988.

First published 2002 by
PALGRAVE
Houndmills, Basingstoke, Hampshire RG21 6XS and
175 Fifth Avenue, New York, N.Y. 10010
Companies and representatives throughout the world

PALGRAVE is the new global academic imprint of
St. Martin's Press LLC Scholarly and Reference Division and
Palgrave Publishers Ltd (formerly Macmillan Press Ltd).

ISBN 0–333–96509–4 hardcover
ISBN 0–333–96510–8 paperback

This book is printed on paper suitable for recycling and
made from fully managed and sustained forest sources.

A catalogue record for this book is available
from the British Library.

Library of Congress Cataloging-in-Publication Data
Challenging subjects : critical psychology for a new millennium / Valerie
Walkerdine, [editor].
    p. cm.
    Includes bibliographical references and index.
    ISBN 0–333–96509–4 – ISBN 0–333–96510–8 (pbk.)
    1. Critical psychology. I. Walkerdine, Valerie.

BF39.9 .C46 2002
150.19'8–dc21   2001059057

10 9 8 7 6 5 4 3 2 1
11 10 09 08 07 06 05 04 03 02

Printed in China

Contents

Notes on the Contributors · vii

Introduction · 1
Valerie Walkerdine

PART I NEW POLITICS, NEW SUBJECTIVITIES

Introduction · 7
Valerie Walkerdine

1 **Identity Politics and Privatisation:
    Modern Fantasies, Postmodern After-Effects** · 11
    Anthony Elliott

2 **Political Subjects, Workplaces and Subjectivities** · 23
    Mary Walsh and Mark Bahnisch

3 **Reflections on Emotionality, Morality, Subjectivity, Power** · 39
    Ute Osterkamp

4 **Refiguring Subjectivity after Modernity** · 51
    Couze Venn

PART II ETHNICITY, HYBRIDITY, TRAUMA

Introduction · 75
Valerie Walkerdine

5 **Uprooted Communities, Silenced Cultures and
    the Need for Legacy** · 78
    Erika Apfelbaum

6 **Troubled Times: Changing the Political Subject in
    Northern Ireland** · 88
    John Cash

7 Racism, Racialised Identities and the Psychoanalytic Other
Stephen Frosh — 101

8 Coping with Plural Identities
Swatija Manorama — 111

PART III SPIRITUALITY, EMBODIMENT AND POLITICS

Introduction — 129
Valerie Walkerdine

9 A Psychophysics of the Imagination
Lisa Blackman — 133

10 Embodying the Spirit in Psychology: Questioning the Politics of Psychology and Spirituality
Helen Lee and Harriette Marshall — 149

11 Synchronicity as a Feature of the Synchronic
Benjamin Sylvester — 161

12 Refiguring the Sacred: Re-enchantment and the Postmodern World
Kathleen McPhillips — 177

Index — 191

Notes on the Contributors

Erika Apfelbaum is Emeritus Professor of Social Psychology at IRESCO, CNRS, Paris. She has published extensively on feminist psychology, intergroup relations, migration, power and trauma.

Mark Bahnisch lectures in sociology in the School of Humanities and Social Science, Queensland University of Technology, and is currently completing his PhD through the Australian Centre in Strategic Management at the same university. His research interests focus on subjectivities and the sociology of organisations, political discourses of public organisation, the sociology of the body, and industrial relations and political economy. He has published book chapters, journal articles, conference papers, book reviews and consultancy reports in these fields (many co-authored with Mary Walsh).

Lisa Blackman is Lecturer in the Department of Media and Communications, Goldsmiths College, London. A critical psychologist by background, she teaches media and cultural studies and researches new forms of subjectivity. She is the author of *Hearing Voices: Embodiment and Experience*.

John Cash is Deputy Director of the Ashworth Centre for Social Theory at the University of Melbourne and an editor of the journal *Critical Horizons*. He has conducted research in Northern Ireland on several occasions, while visiting INCORE and the Centre for the Study of Conflict at the University of Ulster.

Anthony Elliott is Professor of Social and Political Theory at the University of the West of England, where he is Research Director (Development) of the Faculty of Economics and Social Science and Director of the Centre for Critical Theory. His recent publications include *The Mourning of John Lennon* (1999), *Social Theory and Psychoanalysis in Transition* (1999, 2nd edn), *Concepts of the Self* (2001) and *Psychoanalytic Theory: An Introduction* (2002, 2nd edn). He is editor of *Freud 2000* (1998) and *The Blackwell Reader in Contemporary Social Theory* (1999), and co-editor of *Psychoanalysis at its Limits* (2000) and *Profiles in Contemporary Social Theory* (2001).

Stephen Frosh is Professor of Psychology at Birkbeck College, University of London, and previously Consultant Clinical Psychologist and Vice Dean in the Child and Family Department at the Tavistock Clinic, London. He is the author of numerous academic papers and several books, including *Young Masculinities* (2001) with Ann Phoenix and Rob Pattman, *For and Against Psychoanalysis* (1997), *Sexual Difference: Masculinity and Psychoanalysis* (1994), *Identity Crisis: Modernity, Psychoanalysis and the Self* (1991) and *The Politics of Psychoanalysis* (1987; second edition 1999). He is joint author, with Danya Glaser, of *Child Sexual Abuse* (second edition 1993) and co-editor with Anthony Elliott of *Psychoanalysis in Contexts* (1995).

Helen Lee is Lecturer in Critical Psychology at Staffordshire University, Stoke-on-Trent. The chapter 'Embodying the Spirit in Psychology: Questioning the Politics of Psychology and Spirituality' relates to her PhD thesis 'Explicating Spirituality Through Different Knowledge Sites'. Her main research interests centre on the sociocultural and psychological production of spirituality.

Swatija Manorama has been an active member of the Forum Against the Oppression of Women (FAOW), Bombay, since 1983 and is coordinator for a project on pre-adolescent girls for VACHA Women's Resource Centre, Mumbai.

Harriette Marshall is Professor in Feminist and Critical Psychology at Staffordshire University, Stoke-on-Trent. Her main research interests include identities, issues around gender, ethnicity and the role of psychology in relation to inequalities.

Kathleen McPhillips teaches gender studies and social analysis in the School of Humanities, University of Western Sydney. Her particular interest is in the emergence of new forms of spirituality and religion and their connections to processes of cultural and social change. She has been influenced by feminist theory, post-structuralism and post-Jungian understandings of self and world.

Ute Osterkamp is a Lecturer at the Institute of Critical Psychology, Free University of Berlin (FUB).

Benjamin Sylvester is Head of Psychology at Charles Sturt University, Bathurst, New South Wales, where he is co-leading the development of a more experience-based pedagogy in the psychology curriculum. His first contact with critical psychology was through the Centre for Child Care and Development at Cambridge University during the early 1980s. In 1989 he published *Visions of Infancy: A Critical Introduction to Child Psychology* (also available in French, Spanish and Italian). With William Kessen, he co-edited a special issue of *Theory & Psychology* on 'The Future of Developmental Theory' (1993).

Couze Venn is Reader in Cultural Studies at Nottingham Trent University. He is co-author of *Changing the Subject* and a founder member of the journal *Ideology and Consciousness*. His articles on postcolonial theory and on the formation of subjectivity have appeared in several referred journals and in edited collections. He is a member of the editorial board of *Theory, Culture and Society*. His recent publications include *Occidentalism: Essays on Modernity and Subject* (2000) and he has recently edited special issues of *Theory, Culture and Society* on 'Violence and the Sacred' and on 'Intellectuals, Power, Multiculturalism'.

Valerie Walkerdine is Foundation Professor in Critical Psychology and Head of the Centre for Critical Psychology, University of Western Sydney. She is founding editor of the *International Journal of Critical Psychology*, is on the editorial board of a number of international journals and has published extensively on gendered and classed subjectivities and critical psychology. Her most recent publications include *Mass Hysteria: Critical Psychology and Media Studies* (2000) with Lisa Blackman and *Growing Up Girl: Psychosocial Explorations of Gender and Class* (2001) with Helen Lucey and June Melody.

Mary Walsh is Lecturer in Politics at the University of Canberra. She teaches Politics and Democracy, Australian Politics, Women, Politics and Public Policy and Gender and Organisations. She has previously taught at the University of Queensland, Griffith University and the Queensland University of Technology. She is the author of *Introducing Political Theory* (to be published in 2003) and has published several journal articles, book chapters and reviews in the areas of political theory, Australian politics and feminist theory.

Introduction

VALERIE WALKERDINE

In beginning a new millennium we face new challenges and a rapidly changing polity. This volume addresses not the familiar terrain of what is wrong with academic psychology and how critical psychology might be marshalled to address these wrongs, but seeks to explore some of the challenges of the present and the future and to ask both how subjectivity is implicated and what kind of what work might be developed in relation to these issues. The volume grew out of a conference, the Millennium World Conference in Critical Psychology, which took place in Sydney in 1999. The conference had three themes, which are reflected in the three sections of this book: new politics, new subjectivities; psychology, survival and culture; spirituality and the body. The aim was to develop and build new approaches to some of the most pressing issues which confront us and the enduring themes which refuse to go away, to take critical psychology away from simply a stress on the academy and towards politics. To make sense of this move, I want to make reference to an altogether different political moment, the 1970s development of a European politics which stressed the theory of the subject, the moment of Althusser, Lacan and the emerging interest in post-structuralism. Although there is much that is critical to be said about that moment, what it did, for me at least, was to stress the importance not of psychology *per se*, but the significance of the subject and conceptions of subjectivity for politics. Indeed, with the emerging interest in the work of Foucault, psychology came to have a dual place in the political. On the one hand it could be understood as part of the psy sciences, a surveillant power/knowledge (Foucault, 1979) through which what it means to be a subject is produced and regulated and on the other as part of the need to understand how the multiple and conflicting sites of being a subject are lived, how subjectivity is produced and what its place in the political is. This twin task is what I take to be the project of a critical psychology, widely understood. As in the 1970s, this work is undertaken by studies in a number of disciplines and not simply within academic psychology. It is not surprising therefore that the Millennium Conference attracted a large number of people working on those issues from outside academic psychology as well as those within it. That lively and important mixture is deliberately reflected in the chapters that follow. The chapters are diverse in terms of approach, theoretical orientation and subject matter. What joins them together is an engagement with pressing social, cultural and political issues and an innovative approach to the issues of subjectivity contained within them.

Critical psychology can be thought of as an umbrella term which describes a number of politically radical responses to and differences from mainstream psychology; it includes the perspectives I have outlined above, as well as the left, feminism, ethnic and anti-racist politics, ecological movements and new forms of spirituality and radical work more generally conceived. Critical psychology movements can be roughly dated from the counter-cultural movements of the 1960s, the anti-psychiatry movement, the new left, civil rights, women's movements and gay liberation. The events of the late 1960s, like other events throughout the following thirty years, have affected psychologists personally, professionally and politically in diverse ways; no matter how mainstream, all psychologists have been affected in some ways by the changed political and intellectual climate. Critical work is no longer the terrain of the margins, at least, it must be said, within social and developmental psychology. However, it must be said that among all of this good news something has been lost. While there is absolutely no doubt that things have moved to a huge extent in the last thirty or so years, with, for example, theoretical work and discursive analysis as well as psychoanalytic work, anti-racist and feminist work now accepted as legitimate, it sometimes seems as though the political commitment which generated these changes has been lost. It is that concern with the political which guides this volume. However, so much has changed on the political stage that the kinds of political and intellectual interventions made all that time ago will no longer fit. The challenge then is to think about both the present polity and our engagement with it, in a new way. It is that which the Millennium Conference sought to address and it is that concern which has guided the choice of chapters here – not because the authors share any common political position or academic approach but because they all tackle issues that are crucial for us to address within the new political climate.

While the left and feminism have been profoundly challenged and are changing, the crises that confront us are no less stark than they ever were. Globalism and economic rationalism are ravaging a world also caught in the grips of ecological suicide. Psychology and subjectivity are absolutely caught up in these changes. Economic rationalism, for example, demands an autonomous subject who can cope without work, social, family and community supports. Psychology is constantly called upon to support the veracity of this subject and to prop up, through psychological practice, its inevitable failures. This prohibits any other understanding of the production of subjects within any particular polity and any other kind of practice. It is that dual task which sets critical psychology apart. It is not enough to examine the place of psychology in producing the present; it is also necessary to propose alternative ways of understanding and acting. Each of the three sections of this volume deals with a particular topic and explores different approaches to the issues with respect to subjectivity. The three themes, New Politics, New Subjectivities; Ethnicity, Hybridity, Trauma; and Spirituality, the Body and Politics, are designed to address some of the pressing issues that confront us now from a diverse array of theoretical perspectives. The authors in this volume all point to a different conception of subjectivity in a changed polity. Their arguments are both theoretical and intensely practical in that they concern new ways of thinking and intervening in politics as it is lived, creating and being created by subjects both now and in the future.

Bibliography

Foucault, M. (1979) *Discipline and Punish* (Harmondsworth: Penguin).

Part I

NEW POLITICS, NEW SUBJECTIVITIES

Introduction

VALERIE WALKERDINE

Each of the chapters in this section deals with new or changing forms of subjectivity in the public and work sphere. The abiding theme of power, and how to understand the relation of power to human subjects, comes through all of these chapters, though approached in quite different ways. Anthony Elliott (Chapter 1) discusses the politics of the privatisation of the public sphere. The consumer, says Elliott, 'drifts from seduction to seduction, anxious to keep disabling anxieties from breaking into consciousness'. In a context in which there are no longer any certainties, either in work or family life, these anxieties and keeping them at arm's length together assume enormous proportions. Elliott discusses the German sociologist Ulrich Beck's notion of risk in the process of globalisation. He argues that Beck's sociological approach leaves out the psychic costs of privatisation. In particular, the life of choice, signalled by an end of jobs for life as well as lifelong marriage partnerships, suggests that one can be anything one chooses, that the end of safety nets allows in the possibility of a different kind of life – one that we have chosen rather than the one that our social location had waiting for us. This fiction fuels a fantasy of omnipotence, a fantasy of control over a world in which we actually have less control, not the more we are apparently being offered. The chapter attempts to grapple with the political and psychological way forward in relation to the loss of apparent certainty and the increase of risk. As Elliott says, it is the loss of the modernist techno-scientific project which is at issue and the absolute need to find a way out the other side, which is not simply the way of the private but rather a different kind of politics and social organisation which recognises the shifting nature of identity, the subject in process, as the basis for alliances and governance. As Elliott makes clear, that alternative politics has never been more necessary and never seemed more remote. The political and psychological tasks are urgent in the present climate because increasing resources will be called on to shore up globalised privatisation, both economically and personally.

Mary Walsh and Mark Bahnisch (Chapter 2) develop this theme, discussing management discourses about workers' subjectivities, examining in particular the differences between those accounts which stress class relations as the basis for a liberatory politics of the subject and those who work with notions of difference and multiplicity. They discuss the debate between labour process theorists and post-structuralists about the possibility or not of resistance. They argue that the disappearance of resistance mirrors the appearance in the workplace of the Other at work: 'women, non-whites, people with disabilities, people who are not hearing the interpellative call of the transhistorical subject of labour'. It is the appearance of these Others which leads Walsh and Bahnisch to turn to feminist corporeal theory to think about the gendered body/mind of the new worker. In this analysis, it is the identification of masculine knowledge with the mind (especially in its regulation of the feminised body of the male manual worker) which is seen to elide 'the lived and situated experience of male and female bodies'. In this context, the subjectivity of the worker can be understood as learned and reproduced in the 'complex psychical realm where body and mind interact'. Like Elliott's subjects under risk conditions, these workers as subjects are always in the process of becoming and always able to reimagine and reconstitute themselves and therefore to always be in a process of resistance. However, as Elliott made clear, this reimagining and reconstitution is no easy task. However, it is precisely the point that we are talking about Others as workers, workers who did not easily fit into the labour-process category of worker in the first place. It is this lack of fit, which I think makes possible the necessity of constantly having to rethink and reimagine, though it is a precarious project, which needs a great deal of support. Hence the huge importance of a different conception of politics and indeed of what psychological practice might be about within this context.

Ute Osterkamp (Chapter 3) writes about a different kind of resistance, the resistance to fascism in Nazi Germany. The self-control and compliance that she explores relates to the need to purge oneself of any improper impulses and desires to ensure loyalty and meekness. It is this control of one's own impulses which, she suggests, is central to the task of the control of others by those who are allowed to participate in power providing they restrict their own aspirations by efficiently carrying out the controlling and disciplining of the less privileged and less compliant. In turn, she argues, this calls for the need to keep oneself aloof from below and deadening any feelings of sympathy or solidarity with an 'emotional immunisation against the awareness of others' misery and one's responsibility for it'. It was this quality which was understood as essential for the fascist elite in Germany. However, we might also point out its necessity for middle managers carrying out so-called rationalisations in all manner of organisations under globalism and economic rationalism. This emotional immunisation may be less violent than in wartime Germany, but I would argue that it is nevertheless necessary for carrying out the corporate tasks that produce a misery that leaves no organisation immune. The corollary to this, as Osterkamp points out, is the terrible suffering of those inmates of the camps, for example, who had to watch others being killed and suffering terribly while not being able to do anything for fear of their own lives. It is this which brought with it the most terrible burden of guilt and shame for their inability and the inability of the world to stop what they had been forced to witness. It is therefore necessary to understand the mechanisms and function of the processes of demoralisation as both supremely social and psychic. Osterkamp takes the analysis further by thinking about the role of psychology and psychologists and the way in which psychology and its practitioners can become similarly insulated. She calls for us to remove our 'ideological blinkers' in order to question the moral stances and actions that we too are asked to take within our present polity.

Couze Venn (Chapter 4) seeks to refigure subjectivity in the light of the postmodern and postcolonial interrogations of the discourses of modernity. This means that this refiguration begins from a critique outside the space of occidentalism, that is, 'outside the space of the becoming West of Europe and the becoming modern of the world'. He wants to question the privileging of the autonomous subject. Like other authors such as Elliott and Walsh and Bahnisch, Venn talks of the possibility of a different kind of subject, of different ways of being. Echoing also Osterkamp's discussion in the previous chapter, he writes of the necessity to renarrativise and reposition particular selves in order to facilitate the work of healing and rememorialising the past. The subject position is not fixed. Osterkamp's fascists can and could renarrativise their position, though there is no doubt that this would be a momentous emotional as well as political work. How is one therefore to write another history of the subject which would then be another history of modernity, asks Venn. The modern logocentric concept of the subject has a way of erasing history and memory. The refigured subject is produced at the intersection of history, biography and the body. Its intersubjectivity is learned through a system of apprenticeship which is not internalised or willed but rather enfolded, entwined, interior and exterior. Venn goes on to discuss the work of Fanon and out of that to consider the process of subjective change. He argues that the production of dissident discourses is a necessary but not sufficient condition for change. As he says, we know well that counter-hegeronic discourses, for example, to do with racism, do not persuade racists to change their values. What is needed, he suggests, is something that works additionally 'at the level of affect. A discursive practice that plugs into the economy of desire'. That artistic practices can sometimes tap into this economy is important – a poetics of transformation. This transformation needs to tap both into the past and its losses and also into the being-in-the-world, which can move us on and apprentice us into new ways of being, while dealing with that which was left behind. This process relates to the theorisation of the changes in subjectivity in the present polity discussed by all four chapters in this section. For all of the authors, subjectivity is mobile, not fixed, implying a subject in process who has a shifting relation to a past and the creation of a mobile future. Never has the project of working on this concept of subjectivity been more urgent politically as old allegiances and ways of being in the world are constantly shaken and destroyed. This work presents for us the possibility of the profoundly social yet profoundly psychological work which is needed to engage with the transformations that we are all facing in a way which is productive of a new polities and of new possibilities of being.

1

Identity Politics and Privatisation: Modern Fantasies, Postmodern After-Effects

ANTHONY ELLIOTT

Ours is the age of privatisation. From the narcissistic lures of psychotherapy through the technocratic imaginary of cyberspace and virtual reality to the consumerist ideologies of late capitalism (in which, as decentred subjects, we slide blissfully from signifier to signifier), experience today, much like everything else, is essentially privatised.

A deregulation of public institutions is not only on the agenda, but is an increasingly fundamental aspect of politics today. In our culturally cosmopolitan, globalised world, the activities of government are more and more centred on the restructuring of political responsibilities and public institutions, one consequence of which has been an effacing of past commitments and prior values. Out with the old, in with the new: the 'common interest' and the 'public good' have been replaced by the benchmark of individual choice, the freedom of the market and of pleasure-seeking.

At a political-institutional level, this is evident from a range of policy changes that have brought about the demise of the Keynesian welfare compromise in the west. These include:

- the pro-market restructuring of national economies into global economic competition;
- the deregulation of financial and labour markets, currency and banking systems;
- the dismantling or privatisation of public institutions (such as the partial or complete sell-off of banks, gas, electricity, water, airlines, telecommunications, and the like).

Politics has, of course, long carried the burdens of the erratics of the marketplace, its ups and downs. Today's politics, however, deepens the social and moral indifference of the market. For the unquestionable priority given to market competition is itself part and parcel of a relentless process of privatisation. This is a privatisation of politics in the broadest sense: of the individual, citizenship and moral responsibilities.

Privatisation, then, should not only be thought of as an institutional matter. The intended or unintended consequences of deregulation of public agencies has been a thoroughgoing privatisation of life (or life-strategies) in general. In privatised, postmodern society, the individual as consumer drifts from seduction to seduction, anxious to keep disabling anxieties from breaking into consciousness, and revelling in the libidinal *jouissance* of bodily appetites and sensory pleasures. Jobs for life are replaced by individualised contracts; till-death-us-do-part marriages are broken, restaged and broken again; and intimate ties are of the 'until further notice' variety. From one angle, then, privatised culture simply is that sixties' maxim – 'the personal is the political' – lived in reverse. Today's politics is privatised, and privatised to the hilt.

This chapter is an intervention into some current controversies over politics: specifically, the politics of privatisation. I begin by contrasting two broad constructions of identity ideology in the contemporary era. The sketch of these ideologies is primarily psychoanalytic in character. My focus changes in the next section, where I turn from identity disputes to the more structural problem of risk in today's politics and institutions. There I consider the path-breaking work of the German social theorist Ulrich Beck, looking in particular at his thesis that the deregulation of the commonality of risk is an outcome of the process of globalisation. I then analyse what Beck's sociologism of risk leaves out of account: namely, the psychic costs of privatisation. By drawing on the psychoanalytic contributions of Julia Kristeva and Wilfred Bion, I contend that the politics of privatisation is premised upon pseudo-rational fantasies of omnipotence – fantasies that serve to deny the globalised risk we face today as individuals and collectivities.

Strategies of Identity, Modern and Postmodern

Much talk these days is about identity: identity and its problems, the transformation of identity, and, perhaps most fashionably, the end or death of the subject. Nowadays notions of identity seem inevitably to capsize into either modern or postmodern forms of theorising. In modern theorising, the catchword for identity is that of 'project'; in postmodern theorising, it's that of 'fragmentation'.

The 'project' of modern identity is that of identity-building. By identity-building I mean the building up of conceptions of oneself, of one's personal and social location, of one's position in an order of things. It is such restless self-activity that replaces the ascriptions of tradition and custom. Freed from the rigidities of inherited identity, human beings are set afloat in the troubled waters of modernity – in its unpredictability and flux, its global transformations, cultural migrations and communication flows. Modernity, we might say, is much preoccupied with identity as an end in itself: people are free to choose the kind of life they wish to live, but the imperative is to 'get on' with the task and achieve. To put it in another way, the order-building, state-constructing, nation-enframing ambitions of modernity require human subjects capable of picking themselves up by their own bootstraps and making something of life, with no rationale beyond the market-driven imperatives of constructing, shaping, defining, transforming. Perhaps the most comprehensive analysis to date that we have of this modern conception of identity building has been provided by the British sociologist Anthony Giddens (1991, 1992), who lists 'life-planning', 'internal referentiality' and 'colonisation of the future' as defining features. But the paradox of self-construction, if we read Giddens against himself, is that modern craving of identity maintenance or identity preservation results in a drastic limiting of life-stories, the denigration of meaning in the present and its projection into the future. What Giddens calls the future colonised is a spurious form of self-mastery, if only because the predictable, the routine and the determined always involve destructive forms of unconscious repetition.

Indeed, the psychic costs of life lived as project are grave. For the founder of psychoanalysis, Sigmund Freud, the crux of the problem is that of delayed gratification. In *Beyond the Pleasure Principle*, Freud argues that psychic violence erupts in that gap between demand for pleasure and pleasure actually attained. 'What we call happiness', writes Freud, 'comes from the (preferably sudden) satisfaction of needs which have been damned up to a high degree, and it is from its nature only possible as an episodic phenomenon.' The more culture presents itself as future-colonizing and project-orientated, the more life becomes repressive: the very contingencies of human experience are imagined insured against by the promise of future certainty, a certainty always tantalisingly out of reach. Elsewhere, in his magisterial cultural analysis *Civilization and Its Discontents*, Freud speaks of the modern adventure as a drive for order, a drive which he links to the compulsion to repeat. The trimming of pleasure into that of order, says Freud, spares us the painful ambivalence of indecision and hesitation. So too, the French psychoanalyst Jacques Lacan sees the human subject as marked by the impossibility of fulfilment, an empty subject constituted through a primordial lack or gap of the Other. Indeed, such a decentring of the subject is at the heart of 'Lacan's Freud'. Lacan (1977, p. 171) states:

> If we ignore the self's radical ex-centricity to itself with which man is confronted, in other words, the truth discovered by Freud, we shall falsify both the order and methods of psychoanalytic mediation; we shall make of it nothing more than the compromise operation that it has, in effect, become, namely, just what the letter as well as the spirit of Freud's work most repudiates.

Lacanian psychoanalysis is today sometimes represented as a sort of thinking person's *Natural Born Killers*. (Indeed, where else could you find such a bizarre blending of the raw stuff of human experience and the cult of the hero?) In fact, Lacanian theory has often been unproblematically inserted into the whole discourse of postmodernism, as if the critique of the withering of imaginative cultural production could be generated up from unconscious desire itself. But it might be just as plausible to see Lacanian psychoanalysis as symptomatic of the modern adventure in identity-building. For the Lacanian mafia, without knowing it, offer up a superb portrait of the limits and dead-ends of *life lived as project*. A subject marked by lack and gap is, one might say, an accurate portrayal of that brand of modern identity which is always on the move, hungering for new (and better) destinations, but never actually arriving. From the National Socialism of Hitler's Germany to the present-day resurgence of nationalism in Europe, identity-building is framed upon an exclusivist, violent negation of the Other.

Life lived as an identity-project, then, is defined by *pleasure in discontent*. This is a discontent which leads modern women and men to the view that 'things can always be better', to the denigration of the here-and-now, and to the desire for smooth-functioning, regulated identities (always in the future, or around the next corner).

By contrast, in what are increasingly called 'postmodern' times, the status of identity-projects diminishes. Postmodern sentiments recognize that the sociopolitical consequences of modernity clash strongly with its programmatic promises (see Bauman, 1991, 1995, 1997). Instead of the search for the ideal identity (complete, finished, self-identical), we find instead a celebration of cultural heterogeneity and difference. Ours is the age of what Jean-Francois Lyotard describes as 'open space–time', by which he means that identities are liquidated into episodes, a flow of drifting moments, eternal presents, transitory encounters. The postmodern condition – with its globalisation of the market, its proliferation of media simulations, its cult of technologism, its self-reflexive pluralism – unleashes a multiplicity of local identities without any 'central' or 'authoritative' coordination.

The American cultural critic Christopher Lasch (1981) some years ago made a crablike move towards the idea of a postmodern life-strategy, which he summarized as a 'minimal self'. This new self is one drained of ego-strength and autonomy, a narcissistic self focused only on the experience of living 'one day at a time', the comprehension of reality as a 'succession of minor emergencies'. Daily life, in the postmodern, becomes a matter of shifting anxieties and drifting concerns, always changing, always episodic. It is as if we live in a constant state of information overload. Crisis, in short, has become the norm. Living in a world of constant crisis means, necessarily, adjusting one's emotional response level. There is no citizen that can adequately monitor all that is going on; and any attempt to do so can only lead to psychic burnout. So, players in the postmodern game of life develop an air of indifference and aloofness, sure only in the knowledge that all new improvements, social and technological, will create additional problems further down the track.

Postmodern life is episodic, a fractured and fracturing world, with little in the way for continuity or the making of meaningful connections. And yet one can also view the personal consequences of the postmodern in a somewhat more positive light. Imagination, it appears, has been given a considerable boost as a result of new technologies and electronic advances. Computers, word processors, faxes, the internet, DAT: we now have technology which ushers in the possibility of different kinds of pleasures, different thoughts and feelings, different imaginings. In a recent book, *Subject To Ourselves*, I develop the argument that the advent of such new technologies, and of globalisation, is ambivalent in its political implications. It brings new opportunities for personal, aesthetic and moral life, but it also brings new dangers. The debate about the difficulties of censoring hard-core pornography on the internet prorides a case in point.

In psychical terms, one may say that the trademark of postmodernity is a radical 'decentring' of the human subject: the limiting of omnipotence, not in Lacan's sense of a separation of subject and Other, but rather in terms of a *reflexive scanning of imagination* (see Elliott, 1995, 1996). By reflexive scanning, I mean to draw attention to the complexity of fantasy itself, as a medium of self-construction and Other-directedness. This fantasized dimension of our traffic with meaning is underscored powerfully by contemporary theorists such as Jessica Benjamin (1995) who speaks of 'the shadow of the other subject', Christopher Bollas (1995) who speaks of 'personal idiom', Cornelius Castoriadis (1997) who speaks of 'radical imagination', and Julia Kristeva (1991) who speaks of 'open psychic systems'. Viewed from this perspective, the postmodern can promote a heightened self-understanding of imagination and desire in the fabrication of meaning in daily life. Against this backdrop there are risks and opportunities. The risks are that there is no guarantee that the reflexive scanning of imagination will prove solid enough to sustain interpersonal relationships; but the gains are the capacity to proceed in personal and cultural life without absolute guidelines – in short, an increased toleration of ambivalence and contingency.

But perhaps the most important feature to note concerns the durability of human imagination. New technologies and postmodern aesthetics can extend the richness of the sense-making process, furthering the questioning of pre-existing categories by which we make sense of personal and social life. In people's changing attitudes to technology and globalisation, identity has become problematic all over again. From the most intimate, personal relationships through to global processes of political governance (such as the UN), social life has become more and more structured around ambivalence and contingency. The dynamics of mind and world are increasingly treated as puzzling, and simple descriptions and explanations of social processes are discarded.

These identities of which I've spoken, the modern and postmodern, represent different ways of responding to the globalisation, bureaucratisation and commodification of contemporary culture – of which I'll say more about in a moment. But let me stress now that we should not see these identity-strategies as simple alternatives: the postmodern as something that eclipses the modern. Modern and postmodern identities are better seen, as Zygmunt Bauman (1991, 1997) has brilliantly analysed, as simultaneous strategies deployed by contemporary societies. Constructing a self today is about managing some blending of these different modalities of identity: a kind of constant interweaving, and dislocation, of modern and postmodern states of mind. If, for example, the signifier 'America' can today be used to fashion identities framed upon a sense of global interconnectedness, democratic cosmopolitanism and a postnational way of belonging, it can also easily be deployed in a more defensive manner, namely in the production of identities held in thrall to the foetus and the flag.

Individualisation – or, Structurally Necessitated Identity-Creation

What are the broader social transformations underpinning such modern–postmodern identity strategies? And what are the institutional reference points marking out the dimensions within which identities are fabricated today?

There has recently emerged a massive level of interest in the notions of globalisation, globalism and global culture. Indeed theory in the space between globalisation and culture has been on the boil for some time now, having reached a level of pressure which is at once a deepening and a displacement. On the one hand, the discourse on globalisation opens up new political, social and economic flows that classical notions of nation, state and society seem ill-equipped to comprehend. On the other hand, the attention which theory has lavished on globalism has often been at the cost of denying the significance of the regional, local and contextual, the long-running post-structuralist emphasis on difference and otherness notwithstanding.

What's fuelled such interest has been the emergence of a range of socially produced, institutional transformations: these include transnational communication systems, new information technologies, global warming, holes in the ozone layer, acid rain, the industrialisation of war, the collapse of Soviet-style socialism, and universal consumerism. The globalisation of financial markets, the increasing importance of international trade, and the advent of new technologies, in particular, define the contours of an advanced capitalist order, in which general deregulation and the marketisation of culture reign supreme. The political ambivalence of globalism is nowhere more obvious than in the split it introduces between macro and micro levels of social life. In terms of macro considerations, it can be said that if globalism has bulked so large in contemporary theory then it is because the deregulation of society and economy is fundamental to late capitalism. Indeed deregulation begins to invade the fabric of social life itself: there is no such thing as 'society' (a point on which the social theorists Laclau and Mouffe find themselves, embarrassingly, in agreement with Baroness Thatcher). And indeed it's (sometimes) hard not to see the postmodern imperative of 'anything goes' as simply consumerism passing itself off at the level of intellectual discourse. But deregulation is only one aspect. The other side of a labour market that demands complete flexibility and mobility is that of an increasingly regularised and standardised micro world. In this respect, social integration is portrayed as a blending of normalisation (as described by Foucault) and the seductions of the market, the thrills of simulated pleasure-seeking (as described by Baudrillard).

The division between a deregulated public sphere and hyper-regularised private sphere is, however, surely unconvincing. For me, this is really but a variant of the idea of big institutions dominating individual lives, such as we find in the Frankfurt School's concept of the 'totally administered society' or Habermas's thesis of an 'inner colonisation of the lifeworld' by technical systems.

Perhaps the most interesting development in social theory in this context has been around the idea of individualisation, an idea elaborated by the German sociologist Ulrich Beck in his recent books *Risk Society*, *Ecological Politics in the Age of Risk*, *The Normal Chaos of Love* and *The Renaissance of Politics*. Beck's argument, bluntly stated, is that contemporary society is marked by reflexive individual decision-making in a context of growing uncertainty, risk and hazard. At once stripped of its traditions and scarred by all kinds of menacing global risks, contemporary culture radicalises individual decision-making and individual initiative. 'Certainties', says Beck, 'have fragmented into questions which are now spinning around in people's heads.' By this I take Beck to mean that the very definition of social coordinates, ranging from love and sex through marriage and family to politics and democracy, are up for grabs, with new modes of life being worked out, arranged and justified. Quite spectacular individual opportunities arise in this respect, as decisions (sometimes undecidable or painfully ambiguous ones) lead to further questions, dilemmas, problems – indeed, this aspect of individualisation theory often sounds like a lifting of Castoriadis's theory of radical imagination to the second power.

Before anyone concludes that all this is little more than some manic upgrading of the narcissistic illusions of the ego at the level of theory, let me point out that Beck is not suggesting that individualisation processes produce unfettered autonomy. On the contrary, individualisation presupposes the internalisation of social regulations, laws and precepts. Thus the very social conditions which encourage individualisation (such as detraditionalisation and internationally mobile capital) produce new, unintended consequences (such as psychic fragmentation and the privatisation of public, moral issues). But the other side of opportunity is more than simply danger in post-traditional society. It is risk says Beck, and risk on an astonishing global scale. In an age of commodified multiple choice, instrumental rationality, and genetic, chemical and nuclear techno-science, there is a diminishing protection of social life: we live to today in an 'uninsured society'. Whereas expert knowledge was once imagined to offer a sense of security from external risks, today science, technology and industry are seen as deeply intertwined with the very origins of global risk. Global awareness of menacing risks are routinely discussed, interrogated, criticized, made use of, and agonised over. How can anyone know, for example, what possible effects the nuclear meltdown at Chernobyl might have on human bodies fifty years from now? And what, precisely, might be the long-term effects of global warming, psychologically, ecologically and politically?

These are important questions, and experts disagree about the answers. Politically speaking, however, it is near-impossible to predict the likely scenarios, energising and catastrophic, arising from global interconnectedness. The critical point that Beck makes is that risk-management and risk-avoidance are constitutive of personal and cultural life today, if only for the reason that we are confronted by hazards and risks that previous generations didn't have to face: we live with risk on a global scale. After all no one can opt out, says Beck, from the consequences of ecological catastrophe or nuclear disaster.

The Privatisation of Risk – or, Fantasies of Omnipotence

But there are important political limits to the sort of reflexive risk calculation that Beck claims late modernity has ushered into existence.

Perhaps most significantly, what gets displaced here are some of the more pernicious effects of deregulation upon social reflexivity. In a deregulated, market-driven society, significant constraints impinge upon our capacities for risk-monitoring and risk-calculation. Of key importance here is the *privatisation of risk*. Today, risk is increasingly dumped into the individualised world of acting subjects; risk is presented as a series of technical problems to be individually coped with and reacted to through individual effort. More and more, our cultural know-how is shaped by scientifically preselected and predefined risks. But rather than acknowledge the hiatus between global processes of risk production which are largely beyond the control of their victims and the denial of risk in the public sphere, we are returned to the dumping of risk at an individual level, a dumping which produces certain pathological symptoms, of which the current fetishism of the body and body-projects (all the way from Cindy Crawford to Michel Foucault) could be seen as an example.

Deregulation, then, arises out of the gradual collapse of collective risk insurance, and it replaces the supra-individual regulations of modern living with that privatised groundlessness which permeates postmodern existence. This logic of deregulation depends upon a profound fetishising of the commodity form, the restructuration of economic life and culture, the social and the symbolic, in which community (and community action in general) is now cast in the ethical shadow of Las Vegas.

In terms of social critique, however, it is not a question of reducing the political to the private, but of understanding it otherwise. As concerns the interconnections between globalisation and identity-deregulation, the political right stresses the gains to individual freedom and cultural difference that multiple choice brings; it is only when it comes to considering the fate of personhood as such that this discourse reveals itself as embodying the market-driven interests of a Murdoch or a Packer, rather than the more dispassionate, philosophical reveries of a Hayek or a Fukayama. Indeed the wave of 'corporate economism' which has swept over western political culture of late, and which reduces political questions about the future of society to managerial problems about market efficiency, ignores the anxiety-provoking dimensions of fabricated risk at its own peril. For it imagines, in some wildly omnipotent moment, that the unlimited expansion of techno-science can solve the interpersonal and ethical issues which our new global interconnectedness creates. Such political imagination is of the either/or variety: either we have strong foundations (the illusion of self-mastery) or we are confronted with complete fragmentation (the fantasy of being 'wiped out').

What I am suggesting, then, is that globalised risk is *traumatic*, and that one central means of dealing with this trauma is through the dredging up of defensive, modernist fantasies of ordering and enframing the chaos of Otherness which today surrounds us. Here social imaginary significations of 'the hidden hand of the market' provide just such an escape route from the dilemmas of late modernity: such significations re-enact monotonously the trauma connected with the loss of tradition and the loss of techno-scientific certitude. Put this way its easy to see why we might become addicted once again to the idea of 'laws' – after all, the logics of economic efficiency involves a powerful, wish-fulfilling view of the social world as impersonal and lawlike. In effect, this is something akin to the nature of the transference in psychoanalysis, in which unconscious desires and scenarios from the past are projected onto current situations. With respect to late modernity, to the extent that we remain under the sway of a modernist transference that strives for the illusion of mastery and control, we will be unable to apprehend our own imaginative and interpersonal engagements with globalised risk.

Stuck with rationalisation, deregulation and privatisation, some theorists (rather foolishly) have decided to engage in their own privatisation of the world, ruthlessly splitting identity and difference, consensus and heterogeneity, idealising the second set of terms at the cost of running down the first. My own sense, by contrast, is that the repair of damaged communities implies the containment of what Theodor Adorno called the 'torn halves' of society: self and Other, private and public, theory and practice.

The problem of managing and coping with risk ranks as one of the most pressing political issues of our times. But the irony of the current situation is that a thorough-going privatisation of risk is being undertaken at precisely the historical moment that human interdependence on a global scale is far-reaching. What is urgently required, by contrast, is a radical politics capable of resisting this leap from risk to privatisation. What is required is an acknowledgement of the profound and intimate connections between risk in our imaginative and interpersonal worlds and our reflexively steered social institutions and processes of governance.

Such an acknowledgement, however, seems a remote possibility in the present political climate. In the meantime, one of the core tasks of critical social theory is to make a brave stab at working out some of the fundamental difficulties that arise from the repressions and pathologies of privatised risk.

In this context, a striking feature of much current feminist theory is that it has already produced some interesting-sounding answers to the difficulties surrounding political radicalism today. To take one particularly powerful integration of feminist and psychoanalytic currents, Julia Kristeva has recently argued that a *repressed strangeness* is 'the hidden face of our identity'. Emotional contact with this sense of strangeness is for Kristeva central to the enlargement of both psychic space and political imagination. According to Kristeva, we have to be prepared to go all the way through the complex interplay of identity and difference and see, in a working through of the impact of astonishment, whether we can emerge somewhere on the other side.

Kristeva grants a certain emancipatory significance to emotional astonishment and shock, essentially I think because it's the principal psychic process which can actually undo that fantasy of omnipotence which brought about the pseudo-rationality of politics in the first place. Kristeva thus proposes an alternative basis of identity: the *subject-in-process*, a process open to the dimensions of uncanniness, of strangeness, and of Otherness. Now, that this should offer a means of contesting the rigidities of masculinist culture is perhaps clear enough. But what I want to suggest in closing is that the dimension of unconscious strangeness (of which Kristeva speaks) also has particular application to the intertwining of globalised risk and reflexive identities. From this angle, I would suggest the 'risk biographies' that all of us today necessarily live need not be equated with 'privatised biographies', or at least this is arguably so once it is realized that strangeness returns us with full force to the question of Otherness and, in particular, the intersubjective dimensions of self-identity and social relations. (Let me also say – for those still inclined to follow the dead-ends of a Foucauldian critique of psychoanalysis – that to grant some political space to strangeness and astonishment is not to risk a 'surveillance biography' nor a 'breakdown biography'.) The sense of strangeness that arises through the impact of risk is, on the contrary, essential for grasping risk as risk; it is essential for grasping risk as an autonomous individual, as a subject part of a broader political community.

The writings of the psychoanalyst Wilfred Bion are also highly relevant in this context. For Bion paid great attention to the lengths people will go in order to avoid the impact of shock and astonishment. Thinking politics through, we might say after Bion, demands the processing of thought. 'You have to take the risk of finding out something you don't want to know,' writes Bion of thinking; and, as such, 'most people want to closure off what they don't want to see or hear.' The desire not to know, or not to think and feel, for Bion, is itself rooted in a desire for closure – to which we might add that current cost/benefit forms of privatisation offer just such closure in their limiting of freedom for thought and thinking about social alternatives. Thus, it is not just the avoidance of thinking, the political inhibition on knowledge, but also the refusal to entertain thoughts of alternative futures which is crucial here. Baudrillard (1985, p. 585) makes a similar point about the closure of the political unconscious: 'Nothing is more seductive to the other consciousness (the unconscious?) ... than not to know what it wants, to be relieved of choice and diverted from its own objective will.'

Bion and psychoanalysis are highly relevant here, I think, because the politics of risk is, in part, the negotiation of loss – the loss of tradition and the loss of modernist certainties stemming from techno-science. Indeed, the politics of risk, in so far as it is a management of loss, demands encountering (or tolerating) what Bion called 'catastrophic change'. By psychic catastrophe Bion refers to fears and anxieties about dissolution, to alternative forms of thinking and feeling. From this angle, we can say that self-recognition of the fear of 'catastrophic change' is essential to the undoing of the hold of repetition, and also to the opening out of the mind to risk in all its complexity and contradiction.

This is an opening out, not to the riskiness of everyday life, but to the depth of risk: taking seriously how globalised risks impact upon both the self and others. This would be an appreciation of how risk involves financial markets and economic interdependency, but crucially also how risk affects social relationships in the broadest sense.

Bibliography

Baudrillard, J. 'The Masses: The Implosion of the Social in the Media', *New Literary History*, 16(3) (1985).
Bauman, Z. *Intimations of Postmodernity* (London: Routledge, 1991).
Bauman, Z. *Mortality, Immortality and Other Life Strategies* (Cambridge: Polity Press, 1992).
Bauman, Z. *Life in Fragments* (Oxford: Blackwell, 1995).
Bauman, Z. *Postmodernity and its Discontents* (Cambridge: Polity Press, 1997).
Beck, U. *Risk Society* (London: Sage, 1991).
Beck, U. *Ecological Politics in the Age of Risk* (Cambridge: Polity Press, 1994).
Beck, U. and Beck-Gernsheim, E. *The Normal Chaos of Love* (Cambridge: Polity Press, 1995).
Beck, U. *The Reinvention of Politics* (Cambridge: Polity Press, 1996).
Benjamin, J. *Like Subjects, Love Objects* (New Haven: Yale University Press, 1995).
Bion, W.R. *Learning from Experience* (London: Heinemann, 1962).
Bion, W.R. *Second Thoughts* (London: Marsefield, 1967).
Bion, W. R. *Four Discussions with W.R. Bion* (Strath Tay, Perthshire: Clunie Press, 1978).
Bollas C. *Cracking Up* (London: Routledge, 1995).
Castoriadis, C. *The Imaginary Institution of Society* (Cambridge: Polity Press, 1987).
Castoriadis, C. *The Castoriadis Reader* (Oxford: Blackwell, 1997).
Elliot, A. 'The Affirmation of Primary Repression Rethought: Reflections on the State of the Self in its Unconscious Relational World', *American Imago*, 52(1) (1995) 55–79.
Elliott, A. *Subject To Ourselves: Social Theory, Psychoanalysis and Postmodernity* (Cambridge: Polity Press, 1996).
Elliott, A. *Social Theory and Psychoanalysis in Transition* (Oxford: Blackwell, 1992; 1999).
Freud, S. *Civilization and Its Discontents* (London: Hogarth Press, 1950).
Giddens, A. *The Consequences of Modernity* (Cambridge: Polity Press, 1990).
Giddens, A. *Modernity and Self-Identity* (Cambridge: Polity Press, 1991).
Giddens, A. *The Transformation of Intimacy* (Cambridge: Polity Press, 1992).
Giddens, A. *Beyond Left and Right* (Cambridge: Polity Press, 1994).
Habermas, J. *The Structural Transformation of the Public Sphere* (Cambridge: Polity Press, 1989).
Klein, M. *Envy and Gratitude and Other Works* (London: Virago, 1988).
Kristeva, J. *Tales of Love* (New York: Columbia, 1987).
Kristeva, J. *Strangers To Ourselves* (London: Harvester Wheatsheaf, 1991).
Lacan, J. *Ecrits* (London: Routledge, 1977).
Nowotny, H. *Time: The Modern and Postmodern Experience* (Cambridge: Polity Press, 1994).

2

Political Subjects, Workplaces and Subjectivities

MARY WALSH AND MARK BAHNISCH

In recent organisation theory, the constitution of employees' subjectivities at workplaces by management discourses is an important theme. This research arises from a desire to uncover reasons for employee consent to managerial control. Such research draws on Marxist labour process theory. Our chapter outlines the context for the theorisation of workplace subjectivity. Next, we suggest that the theorisation of workplace subjectivity remains within an ontology drawn from readings of Marx and Hegel which asserts that subjectivity originates in an ontological relationship with the natural world, and comes into being through the mediating power of labour.

Recent literature has adopted feminist and post-structuralist accounts to suggest that control at work is secured through the construction of a certain working subject. We argue that this literature relies on an impoverished understanding of feminist and post-structuralist constitutions of the subject. The term subjectivity provides a gloss on understandings that remain within an (often undertheorised) Hegelian and Marxist ontology. What is at work in the politics of theorising the working subject is a desire to preserve class relations as the foundation for liberatory praxis. We critique the politics of theory that elides difference and multiple subjectivities in favour of a normative claim that work is central to identity structured by class relations at the site of production. We suggest an understanding of subjectivity that draws on the concepts of phenomenology and the imaginary that has the potential to move beyond the various impasses in labour process theory.

What does this work have to offer? Why is it important for critical psychology? In the first instance much conventional psychology is situated within the dominant epistemological, ideological and philosophical frameworks of existing social institutions. Critical psychology seeks to challenge mainstream psychology's individualism, scientism and traditional conservatism and develop a conceptual critique of the various theoretical underpinnings and assumptions of psychology as a discipline. Further, it seeks to develop political critiques that situate 'psychology's socioculturally regulative role' and its 'unwitting collusion' in maintaining contemporary social order through normalising and oppressive practices of power. Labour process theorists entrench a notion of the subject as comprising subjective factors opposed to the objective reality of subordination to capital. This focus upon the self, singular identity and individualism obscures the complicity of mainstream psychology in these forms of power by not adequately acknowledging individualisation as opposed to individualism.

Current discussions of social institutions and the social realm more generally implicitly work from an understanding of the social realm as an aggregate of individuals combined with the political as a subset of governmentality in ways that obscure the links between the psychological and the political. Rethinking the social reterritorialises the space of psychology as a discipline. The psychological colonisation of an ethics of individualism and practices of individualisation profoundly depoliticises the space of the political that is already under attack in contemporary liberal democracies in the guise of neoliberal rationalities of governance and 'strong' versions of post-structuralist accounts of subjectivity. As political theorists, there is a particular concern with the implications of modern techniques of government that rule citizens 'through their freedom rather than despite' (Rose, 1998, p. 10). Regulatory practices govern individuals in ways that tie them to their selfhood and identity with the complexities of identity politics achieving increasing salience.

We agree with Rose that it is necessary to go beyond a theory of the subject to specify in what manner the psy disciplines specify the self (Rose, 1998, p. 169), but we do not similarly turn to Deleuze and Guattari in this instance. Instead we are interested in the implications of practices of individualisation that reconfigure the place of the political in a neoliberal millennium. Critical psychology as a discipline situates important theoretical and practical insights regarding the neoliberal and post-structuralist utilisation of the sum of individualist interest equals the field of the social. This moves further away from the kinds of ideals about the social realm and institutions where individual members have some commonality and intersubjectivity as human beings, owing allegiance to each other. It can highlight understandings of the social realm as something more than the sum of individualised interests and rework critical psychology's critical edge by exposing an individualised social order that is a very particular conceptualisation of the social.

This is important for critical psychology as a form of critical engagement. Contemporary changes in the labour market have actually meant a huge loss of conditions for most working people (for example, no employment security, casual work, home work and so on). Individualisation at the workplace demonstrates that the political realm is undergoing transformation and critical psychology as a discipline can assist in understanding the complexities involved here. More generally, the chapter offers reflections on the politics and desires of theory (utilising a notion of the unconscious), as well as an analysis of subjectivities and the resistances to intersubjectivity that are of central concern for critical psychology.

Subjectivity at Work: Labour Process Theory

Labour process theory originated with Braverman (1976), and seeks to locate work 'inside the wider system of production and class relations' (Thompson, 1989, p. 4). Labour process theory studies work in an integrated way (Littler, 1990, p. 47), embedding work organisation in the critical study of social relations, modes of accumulation, the social construction of skill and labour markets, and the interface between managerial strategy, control and the expropriation of surplus value. The initial text in this tradition, Braverman's *Labour and Monopoly Capital*, eschewed a theory of consciousness and social change, and sought to provide an 'objective' scientific account of the degradation of labour, premised on a Marxian ontology of the human. Braverman's inattention to what later theorists have described as the 'subjective' aspect of the labour process (Ezzy, 1997, p. 427) led to a debate over the issue of why workers consent to managerial control. This debate assumed centre stage in the 1990s, following Thompson's call for 'the construction of a full theory of the missing subject' (1990, p. 114). This focus moved the labour process debate some distance from Marxism, particularly as some theorists turned to feminist, post-structuralist and critical theory understandings of subjectivity (Newton, 1998).

The question of why workers consent to managerial control could be answered in a number of ways. A Weberian answer might refer to the secularisation of the work ethic and the status and instrumental rewards available to employees of a bureaucracy (Mommsen, 1989, p. 113). A range of instrumental factors have been studied by industrial sociologists and organisational psychologists (Rose, 1988). The way labour process theory frames this problematic is significant. Burawoy (1980, p. 90) questions how 'workers come to comply with and otherwise advance their own dehumanisation'. The ontological premise of an alienated subject split from labour requires an explanation in terms of 'subjective' factors, which are opposed to the 'objective' reality of subordination to capital. What is at stake is labour process theory's desire to find evidence of the potential for workers to liberate themselves or be liberated from a false consciousness (Tanner et al., 1992). Thompson's attacks in recent publications on post-structuralist understandings of subjectivity are less strident than polemics such as that of Feldman (1997), who equates Foucault with 'evil' and ethical relativism. But Thompson's concern for the dangerous lack of space for worker resistance (Thompson and Ackroyd, 1995, p. 615) highlights a continuing political desire for the articulation of a liberatory discourse which can be counterpoised to alienated consciousness (Thompson and Warhurst, 1998). Theory is being strangely reified: if power is opposed to resistance (as if this is Foucault's understanding) then workers may not have 'space' for developing a political consciousness.

Bordo (1999) is quite correct to point out that political action takes place regardless of whether theory provides a 'space' for agency (see also Le Doeuff, 1989). The anxiety of a certain labour process theory about the space for resistance is a powerful pointer to its (frequently unacknowledged) continuing commitment to a certain Marxian ontological and epistemological position. The question of whether management is successful in winning the hearts and minds of workers (as Thompson complains both management theorists and 'postmodern' labour process theorists believe) is not an empirical question but one which reveals a sense of unease about the continued salience of a normative ontological politics of the working subject. Thompson and Warhurst (1998) are no doubt correct in their argument that Taylorist control and exploitative works have not disappeared in a 'post-industrial' world. Nevertheless, the problematisation of metanarratives of class by theorists of difference seems to have induced a certain (theoretical?) anxiety in the ranks of class theorists. There is a politics in the theorisation of an alienated but essentially unified subject at work. The reinscription of subjectivity in the analysis of work is in itself a normative move of closure.

Spectres of Marx and Hegel Haunting the Theorisation of the Working Subject

In order to reflect on the political ontology of labour process theory, we now outline Hegel's and Marx's theorisation of subjectivity, highlighting the difference between their understandings. Hegel's position on the materiality of the natural world is that the subject through incorporation into the ego comprehends objects. 'As intuited or even in ordinary conception, the object is still something external and alien. When it is comprehended, the being-in-and-for-self which it possesses in intuition and pictorial thought is transformed into a positedness; the I in thinking it, pervades it' (Hegel, 1892, p. 585). This phenomenological perspective has implications for the ontology of the subject in its relation to the external or natural world. Hegelian dialectics describes the relation of the subject to the object. A false consciousness externalises the object, a rational consciousness is an immediate thought perception of the object as internalised by the subject (Hegel, 1892, p. 69).

What unites the subject with the object of its perceptions, the *mediating* term which bridges the two dialectically, is work: the work of perception, the work of teleologically transforming the object. Work expresses the transcendence of consciousness through mediating the universal possibilities of the subject to the objectification of nature, and nature's teleological transformation into purposive ends. Work externalises and objectifies the subject's consciousness (Hegel, 1892). So, for Hegel, the dialectics of labour illustrates the way in which the individual subject participates in the universal social. In *The Philosophy of Right*, Hegel's (1967, p. 271) individual subject participates in the universality of the social through being positioned as a moment of civil society through membership of a particular social class, mediating their identity through work. The work of the subject is 'an integral expression, a consummation where the external reality which embodies us and on which we depend is fully expressive of us' (Taylor, 1975, p. 148). The Hegelian subject is a reaction against Descartes's and Kant's isolated individual subject, a subject whose corporeal being and natural dependency should not be objectified. Rather, the opposition between the individual and the social should be dissolved through dialectics (Weir, 1996, p. 21).

Hegel is misread as a purely idealist thinker not only by analytical philosophy but also by Marx and Derrida (Zizek, 1991). Hegel's dialectic resolves the contradiction between subjectivity and objectivity, between false consciousness and rational consciousness. The Hegelian subject's determination can be abstracted from the real into the universal, but at the point of decision, of the particular, individual subjectivity moves towards the real. The universal is an idea that must be the end of collective labour, the work of the social will, but can only ever be actualised materially (Hegel, 1967). Ontologically, Hegel's argument is that the subject is historically and socially situated through its corporeal being. Hegel does not oppose an epistemologically knowable real to an epistemologically false appearance. This is Marxian dialectic, which continues to be reinscribed in social theory prescribing a subject alienated from its real being and real interests through the externalisation and expropriation of its labour.

Marx's ontology of labour opposes the objective realm of production and a subjective realm of human needs (Marx and Engels, 1956). Labour in

Marx's thought mediates between the ideal and the material (Arthur, 1986, p. 7). Ontologically, the human subject is a universal being who is defined by transformative power over nature. Labour objectifies nature through the subject's purposive transformation (Marx, 1844). The opposition between the objective and the subjective is compounded through the alienation of human labour through capitalist expropriation. Since labour constitutes human subjectivity, the externalising, or making other of labour, alienates the subject from itself. The subject becomes the other, the object. This historically specific capitalist mediation of the ontologically necessary mediation of labour obscures the real interests of the subject. It individualises and objectifies the subject, and disrupts the originally and naturally social nature of the human being (Marx, 1844). So, through the alienation of work from self, the subject is alienated from the social, and from an ontologically prior unified consciousness.

Human subjects are historical subjects and conscious beings. Consciousness annuls itself through the alienation of its object, and, comes to 'know itself as object', and, dialectically, can in a further moment subsume the object into itself, becoming '*at home* in its *other being*'. The third term in this movement is 'the indivisible unity of being-for-itself' (Marx, 1844, p. 147). So consciousness is ontologically and originally unified, but through the moment of alienation becomes split, worthy of interpellation as false. Reification is the consequence of false consciousness, a false or ideological perception of social relations as things. The task of dialectical materialism, of Marxism as science, is precisely to demystify and dereify the objects of false consciousness, and reveal to the material subject its participation in the unity of being-for-itself.

The Spectre Comes Back to Haunt Labour Process Theory

Labour process theory remained close to 'orthodox' Marxist philosophy and theory (Braverman, 1976). The subjectivity debate arose from what Littler (1990, p. 79) defined as the difficulty of applying Marx's concepts to 'historical and empirical studies'. Some labour process writers wanted to apply only certain aspects of Marx, rejecting for instance the labour theory of value (Littler, 1990, p. 79; Thompson, 1983). Two consequences flowed from these theoretical developments. First, as Littler (1990, p. 79) claimed, some theorists tried to rethink the labour process 'beyond philosophical categories' and 'without prior assumptions'. However, this attempt (aside from being impossible) led only to a retreat into empiricism and descriptive studies, contrary to the original theoretical aim of providing an integrated approach to work. Second, labour process theory differentiated itself from earlier British industrial sociology politically by providing a theoretical foundation for a liberatory critique of work (Thompson and Ackroyd, 1995). So, what was needed was the construction of a new philosophical foundation to theorise work so as to 'provide the basis for a theoretically informed praxis' (Wardell, 1990, p. 172).

Mainstream labour process writers defend the control–resistance model while adopting an increasing (strategic or rhetorical?) distance from Marxism (Thompson, 1999). Radical organisational theorists seek to incorporate post-structuralist understandings of the subject into the analysis of the subject at work. Hugh Willmott (1995, 1997) remains closer to Marxism but draws on critical theory understandings of the crisis of the modern subject, and positions his analyses in the Frankfurt School tradition. Willmott (1997) is interested in rethinking the materiality of the human subject in order to reveal the historical specificity of the process of individualising the subject through a both 'allaying and confirming' process of deobjectification implicit in individualised capitalism. Willmott portrays the identity of the subject as mediated by the contradictions of capitalism and an attempt to manage these contradictions.

David Knights (1997) and his collaborators have adopted a Foucauldian understanding of subjectivity, seeking to disrupt the dualism of the control–resistance operation through a conceptualisation of the subject as constituted within discourse and power. Knights (1997) adopts a postmodern epistemology, arguing for local knowledges, and commendably recognising the sexed nature of knowledges. Willmott and Knights have the laudable aim of constructing a politics of work that does not reduce the sphere of social relations to a class dichotomy. Thompson (1989, 1990, 1995) is the most prominent of defenders of the control–resistance analysis. As early as 1983, Thompson moved to distance himself from identification with the full corpus of Marxist theory. Despite an increasing identification with social democracy, Thompson is still committed to theorising work in such a way as to provide for a liberatory praxis. His recent political assumptions are somewhat undertheorised, aiming to 'develop ideas and practices which *empower* workers and their organisations'. Thompson (1990, p. 96) seeks to restore the 'emancipatory intent' of theory while not 'defending' Marxist orthodoxy.

Thompson (1990, pp. 115–21) departs from Marxist theory in his privileging of an antagonistic, resistant working identity over an objective class identity. However, he is concerned to develop a 'politics of production' which would preserve labour as a 'historical subject'. He wants to articulate a 'transitional politics' but nevertheless continues to defend resistance at work as articulating class interests, rejecting only what he believes to be Marx's belief in a strategy which would encompass a class-wide opposition between capital and labour. So Thompson's subject is always receding from a unified consciousness, but teleologically approaching this ideal point. The ontological goal of the subject remains its reunification and deobjectification as the subject-for-itself. This movement is caught in tension between the moment of the subject-in-itself and the subject-for-itself, suspended in history. The sphere of liberatory politics is specific to the realm of work (1990, p. 122). The collapse of the political into the economic is characteristic of a Marxist epistemology which differentiates the social by problematising the place of labour in social relations. Thompson trains his polemical sights on post-structuralist understandings of the subject in his 1995 article, co-authored with Ackroyd, 'All Quiet on the Workplace Front?'. What concerns them is 'the virtual removal of labour as an active agency of resistance' (1995, p. 615), that 'labour as a subject of industrial and political action has been broken'.

Once again the ghost of the transhistorical (reified) subject of labour reappears; a spirit of history if there ever was one, slaughtered this time by post-structuralist theory. Thompson and Ackroyd (1995, p. 618) oppose management agency to labour passivity, as if things were this simple. Willmott (1997) makes it clear that managers often occupy a contradictory position within the workplace, recognising that class identities are not foundational. The transhistorical interpellations capital and labour are not heard unmediated by any working subject. Thompson and Ackroyd complain that post-structuralist writers posit 'a totalising with management discourse', for instance in discussing the construction of new discourses of customer choice and market responsiveness which *materially* effect the management of universities. But Thompson and Ackroyd (1995, p. 620) dismiss the realm of the symbolic as immaterial – literally. Dialectical materialism meets social science empiricism to the point where Thompson and Warhurst (1998, p. 13) lament the difficulty of measuring subjectivity 'empirically'. We are well within a fairly unsophisticated epistemological realism, which is odd as Marx recognised the reality of symbols such as money (or capital, for that matter).

After invoking the spectre of Foucault, they argue that the Foucauldian claim that power is capillary and constituted through knowledge lacks empirical verification. Power, it seems, is everywhere, and there is no escape (1995, p. 625). Resistance is 'effectively eliminated', 'squeezed out', does not threaten power because 'discipline can grow stronger knowing where its next efforts must be directed'. What is (violently) elided here is Foucault's concept of power as productive of new forms of meaning, identification and bodies. Control and resistance might be dualistic, but is not sinful (1995, p. 626). They are 'heuristic devices' without which scholarship is condemned (for its sins?) to 'the confusing and opaque results observed in the work of Foucault and his followers'. Turning to the question of identity,

Thompson and Ackroyd (1995, p. 627) claim that post-structuralist theory errs by suggesting that 'identity and the processes that shape it are not static'. Presumably, what is needed instead is a reductive materialist ontology that defines identity purely in relation to objective relations to labour. They object that Willmott (1993) understands identification as produced by the indeterminacy of the subject of modernity, eliding the specificity of working subjectivity. We would have thought Marxist theory was centrally concerned with the production of subjects of modernity. It is strange that a discourse that claims to analyse work politically would seek to isolate work from political relations, even as a 'heuristic' device. Post-structuralists stand condemned (and the language of sin and condemnation is interesting) for reducing reality to language (1995, p. 624) and for 'taking labour out of the process' (1995, p. 629).

Caricatures of post-structuralist thought as found in Feldman (1997) and Thompson and Ackroyd (1995) are politically troubling. Derrida (1988), a theorist who calls for an ethics of reading but who has been misread more often than not, has drawn attention to the violent political closure inherent in authors such as Habermas (1990) who critique a mischaracterisation of post-structuralism. In terms of the ethics of reading, Derrida defends ethical reading as necessary for productive theoretical and political dialogue. To assert that post-structuralism reduces reality to discourse, for instance, is simply absurd and has been denied in the most emphatic terms by Derrida (1988, p. 157; 1994). Just as Marx misreads Feuerbach and Hegel, and pillories Stirner in the most abusive terms, so theorists of 'ethical' discourse and the 'ideal communicative situation' smear French theorists. Meanwhile, labour process theorists mischaracterise post-structuralist organisational theorists in the name of the spectre of Marx.

Much of this culture of complaint in labour process theory unconsciously derives from not only the apparent disappearance of 'resistance', but also the increasingly salient presence of the Other at work: women, non-whites, people with disabilities, people who are not hearing the interpellative call of the transhistorical subject of labour. Many of us at work are not the subject in question, a male working subject with 'trade union consciousness', if not 'class consciousness'. The politics of the working subject is a politics of nostalgia, hoping that difference can be elided through a performative invocation of structural antagonisms that allegedly determine the subject. As Marx's repeated references to man make clear, the subject at work is a sexed subject. So, in search of a new politics of the working subject we turn to feminist theorising about subjectivity, utilising a typology of feminist theory based on Walsh (1996). We hope to illustrate that feminist corporeal theory can shift the debate on the working subject away from reductive subject positions. Moreover, we are not saying that the politics of the workplace is no longer important (quite the opposite) but rather that it can no longer be constructed on the basis of an opposition that totalises the structuration of the social – that is, the Marxist view assumes a fixity of the social field (see Laclau and Mouffe, 1985) and also divides people into classes according to their position on either side of the social relations of capitalist society at the point of production.

Becoming a New Subject Position: Recent Feminist Theorisations of the Subject

Just as post-structuralist thinkers are reduced to parodies of their thought, theorists of sexual difference are attacked as essentialist, even though *gender* theorists neglect an active understanding of the body (Walsh, 1997, p. 53). Writing gender into theory implies that there is a universal, unsexed human subject, that the mind and body are essentially blank or neutral with social inscriptions working from the outside in to actively shape individual consciousness. Both body and mind are 'postnatally passive *tabulae rasae*' (Gatens, 1996, p. 4). This position posits an 'alleged neutrality of the human body, (a) postulated *arbitrary* connection between femininity and the female body, masculinity and the male body' (Gatens, 1996, p. 4). Although such theorists aim to create theoretical space for feminist political practice, their rejection of ontological understandings of sex as essentialist leads to a rationalist view of the *mind–body* opposition identical to Cartesian dualist western thought. The thinking subject is disembodied and unsexed. In the 'Speaking-with' position, which is consonant with male theorising,[1] subjectivity is identical with consciousness and the body and its sex are largely understood as the passive object or objects of consciousness. There are clear resonances with organisational theory understandings of the subject as a thinking subject shaped by consciousness and discourse.

Speaking-with theorists have largely displaced those who hold to biological essentialism, a position characterised as 'Speaking-otherwise-within'. Speaking-otherwise-within relies on a closed ontology, and an understanding of sexual difference as a brute prediscursive anatomical facticity, sex as mediating sexuality and sexual practice or sex as reproductive (Walsh, 1997, p. 54). Until recently, the problematic of subjectivity in feminist thought polarised around the contestation of these two positions (Gatens, 1996; Walsh, 1997). More recently, an understanding of subjectivity as corporeal has emerged, namely 'replying-elsewhere'. Replying-elsewhere, exemplified by the texts of Australian theorists such as Moira Gatens (1991, 1996) and Elizabeth Grosz, does not juxtapose mind and body because the subject is not understood as a thing but a process (Walsh, 1996, 1997). Australian feminists have appropriated French thought from a historical and philosophical perspective, in contrast to the dominant disciplinary lenses through which American feminists have read French authors (Schor, 1994; Walsh, 1998). The replying-elsewhere position can be usefully employed in organisational theorists' understanding of subjectivity.

Replying-Elsewhere: Corporeal Subjectivity in Recent Feminist Thought

Much recent feminist corporeal philosophy seeks to reclaim the body from its identification as the not-mind in the binary categories characteristic of western thought (Grosz, 1990, p. 81). The binary style of thought, which establishes an active concept A, and a passive, residual concept non-A (Grosz, 1989, p. 106), constructs the body as the other, the passive residue which is subject to conscious action by the thinking mind. Instead of opposing the facticity of the body to the thinking mind of the subject, a position originating in the Cartesian duality between the mind and the body (Grosz, 1989, p. 27), replying-elsewhere exposes the conflation of the corporeal with the feminine and the implicit devaluation of the latter categories.

It is politically imperative to refuse this opposition and constitute the body as an active determinant of human subjectivity. Replying-elsewhere deconstructs the opposition *mind–body* in order to displace the term *mind* and reinscribe the body as constructed linguistically, historically and culturally. Building on Irigaray's insight that there can be no speaking position outside established discourse (Grosz, 1989), this deconstructive move revalorises the identification of the feminine with the body and exposes masculine knowledge which identifies itself with mind as partial (Gatens, 1991). Subjectivity is not constituted by a neutral mind, but by the lived and situated experience of male and female bodies. We argue that the relationship between masculinity and the male body and femininity and the female body is historically and culturally contingent (Gatens, 1996, p. 13), not the arbitrary relationship of speaking-with theorists.

The subject must be understood as exceeding the opposition between consciousness and body. The embodied subject is always a sexed subject. In Gatens's thought, *mind–body* dualism is displaced by a Spinozist parallelism where the body is its 'total affective context' (Maras and Rizzo, 1995, p. 54). Subjectivity is not a product of a neutral mind but of a sexuality that is learned and reproduced in the complex psychical realm where mind and body intersect. The sexed subject cannot be reduced to genital sexuality or reproductive capacity, and at the same time there is not a subject who enjoys a stable consciousness or *ego*. Rather, subjectivity is inherently unstable and always in the process of becoming. The subject is never simply 'fleshy matter' as the subject is mediated through language. The subject is both historically and culturally located and sexually specific in an ontology of becoming rather than essence (Walsh, 1997, p. 55).

This position, informed by Irigaray's reading of Freud and Lacan, exceeds labour process conceptions of subjectivity which posit an ontological separation of consciousness and the real, conceived as the historical materiality of the objects of human labour. Corporeal subjectivity draws on both phenomenological understandings of the body as constituted by (different but socially situated) lived experience and post-structuralist understandings of the subject as processual and ontologically split. While Lacan (1968) posited subjectivity as constituted through the unconscious structured like a language, corporeal theory refuses the opposition of consciousness to embodiment. Because embodiment is lived experience and constituted through difference, there can be no ontological distinction between consciousness and the (material) realm of the real. Gatens (1996, pp. 68–9) argues that embodied subjectivity is constituted by historically and spatially specific activities and practices which produce particular capacities, desires and bodies. Bodies are always already signified bodies, produced and constituted by discourses and technologies of power (1996, p. 69).

While Gatens appropriates Foucault's insights on the micropolitics of the body, she supplements them with psychoanalytic concepts which can, read together, produce an analysis of the imaginary body which produces emancipatory practices and discourses of a multiplicity of differences (1996, p. 73). The signified or imaginary body, constituted by its relationship with other bodies and inscribed historically, linguistically and culturally, cannot be opposed to the biological or natural body as the concept of the biological body is already in language and culture. The subject is not disembodied or psychical consciousness, and indeed the ego is only conceivable in relation to the signification of its corporeality, which is a complex and ongoing process of the mediation of the body image through the imaginary body (Grosz, 1990, p. 85). So subjectivity cannot be ontologically reduced to essential interests mediated through the social realm.

While the concept of identity is now usually politicised as an essence without an identity, corporeal theory privileges the (multiple) identifications that circulate through and within the corporeal subject. A corporeal politics of the subject, then, can recognise the specificity of both difference and the phenomenological (and ethical) constitution of the subject intersubjectively in relationship with other embodied subjects. Replying-elsewhere provides an enunciative position for theorists to deconstruct binary thought, exposing the performative as well as constative communicative function of oppositions such as *mind–body* and *man–woman*. Understanding subjectivity as constituted in the complex imaginary realm where mind and body interact enables us to conceive of bodies always in the process of becoming and always able to reimagine and reconstitute themselves. While discourses are played out through the embodied subject, the subject always has the potential to resist through contesting these discourses in its process of becoming, to reimagine herself and write her own discourse.

Corporeal Organisational Theory: Towards an Ethics of Work

Thompson remains attached to a dualistic subject alienated from the materiality of the objective through a process of reification. A corporeal understanding of subjectivity refuses these oppositions by a complex understanding of embodied subjectivity constituted through an imaginary body constructed by discourse but also by lived and embodied experience. Subjectivity is always constituted in relation to other bodies. Bodies are relational: different bodies will affect and be affected by others in qualitatively different ways. Bodies are always already embedded in relations with other bodies, power relations that are necessarily contestable, at least in principle. The isolated individual constituted by totalising management strategy is a misunderstanding, as is the working subject alienated by the objectification of labour. The subject is always in a process of becoming, and can actively negotiate power relations and reimagine itself as a new political subject; and as subjectivity is always constituted in relation to an (other) or others, we can rethink an intersubjective political imaginary of work.

Replying-elsewhere specifies a relation between discourse and materiality which is 'a non-reductive materialism, a materialism, which rather than mere brute physicality, also includes the materiality of discourses' (Grosz, 1990, p. 81). Grounding subjectivity in corporeality discloses the (non-reductive) materiality of subjectivity, the intersection of a culturally and historically shaped signification and a dynamic subjectivity always in the process of becoming. This position has the potential for the theorisation of how work and the organisational labour process constitute particular bodily subjects with particular desires, affects, powers and capacities (Gatens, 1996).

Knights and Willmott respond to the increasing individualisation of the subject through the processes of late capitalism. The politics of the working subject transcends simplistic class dichotomies or oppositions between control and resistance. Willmott (1997, p. 1343) adopts Habermas's formulation of a subject in tension with the natural, working to construct a purposive identity. Thompson, by contrast, is influenced by a political desire to find a space for resistance by reinscribing class or antagonistic oppositions at work. His subject is in principle unified, but in practice alienated from the social through the expropriation and objectification of labour. In our view, we need a subject that can provide a basis for a politics of work that responds to the multiplicities of differences and subject identifications found in the social realm. The subject is always in a process of becoming, and power relations are contestable in the psychosocial realm of the political imaginary.

The replying-elsewhere position, with its ontology of becoming and understanding of the constantly shifting imaginary body, can lay the foundations for a politics and an ethics of liberatory work, and even of a praxis appropriate to such a project. A politics of the working subject or subjects that recognises that multiple identifications are played out on the discursive and material sites of contestation of working bodies and the lived experience of working subjects overcomes dualist ontologies. Since identification always fails (Lacan, 1968), it is the sites of this failure which provide the imaginary remainder open to contestation through the political imaginary. Escaping the spectre of Marxist ontology, the politics of work is no longer reducible to a class opposition. It becomes possible to rethink the political specificity of working subjects in a way that does not elide difference. Refiguring subjects at work as ethical, intersubjective subjects provides the basis for a politics of work that respects the specificity of different working subjects.

Acknowledgements

We would particularly like to thank Professor Anthony Elliott for his thoughtful comments on an earlier version of this chapter, and also Professor Valerie Walkerdine and the staff of the Centre for Critical Psychology for their initiative in organising a stimulating conference at which the first version of this chapter was presented.

Note

1. This categorisation of feminist theory and much of our chapter draws on a larger work in progress by Dr Mary Walsh, *Elusive Subjects: Ontology against Performativity* and research reported in Walsh (1996; 1997). We are also indebted to Dr Michelle Boulous Walker for aspects of this typology (see Boulous Walker, 1998).

Bibliography

Althusser, L. *For Marx* (London: Verso, 1970).
Arthur, C.J. *Dialectics of Labour: Marx and His Relation to Hegel* (London: Basil Blackwell, 1986).

Bordo, S. *Twilight Zones: The Hidden Life of Cultural Images from Plato to OJ* (Berkeley: University of California Press, 1999).

Boulous Walker, M. *Philosophy and the Maternal Body: Reading Silence* (London: Routledge, 1998).

Burawoy, M. *Manufacturing Consent: Changes in the Labour Process under Monopoly Capitalism* (University of Chicago Press, 1980).

Braverman, H. *Labour and Monopoly Capital* (New York Monthly Press, 1976).

Derrida, J. *The Ear of the Other: Autobiography, Transference, Translation* (Lincoln: University of Nebraska Press, 1988).

Derrida, J. *Points: Interviews, 1974–1994* (Stanford University Press, 1994).

Ezzy, D. 'Subjectivity and the Labour Process: Conceptualising "Good Work"', *Sociology*, 31(3) (1997) 427–45.

Feldman, S. 'The Revolt Against Cultural Authority: Power/Knowledge as an Assumption in Organization Theory', *Human Relations*, 50(8) (1997) 937–55.

Gatens, M. *Feminism and Philosophy: Perspectives on Difference and Equality* (Cambridge: Polity Press, 1991).

Gatens, M. *Imaginary Bodies, Ethics, Power and Corporeality* (London: Routledge, 1996).

Grosz, E. *Sexual Subversions* (Sydney: Allen & Unwin, 1989).

Grosz, E. 'The Body of Signification', in J. Fletcher and A. Benjamin (eds), *Abjection, Melancholia and Love: The Work of Julia Kristeva* (London: Routledge, 1990).

Grosz, E. *Volatile Bodies: Towards a Corporeal Feminism* (London: Routledge, 1994).

Habermas, J. *The Philosophical Discourse of Modernity: Twelve Lectures* (Cambridge: Polity Press, 1990).

Hegel, G.W.F. *The Logic of Hegel* (Oxford: Clarendon Press, 1892).

Hegel, G.W.F. *The Philosophy of Right* (Cambridge University Press, [1821]1967).

Knights, D. 'Subjectivity, Power and the Labour Process', in D. Knights and H. Willmott (eds), *Labour Process Theory* (London: Macmillan – now Palgrave, 1990).

Knights, D. 'Organization Theory in the Age of Deconstruction: Dualism, Gender and Postmodernism Revisited', *Organization Studies*, 18(1) (1997) 1–19.

Knights, D. and Willmott, H. 'Power and Subjectivity at Work: From Degradation to Subjugation in Social Relations', *Sociology*, 23(4) (1989) 535–58.

Lacan, J. *Ecrits* (London: Routledge & Kegan Paul, 1968).

Laclau, E. and Mouffe, C. *Hegemony and Socialist Strategy: Towards a Radical Democratic Politics* (London: Verso, 1985).

Le Doeuff, M. *Hipparchia's Choice: An Essay Concerning Women, Philosophy, etc.* (Cambridge: Basil Blackwell, 1989).

Littler, C. 'The Labour Process Debate: A Theoretical Review, 1974–1988', in D. Knights and H. Willmott (eds), *Labour Process Theory* (London: Macmillan – now Palgrave, 1990).

Maras, S. and Rizzo, T., 'On Becoming: An Interview with Moira Gatens', *Southern Review*, 28 (1995) 53–67.

Marx, K. *Economic and Philosophical Manuscripts* (Moscow: Progress Publishers, 1844).

Marx, K. *Capital, Volume 1* (Moscow: Progress Publishers, 1954).

Marx, K. and Engels, F. *The Holy Family* (Moscow: Progress Publishers, 1956).

Mommsen, G. *The Political and Social Theory of Max Weber* (London: Polity Press, 1989).

Newton, T. 'Theorizing Subjectivity in Organizations: The Failure of Foucauldian Studies?', *Organization Studies*, 19(3) (1998) 415–47.

Rose, M. *Industrial Behaviour* (London: Penguin, 1988).

Rose, N. *Inventing Ourselves: Psychology, Power and Personhood* (Cambridge University Press, 1998).

Rothfield, P. 'A Conversation Between Bodies', *Melbourne Journal of Politics*, 22 (1994) 30–44.

Schor, N. *Bad Objects: Essays Popular and Unpopular* (Durham North Carolina: Duke University Press, 1994).

Sturdy, A., Knights, D. and Willmott, H. (eds), *Skill and Consent: Contemporary Studies in the Labour Process* (London: Routledge, 1992).

Tanner, J., Davies, S. and O'Grady, B. 'Immanence Changes Everything: A Critical Comment on the Labour Process and Class-Consciousness', *Sociology*, 26(3) (1992) 439–54.

Taylor, C. *Hegel* (Cambridge University Press, 1975).

Thompson, P. *The Nature of Work: An Introduction to Debates on the Labour Process*, 1st edn (London: Macmillan – now Palgrave, 1983).

Thompson, P. *The Nature of Work: An Introduction to Debates on the Labour Process*, 2nd edn (London: Macmillan – now Palgrave, 1989).

Thompson, P. 'Crawling from the Wreckage: The Labour Process and the Politics of Production', in D. Knights and H. Willmott (eds), *Labour Process Theory* (London: Macmillan – now Palgrave, 1990).

Thompson, P. and Ackroyd, S. 'All Quiet on the Workplace Front? A Critique of Recent Trends in British Industrial Sociology', *Sociology*, 29(4) (1995) 615–33.

Thompson, P. and Warhurst, C. (eds) *Workplaces of the Future* (London: Macmillan – now Palgrave, 1998).

Walsh, M. 'Sexual Difference, Feminisms and Political Theory', PhD dissertation (Brisbane: University of Queensland, 1996).

Walsh, M. 'Ontology against Performativity', *Melbourne Journal of Politics*, 24 (1997) 52–68.

Walsh, M. 'Butler, Gender Difference and Subjectivity', in M. Alexander, S. Harding, P. Harrison, G. Kendall, Z. Skrbis, and J. Western (eds), *Refashioning Sociology: Responses to a New World Order, TASA Conference Proceedings* (Brisbane: Queensland University of Technology, 1998).

Wardell, M., 'Labour and Labour Process' in D. Knights and H. Willmott (eds), *Labour Process Theory* (London: Macmillan – now Palgrave, 1990).

Weir, A. *Sacrificial Logics: Feminist Theory and the Critique of Identity* (London: Routledge, 1996).

Willmott, H. 'Strength Is Ignorance; Slavery Is Freedom: Managing Culture in Modern Organizations', *Journal of Management Studies*, 30(4) (1993) 515–53.

Willmott, H. 'Managing the Academics: Commodification and Control in the Development of University Education in Great Britain', *Human Relations*, 48(9) (1995) 993–1028.

Willmott, H. 'Rethinking Management and Managerial Work: Capitalism, Control and Subjectivity', *Human Relations*, 50(11) (1997)1329–59.

Zizek, S. *For They Know Not What They Do: Enjoyment as a Political Factor* (London: Verso, 1991).

3

Reflections on Emotionality, Morality, Subjectivity, Power

UTE OSTERKAMP

Emotions are usually seen in contrast or opposed to thought, cognition and so on. This dualism, in turn, is based on a dichotomy, either of individual and society or of nature and culture; both, however, imply naturalising people's subjection to the given order and a corresponding general devaluation of emotions as such. Thus, the dualism of cognition and emotion is a fundamental ideological element to justify suppressive conditions. As Solomon (1993) for example points out, it has pervaded western thought from ancient times until today. The most enduring metaphor describing the relation between reason and emotion has been, as he states, that of master and slave – an image already used by Aristotle to vindicate the institution of slavery. According to this view, those in power are bestowed with the gift of self-control, which implies not only the right but also the obligation to control those who are thought of as naturally lacking this quality.

The general devaluation of emotion, its alleged inferiority to reason, entails self-control becoming the main criterion for an individual's morality, simultaneously allowing official control to blend into the background and thus maintain the illusion of individual autonomy. Foucault (1997) has traced this relationship between self-control and morality in the history of philosophy. In Epicurean ethics morality was seen as the mastery of one's own desires and restricted to a male elite. It was subordinated to the striving for a good life, lending it beauty and intensity. A good life, in the Epicurean view, requires moderation in the pleasures of life. This moderation, however, is not dictated by external norms but experienced as the heightening of the enjoyment of one's own desires. The elite's 'care for oneself' and its orientation towards a 'good life', however, included as well, as Foucault points out, the recognition that such aspirations can be realised only between equals – an insight which had to be reconciled with the reality of slavery and patriarchism by denying the humanity of slaves and women.

The Stoic ethic has been 'democratised' or 'normalised' in so far as it is no longer restricted to a small elite and its concern with a 'good life' but appears as a dictate of reason which should govern all people's lives alike – independent of their particular societal position and prospects. In this view, internal autonomy does not presuppose external independence, that is the disposal over the means one needs, but, on the contrary, self-control ensures individuals' independence from society: if one has not developed any expectations about life, one cannot become disappointed or suppressed. Since the majority of the Stoics themselves were rather rich and influential, the psychologically decisive question of whether such a renunciation of life's possibilities is freely chosen or enforced did not arise as a problem.

In Christian ethics, self-control is, as Foucault points out, largely replaced by the notion of selflessness, and the care for oneself is replaced by the care for others or, more precisely, by the concern with others' morality and their submission to God's purported will. This implies a crucial psychological shift since the individuals are thus deprived of any means of preserving a sense of integrity as an essential precondition for keeping and defending their aspirations against external constraints. In the wake of this shift, it is no longer sufficient merely to control one's own desires and emotions; rather, 'critical' desires as such are enough to prove one's own moral insufficiency. Self-control is, as Foucault points out, replaced by self-purification – a never-ending task of tracing and expunging of any 'improper' impulses and desires to ensure the individual's inner loyalty and meekness.

Freud, in a way, transferred these ideological changes to the individual level in differentiating between 'social' anxiety and the anxiety of the super-ego as two separate developmental stages. While 'social' anxiety is restricted to the danger of being caught doing 'wrong', after establishing the super-ego (the internalisation of the dominant norms) the situation has fundamentally changed: 'critical' insights and desires themselves (whether put into action or not) cause feelings of guilt, doubts of one's own moral acceptability. Renunciation of instinctual satisfaction does not bring any relief, but, on the contrary, strengthens the super-ego's aggressiveness – that is, weakens our resistance from within. Instead of fighting against the manifold social curtailments of our desires, insight, interests and so on, our aspirations themselves appear as the problem to be dealt with as soon as they touch given 'normality' or power structures. Though Freud himself rather justifies suppression with his notion of people's 'natural' asociality, he nonetheless takes a subjective view in so far as he exposes the personal costs of suppression, usually ignored in academic discussion. Since suppression can work smoothly only as long as it remains hidden from sight, his very concern with its subjective price contains already partial 'subversive' implications. The internalisation of prevailing norms as the essence of the super-ego already bringing in its wake individual feelings of shame and guilt for inappropriate desires (whether one gives in to them or not) is, as Freud points out, only to be expected from '*Kulturträger*' ('vehicles of civilization'), that is from those persons who do not possess power themselves but are allowed to participate in it providing they adopt the dominant norms and interests and restrict their own aspirations to the pursuit of their personal career by efficiently carrying out the tasks they have been entrusted with. These tasks include controlling and disciplining those who are less privileged and hence less compliant. Yet, this control task imposed on the *Kulturträger* seems to meet their own interests too, since the refractoriness of those they have to control could question their own superior position. Simultaneously, however, because of the explosive force which could develop if the *Kulturträger* and the masses became aware of their common though – depending on their particular societal position – differing or even seemingly contrasting constraints, any rapprochement between them has to be undermined and prevented. Participation in power, hence, requires according to Freud both compliance towards those 'above' as well as the necessity of keeping oneself largely aloof from those 'below' and a deadening of any possible feeling of sympathy or solidarity with them (1981).

This emotional immunisation against the awareness of the others' misery and particularly one's responsibility for it was, as Raul Hilberg (1982) points out, an especially essential quality for the fascist 'elite' in Germany. 'Toughness' or callousness was seen as a virtue, 'kindness' – at least towards the 'enemy' – judged as treason to one's own people. This logic is particularly apparent in a 1943 speech given by Himmler, Hitler's deputy, to SS leaders:

> Most of you will know what it means to see 100 bodies, 500 bodies or 1000 bodies. To have gone through this and, apart from some human weakness, have remained respectable – has made us hard. This is a never written and never to be written page of our history ... We can say that we have fulfilled this hardest task in love for our people. And we have suffered no damage in our inmost, in our souls, in our character. (Hilberg, 1982, p. 685)[1]

In the face of such 'patriotic duty', Rudolf Höss, too, the commandant of Auschwitz, did not dare to give in to his feelings of compassion:

> I didn't have the courage for it: because I didn't want to lay myself open to attack, because I didn't want to divulge my weakness, because I was too obstinate to concede having chosen the wrong path ... The admission of being too soft for

SS service would inevitably have led to my expulsion or at the very least to being discharged. And I couldn't bring myself to do that. (Broszat, 1979, p. 69)

One of the most effective methods of silencing one's own scruples in face of the inhumanity one became involved in was to throw oneself into one's work. This promised triple gain: approval from above; no time for reflection on one's own conduct; and a prophylactic absolution for it – followed on the basis that since one wasn't concerned with one's own welfare, one couldn't be blamed for neglecting the welfare of others. Thus Höss, for example, states:

> The constant stress – generated by the RFSS (Himmler as 'Reichsführer der SS'/U.O.) himself as well as war-related difficulties, near daily problems in the camps and, most of all, by the ceaseless inflow of detainees – made me only think of my work. Being so much under pressure myself, I put those under me under pressure too – whether members of the SS, civilian employees, associated administrative departments, firms or detainees. Only one thing counted for me – to get on, to drive others on, to make it easier to carry out the task I was entrusted with. The RFSS insisted on complete fulfilment of one's duties and total devotion to the task at hand to the point of self-sacrifice. Any reservations had to be put aside ... I had to become still harder, colder and more merciless in the face of the plight of the detainees. I saw everything in detail, often far too real, but I could not allow myself to give in to it. I couldn't allow whatever became destroyed in this process to stop me. It had to become irrelevant in face of the final goal to win the war ... The RFSS's wanted Auschwitz to become the largest ever-existent extermination project ... His order to implement it was indeed something unusual, something monstrous. But the explanation given to us made me accept this process of extermination as *right*. At that time, I didn't waste much thought on that – I had received an order and I had to execute it. Whether the mass extermination of the Jews was necessary or not I wasn't competent to judge. (Broszat, 1979, pp. 123 f)

Having had to overcome 'inner' resistance or scruples in doing their murderous 'job' evidently allowed even convicted fascists to view themselves as victims. In complaining of his 'fate' in having to watch the gassing he had had to organise, Höss, for example, completely loses sight of what it meant for the detainees. The prisoners only attracted his attention if their behaviour seemed to confirm the ideology of their moral inferiority and hence the 'human' character of the fascist 'cleansing' policy. His description of the 'interesting' insensitivity and indifference of prisoners towards their fellow-sufferers allows him to simultaneously contrast his own 'minor' inhumanity with their seemingly major lack of feeling. While, for example, the Sonderkommandos, that is the Jews who were forced to gas their fellow-sufferers, in Höss's view, remained completely 'unmoved', he had, as he assures us, to exhaust himself in long, lonely rides through the dark night in order to regain his inner peace.

The ideology of the purging character of one's personal unease about what one feels compelled to do seems to release us from any responsibility for our behaviour. Dissociating our emotions from our actions (the dehumanising effects of it are clearly shown in Höss) is given its blessing by the dualism of cognition and emotion, which serves not merely as an ideological mainstay of given power relations but also as a proven means of eliminating our responsibility for the consequences of our behaviour. This dualism guides the general way of dealing with the past. Taking one's inner repugnance towards one's own actions as a proof of innocence or purity of heart was not merely spontaneously assumed when being called to account, but was publicly fostered, as for instance Peitsch (1990) has demonstrated using the example of how autobiographies were received in postwar Germany, and also Friedrich (1985) has shown using the example of sentences against former German fascists. Thus, for instance, all reports questioning the prevailing narration of fascism as an incomprehensible trial of humankind but hinting instead at its societal background and backing were dismissed by cultural and educational policy as politically motivated and hence morally untrustworthy (Peitsch, 1990). Concerning jurisdiction, Friedrich summarises his observations as follows: every agent of the 'Final Solution' performed their task of extermination with a certain personal attitude – one displayed sadism, another indifference, the third compassion. This personal attitude towards the executions rather than actual participation in them was decisive in whether the defendants were classified as 'murderers' or 'accessories' or simply acquitted.

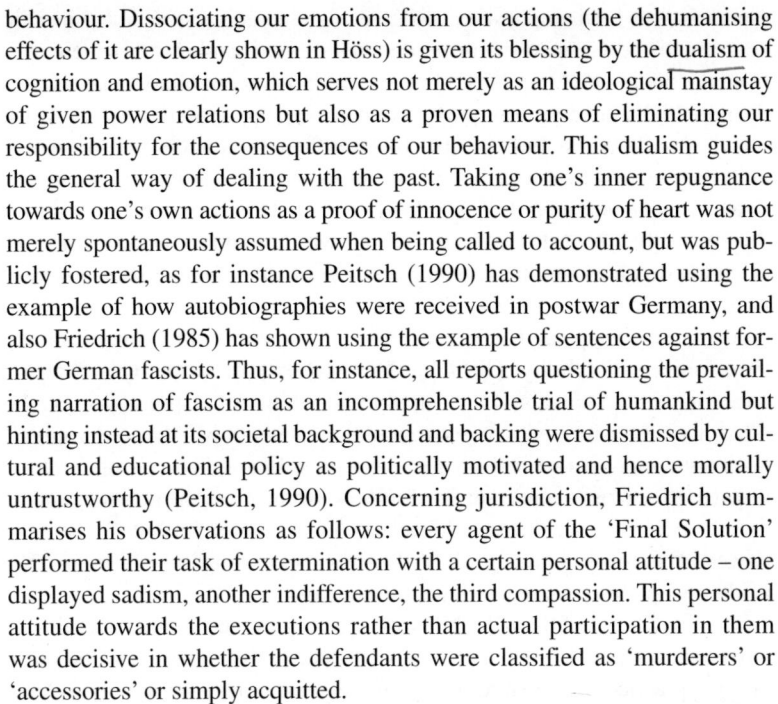

Another mechanism of denying any responsibility for fascism was to limit it to its 'extremes', that is to ignore its factual embeddedness in everyday life. The 'normality' of one's behaviour, in this view, seems immediately to prove its morality. In face of the majority's protests of their innocence by pointing to their inner repugnance towards the fascist brutalities and/or the 'normality' of their own behaviour, it was left to those who had systematically been excluded from this 'normality' to point to its inherent inhumanity. Moreover, the fascists' efforts to kill not merely the bodies of their victims but also their souls, as Levi puts it (something that was realised in the extermination camps with unconcealed brutality), subjected many detainees too to the 'normal' forms of popular demoralisation, that is, of being made to participate more or less consciously in others' suppression and humiliation; simultaneously, however, they also voiced the humiliating effects of being made a party to others' humiliation.

The most humiliating experience was, as many of them agree, the experience of being totally exposed to the arbitrary rule of others and the dehumanising impact of this situation on one's own behaviour, which immediately seemed to prove the fascist ideology of their victims' moral inferiority. Simultaneously, having to stand helplessly by while witnessing others' corporal 'punishments' or torture (or even experiencing relief at not being in their place) was, as Levi emphasises, a source of an ineradicable shame. Since, in contrast to the German majority, detainees could neither avert their eyes from the omnipotent murderous brutality of fascism nor blind themselves to the potentially deadly consequences of denying support to those even worse off, they suffered, as Levi summarises, all their lives under an irrevocable guilt they were drawn into though not responsible for; it was, as he emphasises, a shame not only of oneself but of the world darkened by any injuries done to every one of its creatures – a guilt which could never be washed off or undone again. Though these feelings of guilt and shame remained largely in the background as long as the immediate struggle for life occupied all thought, they reappeared as soon as 'normal' standards of morality regained their 'universal' validity. The subjective necessity of solidarity and resistance, on the one hand, and the actual impossibility of it in practice, on the other, were transformed into permanent doubts about whether one couldn't have done more if one had tried to, he writes. Elaine Scarry's observation that it seems to be 'a universal fate for those from whom the power to author their own fate has been retracted that later populations reattribute to them the power of authorship and speak of them as "permitting" it' (1985, p. 157) evidently applies even to survivors themselves.

The knowledge of the indelibility of injuries and the general darkening of our lives it brings in its wake stands fundamentally opposed to the usual purging practices aimed at restoring our personal innocence. It implies too a radical questioning of the traditional understanding of morality, which naturalises a normality where people are made to suppress all 'deviant' insights and emotions in order to be accepted. As Imre Kertész puts it in summarising his experiences of Auschwitz and Buchenwald: 'All debacles result from having to submit to higher values and norms and to consider their own ones as insignificant or inferior' (1997, p. 37).

The general focus on the individual implies the focus on emotions and simultaneously deprives emotions of their objective references, making them appear primarily as both an 'internal' matter and the site of morality (Foucault, 1994), which some individuals possess more than others. In contrast to such a notion, former detainees advanced a broader understanding of morality, not reducing it to one's own acceptability but questioning conditions where people's acceptance is at stake and where the others' 'immorality' seems to confirm one's own moral superiority. Such a broader understanding is tantamount to overcoming the personalising view, that is, the tendency to exclude others from the scope of our responsibility if they do not meet our expectations. It reverses the prevailing reversal of causes and consequences of suppression: it is not individuals' morality which is being put to the test, but the mechanisms and functions of people's demoralisation. This implies a fundamental reinterpretation of immorality, too. Instead of being viewed as an expression of our alleged asocial instincts necessarily to be suppressed by society, it is discussed as a consequence of our imposed self-denial and a proven source of our manipulability as well as our suffering from it.

From such a perspective, the Sonderkommandos, for example, were not seen as a 'proof' of the detainees' inhumanity, but as the Nazis' most demonic crime and merely the peak of a vile complex of strategies systematically aiming at their humiliation to deprive them, as Levi emphasises, of any dignity and thought of resistance.

The prevailing tendency to individualise fascism in particular persons or groups means that former detainees' attempts to point to its normality were condemned to failure from the very start. Their emphasis, for instance, on the systematic relationship between the Nazis' 'lawful' expulsion of Jewish people from public life (which the majority had accepted and may have even approved of) and the death camps as the final step (which they were shocked about but denied having known about) was evidently experienced by the German majority as a threat to their 'innocence' and dismissed out of hand as a kind of blackmailing motivated by morally dubious interests or resentment: psychology especially distinguished itself in these matters, as Améry, embittered, states, by inventing the 'concentration camp syndrome' which pathologised all those who opposed the publicly enforced forgetting of the past and one's own involvement in it.

The united front former detainees were faced with when trying to point to the 'normal' preconditions of fascism, however, had forced them back, as for instance Améry points out, just into the isolation and loneliness they had already suffered from most during fascism and which made them feel, indeed, as 'survivors', that they were the remains of a past that 'normal' people wanted to get rid of as soon as possible. (And which they had, after all, survived!) 'What I resent[2] –' Améry (1977, p. 100) writes:

> certainly for my own personal benefit but also for the benefit of the German people – is something nobody is interested in – except for the public media who actually buy it. What had dehumanised me has become a commodity I am selling.

Kertész describes his experiences in a similar way: 'All experiences', he resignedly notes, 'are futile; Auschwitz and Siberia have passed (if they have), and nothing had ethically changed' (1997, p. 132).

But nevertheless he too felt compelled to continue his attempts of making himself heard:

> I am too late with this issue, I hear. It is no more relevant. 'This issue' should have been put forward earlier, ten years ago at the latest. I, however, had to recognise once more that I am interested in nothing else but in the Auschwitz-mythos. When I think of a new novel, I am thinking once again only of Auschwitz.

Whatever I am thinking of, I am always thinking of Auschwitz. Even when I am apparently talking of quite different things, I am talking of Auschwitz. I am a medium of Auschwitz, Auschwitz speaks through me. In comparison with to it anything else appears to me nonsense, and surely, quite surely, not merely because of personal reasons. Auschwitz and anything concerning it (and what doesn't?) is the greatest trauma of humankind since the Cross even though it may possibly take decades if not centuries to become aware of it. If not, nothing matters anyway. But why then write? And to whom? (pp. 32 f.)

In a similar way to the majority in West Germany, social sciences too did not reflect on their role in the past but preferred, as, for example, Bauman (1989) puts it, either to pass fascism wordlessly over as if it hadn't happened or were not worth considering, or else to play it down by pressing it into familiar categories such as 'prejudice', 'ideology', and so on. Another variant of diverting attention from fascism's 'normal' preconditions was, as Bauman states, to view it as a particularly dense network of morally deficient individuals released from civilised constraints by a criminal and, above all, by an irrational ideology.

Bauman's statements on social sciences in general apply even more to psychology with its immanent neglect of the societal context of people's behaviour. Even the fact that German psychology was established as an independent vocational subject, that is as a specific academic training, under the fascist regime was evidently no reason for further reflection on the role it played within it. On the contrary, after German fascism's defeat, psychologists were as eager as the rest of the population to rigorously turn their backs on their past – thus uncritically continuing their former submissiveness to present 'normality' and prevent themselves from learning anything from it.[3]

Although, for example, fascism had quite clearly shown its inherent inhumanity – personified in the majority's 'deadly' indifference (see Kershaw, 1981) towards those being 'removed' from sight and Höss' self-pity because of the cruelties he had to perform – psychologists still keep to the dichotomy of cognition and emotion and hence absolutise the necessity of people's suppression. By doing so they systematically ignore the specific human potentiality of exceeding our personal limits through cooperation with others in a process of 'humanising' the external world through objectifying our needs and desires, which will in turn – via reciprocation of their objectification of them – develop, amplify and differentiate themselves (see Holzkamp, 1983; Scarry, 1985; Tolman, 1994). Since in the dualistic view the restriction of people's influence on their relevant life-conditions appears as a matter of course, the crucial subject science question of how our powerlessness is produced, what it means subjectively and how it can be overcome cannot emerge at all. Conflicts arise in this notion between (rational) societal demands and (irrational) personal interests; they are normally 'solved' by compromises – recommending themselves as proven means of ensuring people's loyalty by granting them (despite their moral insufficiencies) some degree of 'tolerance' which they should then be appropriately grateful for.

The rigid insulation that psychologists and other social scholars pursue towards any insight into the problematic nature of their own role and into the 'normality' they accept as a matter of course, however, is evidently less an expression of our mental inflexibility than an anticipatory obedience to the taboo of exposing power relations by pointing to the societal mediatedness of our personal behaviour. Since the dualism of cognition and emotion serves to justify given power structures (by the alleged moral superiority of those being at the controls and the 'irresponsibility' of those being controlled) it will not be overcome 'academically' but only by exposing and fighting its political function (see Lutz, 1988; Osterkamp, 1999). This however implies above all scrutinising also the manifold occasions where we ourselves relapse, notwithstanding our better insights, into blaming people for what we do or let happen to them.

In the face of the general prevalence of a dualistic thinking it is little wonder that even scholars explicitly sharing the detainees' reservations towards the individualised concept of morality finally remain caught in it. Thus, for example, Bauman (1989) explicitly criticises the prevailing tendency of ignoring fascism's 'normality' as well as the problematic nature of a morality so easily made use of by a fascist regime. Since, however, he does not view people's demoralisation from a subject's standpoint as an injury of our moral integrity and proven means of undermining our subjectivity and resistance, he too relapses into the usual practice of judging morality from an external moralising–demoralising standpoint. Though he proceeds from our 'Other-directedness' as a main source of our demoralisation, in his further argumentation people's 'immorality' appears less caused by societal suppression than by our natural moral short-sightedness, hindering us from catching up with society's complexity. Bauman 'dissolves' this contradiction by limiting morality to 'proximity' – people's immediate social relations, which are evidently untouched by any societal power structures in his view. Morality manifests itself, as he points out with reference to Levinas, in our responsibility for concrete others – finding its uppermost expression in our readiness to die rather than to live at their costs. By severing morality from society, however, it appears once again mainly limited from within – by our own self-preserving tendencies, as Bauman puts it. Instead of enquiring into the conditions restricting people's interests in their own self-preservation and exposing the humiliating character of our own demoralisation as well as its societal function (explicitly pointed out by Améry, Kertész, Levi), Bauman then ponders over the 'philosophical' question of whether at least some moral models can be found even under the inhuman conditions of fascist death camps. However, such a quest for a morality independent of any conditions whatsoever seems primarily to be designed to soothe our own fears that we might be deprived of our 'superior' morality as a main means of ensuring our social acceptance.[4] By searching for proofs of morality even under the most extreme inhuman conditions, Bauman unwittingly violates his own moral standard of rather suffering than doing harm – that is, lends credence to many survivors' self-doubts (voiced, for instance, by Levi, 1993, p. 84) about having possibly survived at the cost of more moral fellow-sufferers. With this insistence on an individual morality, however, he disregards the societal production and function of individuals' 'immorality' and deprives his perspicacious observations of their potentially 'revolutionary' character. Thus, for example, he points to the most important mechanism of how our unwillingness or inability to admit the problematic nature of our behaviour makes us continue with it when he states:

> The unwillingness to re-evaluate (and condemn) one's own past conduct is a powerful, and ever more powerful, stimulus to plod on, long after the original commitment to 'the cause' had all but petered out. Smooth and imperceptible passages between the steps lure the actor into a trap; the trap is the impossibility of quitting without revising and rejecting the evaluation of one's own deeds as right or at least innocent. The trap is, in other words, a paradox: *one cannot get clean without blackening oneself*. To hide filth, one must forever draggle in the mud (Bauman, 1989, p. 158).

Since, however, he does not ask what are the conditions that make us behave in this way he surrenders the chance of resolving the vicious circle he has so impressively described: that of continuing our immoral behaviour to keep the semblance of our morality.[5]

Like Bauman, Tzvetan Todorov (1993) agrees with the survivors' statements that people's demoralisation can be overcome only by humanising their living conditions – and nevertheless he also obviously feels urged to find some moral models as an exception to this rule. Not least the survivors themselves, he states, contravened their assertion that the extermination camps had extinguished any morality. This argument, however, fundamentally misses the survivor's claim for a 'meta-morality' – a morality not reduced to our own morality but taking responsibility also for the others' morality by exposing the mechanisms of their demoralisation. Though Todorov himself quotes the statement of Tadeusz Borowski (who too had survived Auschwitz) that morality implies our responsibility for any humiliation done to others, he then reduces this insight once again to the prevailing understanding of morality as perfecting our personal blamelessness. Evidently, it doesn't suffice to feel fully sympathetic with the survivors' concern with the prevailing morality: what is required are 'appropriate interpretative categories' (Scarry, 1985, p. 279) to enable us to grasp the revolutionary implications of their insights and to recognise as the essential problem our own unquestioned acceptance of given normality and the 'narrowness' of our own scientific tools. Instead of yielding to our desire to convince ourselves and the world of our morality (if necessary by silencing, in one way or other, all those questioning it), what is required is rather 'self-distrust' as Améry (1988) calls it, enquiring into our own ideological blinkers as well as our interests in keeping them in place. Only then can there will be a possibility that we might resist any possible fascism more than our parents and grandparents did.

Notes

1. Quotations from German sources have been translated by the author.
2. Améry uses here the German word '*Nachtragen*' as a synonym for resentment, meaning carrying a message – in his case the 'subjective truth' of the fascist 'normality' – which no-one is ever willing to receive and thus, as he writes, 'nailing each of us inescapably down to the cross of his destroyed past' and blocking the exit into the genuinely human dimension, the future (*ibid.*, p. 88). Améry too vehemently opposes an abstract forgiving and forgetting which in his view has nothing to do with morality, but is contrary to it.
3. In the case of psychology this entailed the uncritical adoption of Anglo-American psychology, which was at least seemingly neutral and above suspicion.
4. Equally, discussions in university seminars are often predominated by the students' concern with their own morality, as for instance manifested in the pseudo-critical, and in this abstract form unanswerable, question of how they might have behaved themselves under fascist conditions.
5. Another mechanism of defending against becoming aware of what we are doing, is described by Hilberg's notion of the vanishing horizons: people persuade themselves into continuing their dubious actions by making themselves believe that they will not overstep a certain line – only to push it back once it has actually been reached.

Bibliography

Améry, J. *Ressentiments. In Schuld und Sühne. Bewältigungsversuche eines Überwältigte* (Stuttgart: dtv/Klett-Cotta, 1988) 81–101.
Bauman, Z. *Modernity and the Holocaust* (Ithaca, New York: Cornell University Press, 1989).
Broszat, M. (ed.) *Kommandant in Auschwitz. Autobiographische Aufzeichnungen des Rudolf Höss* (München: DTV, 1979).
Foucault, M. 'On the Genealogy of Ethics: An Overview of Work in Progress', in P. Rabinow (ed.), *Michel Foucault. Ethics, Subjectivity and Truth*, vol. I (New York: The New Press, 1997) 253–80.

Freud, S. *The Future of an Illusion. The Standard Edition of the Complete Psychological Work of Sigmund Freud*, vol. XXI (London: Hogarth Press and the Institute of Psycho-Analysis, 1981) 5–56.

Friedrich, J. *Die kalte Amnestie. NS-Täter in der Bundesrepublik* (Frankfurt am Main: Fischer, 1985).

Hilberg, R. *Die Vernichtung der Europäischen Juden. Die Gesamtgeschichte des Holocaust* (Fulda: Olle & Wolter, 1982).

Holzkamp, K. *Grundlegung der Psychologie* (Frankfurt/M.: Campus, 1983).

Kershaw, I. 'Alltägliches und Außeralltägliches: Ihre Bedeutung für die Volksmeinung', in D. Peukert und J. Reulecke, *Die Reihen fest Geschlossen* (Wuppertal: Peter Hammer, 1981) 273–92.

Kertész, I. *Galeerentagebuch* (Reinbek: Rohwohlt, 1997).

Levi, P. *Die Untergegangenen und die Geretteten* (München: DTV, 1993) 33–69.

Lutz, C.A. *Unnatural Emotions. Everyday Sentiment in a Micronesian Atoll and their Challenge to Western Theory* (Chicago University Press, 1988).

Osterkamp, U. 'Emotion, Cognition, and Action Potence', in Ch. W. Tolman and W. Maiers (eds), *Critical Psychology. Contributions to an Historical Science of the Subject* (Cambridge University Press, 1991) 102–33.

Osterkamp, U. 'Gefühle/Emotionen', in W. Haug (ed.), *Historisch-Kritisches Wörterbuch des Marxismus*, vol. 4 (Hamburg: Argument, 1999) 1329–47.

Peitsch, H. *Deutschlands Gedächtnis an Seine Dunkelste Zeit. Zur Funktion der Autobiographik in den Westzonen Deutschlands und den Westsektoren von Berlin 1945–1949* (Berlin: Sigma, 1990).

Scarry, E. *The Body in Pain. The Making and Unmaking of the World* (Oxford University Press, 1985).

Solomon, R.C. 'The Philosophy of Emotions', in M. Lewis and J.M. Haviland (eds), *Handbook of Emotion* (New York: Guilford Press, 1993) 3–14.

Todorov, T. *Angesichts des Äußersten* (München: Wilhelm Fink Verlag, 1993).

Tolman, Ch. *Psychology, Society, and Subjectivity. An Introduction to German Critical Psychology* (London: Routledge, 1994).

4

Refiguring Subjectivity after Modernity[1]

COUZE VENN

Subjectivity, Historicity, Narration

The ideas I am developing here are part of a bigger project (Venn, 2000) concerning the refiguration of modernity and its subject in the light of the postmodern and the postcolonial interrogations of the grounds which underpin the discourse of modernity. Two kinds of questioning are triggered as soon as we attempt to abandon the old terrain of the logocentric subject and the project of modernity which has sought to institute such a subject. One set addresses the foundational narratives that constitute the subject as phallogocentric and inscribe the view of history as the process of becoming of that subject. The Other reveals the history of colonialism and the Othering of the Other to have been intrinsic to the history of modernity. The engagement with these questions means that one must try to seek a purchase for critique from a space outside occidentalism, that is, outside the space of the becoming-west of Europe and the becoming-modern of the world.[2] This task is made more difficult because there are neither privileged terrains nor originary or uncolonised spaces from which to speak, including something called postcolonial theory. One is left with the option of a deconstructive strategy relying on a number of dissident theorisations of subjectivity and modernity, and a refigured narrative of emancipation driven by the spirit of resistance to all forms of oppression.

A central issue that arises concerns how we are to understand subjectivity if we reject the epistemological privilege which has characterised the era of the 'philosophy of the subject' and what Lacan called the 'ego's era', that is to say, the period in which became privileged the discourses that promote the idea of a self-sufficient, self-centred subject, doubling as the autonomous, objective agent of cognition and of history. The break with such a position is in solidarity with the rejection of occidentalism. My argument in *Occidentalism* (Venn, 2000) is that such a break has profound implications for rethinking the ethical basis on which new forms of subjectivity can be legitimated. This is because the question of who comes after modernity triggers the problem of different ways of being, of unprecedented modes of existence beyond those that have emerged in the history of humanity so far. It thus calls for different principles that could function as the foundation for the possibility of an heteronomous and transmodern ethics – that is, beyond the postmodern and the postcolonial but reached by way of the anticipation of the different and hopeful futures they harbour.

This is the broader context. The connection with this chapter is that the specific issue here is the theorisation of subjectivity which emphasises the primacy of the relation to the other in the process of constitution, that is, the idea of the co-emergence or compossibility of the I and the Other. It will become clear that this narrative of the subject and the problem of subjective transformations as well as that of subjectivities to come are correlated. The social sciences and psychoanalytic theory, because they share some of the key assumptions about the subject that are encountered in the dominant, occidentalist, discourse of modernity, provide a limited purchase in articulating the different principles implicated in the project I have outlined.

My approach is to operate a shift to the terrain of phenomenology's attempt to ground the subject, and the notion of interiority, away from Cartesianism, and to avoid solipsistic or egological accounts of the subject, so ingrained still in a good deal of psychology and psychoanalysis. The reason is that phenomenology, especially from Husserl's critique of Cartesianism in the *Cartesian Meditations*, and Heidegger's engagement with that critique in *Being and Time*, inaugurates a different problematic of being, as a rejection of classical ontology and any philosophy which posits the givenness of the 'I'. One implication is the radical historicisation of the process of becoming, so that the subject is conceptualised as coupled to the lifeworld, understood in terms of social and material constituents that are historically constituted. This is not a major shift if we remember that poststructuralist critiques of the subject have their basis in the encounter with phenomenology and its critique of the discourse of modernity, especially by way of the work of Heidegger. So, we are talking about positions associated with Derrida, Foucault, Levinas, Lyotard, Merleau-Ponty, Ricoeur. I would include even Lacan because of his references to Husserl and what he borrows from Heidegger's critique of phenomenology in displacing psychoanalysis away from its appropriation within 'ego psychology'. My aim is to propose an analytical framework for the constitution of subjectivity which is oriented towards the problem, central for postcolonial theory and radical politics alike, of the reconstitution of subjectivity/identity. I will use a reading of Fanon's reflections on the lived experience of blackness in *Black Skin, White Masks* to explore the implications for both theory and practice. There are, besides, clear implications for psychological theory.

The Subject in Question

It could be pointed out that critiques of the subject have already dethroned the notion of a self-centred, rational, unitary subject. Have they not emphasised instead the constructed and performative character of subjects, their imbrication in and constitution through discourse and through practices of formation? Have they not pointed out the centrality of difference, of the body, the importance of the relation to the Other in the psychic mechanisms determining the 'who' of subjectivity?

I am claiming that on closer inspection we discover that traces of the old model survive even in the radical critiques of the logocentric/Cartesian/ or monadic subject. There is a relative neglect of heteronomy and alterity in theorisations of the constitution of subjectivity. This is evident in the model of power which many authors put to work that implies the foregrounding of the oppressive and subjugative aspects of power, so that theorisations of the relation of the subject and the other are framed in terms of oppositions and exclusions. Let us briefly look at this tendency. Stuart Hall (1996), in his instructive analysis of the problems, reconstructs the route from Althusser and Lacan through Foucault and Derrida to feminist and postcolonial interrogations of the mechanisms whereby subjects are constituted by reference to discursive practices and to the effects of power operating through them. He shows how earlier approaches to subjectivity have been followed by analyses that, while still putting to work post-structuralism and psychoanalytic theory, now emphasise difference, embodiment, historicisation, contingency, phantasy and ambivalence in accounting for a 'subject-in-process'. The problems now concern the 'complex transactions between the subject, the body and identity' (1996, p. 14). He cautions against privileging either the psychic level or the discursive, thus the social field, in theorising constitution; it is more a matter of mutual constitution and articulation between the psychic and the social. In any case, following the later Foucault, we need to add the 'hermeneutics of desire' to the idea of a 'correlation between fields of knowledge, types of normativity and forms of subjectivity' (1996, p. 12). Hall draws from Butler the argument about how 'certain regulatory norms form a "sexed" subject in terms that establish the indistinguishability of psychic and bodily formation' (Butler, 1993, p. 23).

Furthermore, the effects of power mean that identities operate through the 'discursive construction of a constitutive outside and the production of abjected and marginalised subjects' (Hall, 1996, p. 15). This point of view, when extended to consider the question of the racialised other, given that the normative ideal of the subject is a Eurocentric one, brings up issues to do with the historicisation of the process of subjectivity. It becomes a matter of both roots and routes, as Paul Gilroy (1993a) has expressed it. The analysis that Hall makes leads us to surmise that the route must pass through a history and a narrative of modernity. So, the problems are not only those of accounting for the suturing of the psychic and the social and discursive, but a historicisation, already initiated by Foucault, that implicates certain kinds of departures from not only what Derrida calls phallogocentrism, but also from the terrain of orthodox psychology and psychoanalysis.

Without going into details, I will claim that one of the striking features of the theorisations of subjectivity in the positions that Hall examines is the emphasis on a narrative of the subject that seems to assume that the 'outside', namely, other subjects, culture, and so on, although constitutive of something called interiority, is in some way inimical or constraining for the subject. That is to say, the relation of the subject to its 'outside' is thought of in terms of a violence which is done to the subject, or by reference to a dispossession of the subject. It is as if there remains a nostalgia for the self-present autonomous, 'free', subject. For instance, in Butler's account of subjection as 'both subordination and becoming of the subject' (1997, p. 13), power is consistently thought of in terms of subordination, even though her account starts from the recognition of the double-bind and paradox of subjectivity, whereby the subject appears to be both the effect of a 'prior power' and yet also 'the condition of possibility' of agency. Within her problematic of the psychic life of power, the 'subject is neither fully determined by power nor fully determining of power' (1997, p. 17).

My position is not to deny that power and the process of identification do indeed produce these effects. It is, on the one hand, to point to the heterogeneity of power, so that it is not immediately conceptualised by reference to subordination alone, but equally in terms of a capacity for action of a non-coercive kind, reminiscent of Ricoeur's notion of the 'I can', with its ethical inflection. Briefly, the 'I can' in Ricoeur is associated with the 'power-to-act' in the sense of the possibility of an action that enacts being as potentiality. The meaning of the terms are constructed within the horizon of an ontology which is premised on notions of 'oneself as another', thus of care and solicitude, on the recognition of the being of the other as potentiality so that we are each convoked to a justice that must respond to the other's suffering. I mean suffering both in the sense of ordinary everyday suffering as well as in the sense of the anguish that arises from the consciousness of the human condition as one circumscribed by finitude, lack and loss, that is to say, aspects of existence that are intrinsic to the recognition of our beingness in time and that one is powerless to alter. A decrease in the power to act – for instance, the inability to tell one's story, or to attest to an injustice or to a suffering (say, because of a constraining power, that is, a violence) – is itself a modality of suffering and should trigger appeals to values like solicitude and care, and an ethical injunction to act to end the injustice. Power, thus, is not *a priori* on the side of either the ethical or of violence, but open to a judgement that itself participates in the questioning of being as to its way of being (see Ricoeur, 1992, 1996; Venn, 2000).

The canonical example of the non-oppressive power-to-act would be that involved (ideally) in the infant–mother relationship, which I will conceptualise in terms of a choreography, in order to signal the interdependent, dynamic, mutually constitutive, dialogical character of the relationship. It relates to compossibility, which I discuss later by reference to Merleau-Ponty's work. My aim is to counterpose or make visible the fact that, and the manner in which, the other (ideally) inhabits the interiority of the subject as host. One implication is that psychic well-being depends on being able or ready to harbour alterity within the self, as Jessica Benjamin (1998), for example, has argued.

Interestingly, some of the voices which are beginning to problematise the egological paradigm come from the 'unhomely' space of a critical theory that locates itself in an 'in-between' space relative to western thought and the 'theoretical jetty' (Derrida, 1990) of postcolonial theory. I'm thinking here of someone like Homi Bhabha, whose reflections on 'identity' indicate that the other, or the 'we', is not necessarily an adversary, or that in opposition to which the subject understands itself. Instead, drawing from Levinas, he proposes the idea that the 'subject is inhabited by the radical and an-archical reference to the "other" ' (1996, p. 58). The Other, thus, is a participant in the work of healing and of rememorialising the past, since the refiguration of the subject must then require a different historicisation and narrativisation of particular selves, so that the process necessarily repositions the 'who' (of action and discourse) within an intersubjective network of interactions, as I have explored elsewhere (Venn, 1997, 1999, 2000). Furthermore, there are disjunctures of time, or different temporal routes, that different belongings or different roots produce. They have implications for the volatility and heterogeneity of subjectivities in lifeworlds characterised by (post)modernity.

The Relation to Alterity: The Heteronomous 'I'

So, how is one to write an Other history of the subject that would also be an Other history of modernity? Let us consider a series of propositions. I will start with the idea that being is the entity that questions itself as to its way of being.[3] Although this is a fundamental proposition of modern ontology, it does at the same time provide a leverage for moving outside the periodisation bounded by modernity, so that a genealogy of the subject can be located by reference to a longer time-span and a longer history of being. This self-questioning of being about its way of being – and the intimation of a search for a way – reveals being as a being in time, and reveals that it is the dimension of temporality, and thus the consciousness of finitude, that motivates and makes possible such a questioning in the first place.[4] We know ourselves to be fateful and fatal beings, measuring our presentness by reference to the trace and spacing of time, or, if you wish, by reference to duration understood as the space of becoming. I draw attention to the space of becoming because I want to signal the need to move away from any (logocentric, Cartesian, occidentalist) thought of being as origin or as presence; that is to say, as present to itself, requiring no guarantee (transcendental or otherwise) outside the subject. My approach breaks with any affiliation with traditional ontology's assumptions about the horizon of being which grounds the self-sufficient subject of Cartesianism (and cognitivist psychology). Instead I am indicating a sense of temporality in which we live the 'now' as a movement from a becoming-past to a coming-towards, so that the consciousness of the present always leaches into the memory of the having-been and the anticipation of a to-come. The point, once more, is that temporality is a fundamental dimension of being.[5] The way it is lived is tied to loss and to anticipation, that is to say, to the echo of what has been, and to the imagination of the to-come as a time of emancipation and redemption – that is, as the modality of hope, for instance, imagined as the space of the recovery of (fantasised) presence – fantasised if we associate presence with plenitude and *jouissance*, and thus harbouring the (projected) moment of the recovery of loss and the overcoming of lack and the insufficiency of being.[6] An implicated proposition which is worth signalling is that the unity, or seeming unity, of the subject (and of the community) is a projected unity, beholden to an imagined ideal subjectivity, awaiting its always deferred realisation. It follows that Foucault's (1984) question, 'Who are we in the present?', is a question that exceeds genealogy, since the subject is located by reference to a memory and an historicisation, as well as to a narrative of emancipation, and to a sense, therefore, of futurity. It could be noted in that respect that the notion of the subject as presence, that is to say, as a self-present, egocentric consciousness, as in the modern, logocentric concept of the subject, has the effect of erasing the fundamental historicity of beings. That philosophical discourse of the subject, along with the philosophy of the Same affiliated with it, has plagued the human sciences ever since, as we all know, since it posits a subject–object polarity whereby the (epistemic) subject of knowledge can be conceptualised as qualitatively distinct from the object which it can unilaterally determine, as in forms of cognitivism and positivism.

Second, I will introduce the proposition that the way in which, and the means by which, being questions itself as to its way of being is through language.[7] Narrative is the form in which being comes to know itself as a being in time, for time is not a thing, it cannot be directly represented, but is indirectly communicated and experienced in the form of narrativity, a thesis central to Ricoeur's work. Narrative in that sense is the 'guardian of time', as he puts it (1988, p. 241). Specifically, the existence of a self as a being in time takes the form of the emplotment of the events of a life in the form of a narration. Thus, every self is a storied self. And every story is mingled with the stories of other selves, so that each one of us is entangled in the stories we tell about ourselves and that are told about us. The understanding of subjectivity cannot be separated from the way selves are narrated, so that we can conceptualise the 'who' as narrated identity.

Third, the entanglement of identities means, too, that every subject exists as a relation to an other or others, that is, every subject is intricated within an intersubjective web: the I is plural: 'An I by itself does not exist,' says Ricoeur (1992, p. 18). Our inscription in language, and the narrative character of identity, instantiate the intersubjective ground of subjectivity, and point up once again the primacy of the social. (It could be noted that the idea of the primacy of the social for the constitution of subjectivity is reinforced in the (relatively neglected) work of thinkers like Vygotsky, Luria, Volosinov and Bakhtin on the development of consciousness and language).

The embodied and performative character of the human relation amplifies the idea of the subject as a heteronomous, rather than autonomous, 'I'. The world of other bodies and the world of objects constitute the 'dwelling' for subjectivity (see also Grosz, 1994, for the elaboration of the standpoint of embodiment). I am trying to say that it is not enough to say that the 'self' or the 'I' emerges in relation to or in opposition to an Other – for instance, in Lacan's metaphor of the mirror stage, implicating separation from the *Other* in the formation of the ego and recognition of the difference of the Other as an Other. I am stressing the idea that the 'I' is 'more than one but less than two', as Irigaray (1984) would put it. This understanding expands the idea of being as being-with, and as being-in-the-world. It is in evidence in the notion of choreography that I introduced earlier by reference to the mother–infant dyad whereby each element produces the other in terms of activities marked by hospitality, generosity, pleasure and attachment, as well as conflict, mingling the time of the body with the 'time of the soul'. So, the position cannot be collapsed into the either/or of good and bad objects, but suggests dynamics that already diffract subjectivity into the ambivalence of and/and while filling with content the liminal and sublime dimension of beingness.

Fourth, the models for the emplotment of experience already exist in the culture, inscribed in the practices of the everyday, dispersed in tales, novels, films, parables, stereotypes and so on. That is to say, the models or plots or scripts which we use to make sense of our experiences exist as a given in the culture; we do not invent them from scratch or choose them as 'free' agents, though clearly new models and emplotments are constantly generated, especially in modernity. They include narratives that construct the horizon of expectation, instructing us about what we should anticipate and desire. Culture, therefore, delimits the space of experience and the horizon of expectation. The problem of refiguration involves the articulation of the space of experience with the space of expectation. The plots or scripts in discourses of 'identity' provide the elements for the figuration and the refiguration of experience, so that every named subject is not only a figured self but also one who is constantly refigured in the light of the narratives that each of us applies to ourselves in the process of questioning ourselves in relation to acts and deeds; for instance, what it means, by reference to what we do and say, to be a man, or a mother, or a friend, or a black person, and so on. The process of refiguration, we can see, rectifies previous identities as a result of a self instructed by the norms and values that are constructed in discourses of identity, although the who, as singularity, remains the same, as the named person, the one who is called to responsibility.[8]

At the analytical level, the coarticulation of the space of experience and the horizon of expectation refers to the process whereby the historical dimension of narration is interlaced with the biographical dimension. Two temporalisations cross each other to constitute a particular subjectivity at the point of intersection. A who or 'self' 'happens' at the relay point or points where the history of a culture, sedimented in its stock of knowledge, its narrations, its 'texts', joins with the history or biography of a particular individual. In this way every self is sutured in history. But this suturing, or folding, requires the participation of others: as interlocutors, imagined or not, as models or ideal egos, as those in the gaze of whom recognition is bestowed or refused, as elements of the lifeworld that validate particular selves. The subject, besides, is always in process – unless we are speaking about the situations in which the two temporalisations are fused, as in fundamentalist or totalitarian discourses, closing off the possibility of being otherwise.

I use the term apprenticeship to refer to the self-reflective, but learned, autopoetic character of the figuration and refiguration of subjectivity. It is not reducible to the model of internalisation or to a Nietzschean 'willing'. It is in part a way of appropriating, making one's own what belongs to the 'we' or intersubjective dimension of culture, a way of folding the outside inside oneself, a folding that changes the self. However, identification involves not only the folding of an outside to form an interiority, as Rose (1996) has argued. It is closer to what Foucault (1984) suggests in the notion of an ethics and an aesthetics of the self, or the notion of a 'hermeneutics of desire', but without the volitional slippages in Foucault. Apprenticeship suggests that it matters what kind of narratives we are talking about, for instance whether they are religious, secular, ethical, political, critical and so on. We know for example that particular narratives, particular forms and 'texts', are more conducive to critical self-questioning than others. The problem of ideology and that of the 'way of being' belong to this exploration of subjectivity. Ricoeur's thesis about the mimetic function of narrative indicates the broad shape of the mechanisms involved, though there remain many aspects of the mechanisms involved that only ethnographic work can uncover.

Finally, I must clarify the sense of embodiment which I have in mind. The orientation I want to highlight is informed by all the work which has drawn attention to the fact of difference, specifically, of gender and race, and by the standpoint expressed in Merleau-Ponty's radically anti-Cartesian view that the body is the mind's body and the mind is the body's mind. This view clearly rejects the dualism of body and mind and the dualism of psychic and bodily phenomena. It proposes a dynamic interrelation between them. The relationship is a diachronic one, so that the body is altered in the course of its encounters with the phenomenal world of objects and people.[9] Furthermore, Merleau-Ponty says: 'The experience of my own body and the experience of the other are two sides of the same Being ... the other is the horizon or other side of this experience' (1968, p. 225). He argues that there is an articulation of the other's body with mine which 'does not empty me ... but on the contrary redoubles me with an alter ego' (1968, p. 233). The idea, then, is of an intertwining of the world and the human, of interiority and exteriority, of the I and the Other; it evokes, analogically, the relation of a curve to its hollow. Such a relation is not representable as such; it can be apprehended only in the mode of the sublime, if – developing some indications in Lyotard (1994) – we understand the sublime to be the experience through which the invisible part of the visible is disclosed to being, so that the sublime makes present the absent-presence which inhabits it, the elements beyond representation, and which thickens and endows what appears with a transcendent yet ontic or phenomenal dimension. The sublime, it could be said, is a passionate experience of the 'thrownness of being'; that is, the fact that we find ourselves thrown into and abandoned in the world from the beginning and have to live that experience as an aspect of the questioning of ourselves (Heidegger, 1962). Equally, one can understand it as an effect, at the aesthetic-expressive level, of the apprehension of the ungrounded aspect of being. To that extent, the sublime is an intimation of the 'there is', in the Levinasian sense.[10] Embodiment, then, according to my analysis, inscribes a relation to the other, a relation to mind and psyche, and a relation to the objectal world. A different conceptualisation of the subject begins to emerge with this approach, consistent with a critical phenomenology, far from the modernist (or the religious) projection of being into the endlessly deferred moment of a plenitude to come, and its inherently totalising temptations.

The notion of the Other as host opens up a relation to history and to the intersubjective such that it is possible to imagine the body as the monument in which the time of one's life and the time of the community are 'inscrypted'; that is, we can propose that the body functions as both text and crypt, the site of inscription as well as of burial, the at once legible yet secret place in which are recorded the events and experiences of a life. So, like narrative, corporeity too is a guardian of time in that it is the field (or 'clearing', to use Merleau-Ponty's terminology) in which space and time interpenetrate to produce 'a historical landscape and a quasi-geographical inscription of history' (Merleau-Ponty, 1968, p. 259).

At the level of description, then – as opposed to the level of the economies involved – the process of subjectivity involves three dimensions that are analytically distinct but experientially triune. The question of affect is relevant to the analysis of the details. I will deal with that later. For now we can distinguish the three modes of temporality involved in subjectivity according to, first, historical time or intersubjective time, which is also the time of the community (and its metonymies, like nation, race, and the implications for how concepts like nation and race gather to themselves the swollen symbolisms of the authentic community, erasing differences). Second, the temporal dimension of subjectivity refers to memory time and biographical time, it being understood that memory is the form in which subjective as well as intersubjective experiences and narrativisations of events and action are folded into the interiority of particular selves. Lastly, my arguments so far indicate that the body too functions as archive and monument, the living and material repository of the time of one's life: the body remembers everything, but in codes and folds and capacities. For example, there is a sense in which the hand that has learned to play the piano is no longer the same hand. An associated point is that it is in the intertwining of body and objectal world that newness is grounded.

The three are coarticulated in the process of constitution of every particular subjectivity. The relays and mediations linking the different dimensions of being-in-the-world are established through tropes, chains of signifiers, displacements, 'fleshy' memories, activities and so on, each with their affective charge, that construct the symbolic and semiotic universe of signifying practices.

Becoming Otherwise

I will use the chapter from Fanon's *Black Skin, White Masks* (BSWM) entitled 'The Fact of Blackness' to unpack and problematise this process.[11] This will enable me to consider the question of subjective change, and to suggest modifications of the analytical apparatus.

Fanon's language is deceptively complex, if one pays attention to the underlying philosophical and psychoanalytic discourses that inform the text. The chapter begins with an instance of Othering which brings to crisis the economy of identification for the colonised subject. The chapter basically presents three different modalities of subjectivity, corresponding to three modes of being a black person in a racist white culture. The first 'identity' to appear is that of Fanon the French-educated Martinican scholar, 'civilised', 'clever', 'handsome', the cosmopolitan intellectual who is supposed to be able to rise above prejudices, convinced about the equality of all human beings asserted in humanist philosophy. These assumptions are invalidated by the encounter with the fact of racism, inscribed in the objectifying gaze of a little boy who points him out to his mother. Fanon uses the iteration of the phrase 'dirty nigger', 'Look mother, a Negro', coupling it with expressions of fear and loathing (BSWM, pp. 77–81), to disrupt the seeming ontological security of the black man and to precipitate the crisis of identity. The black body becomes the intransigent signifier of savagery, defectiveness, lack, the colonialist stereotypes graven on the black body which upset the performative mimicry of the 'civilized man' that the colonized have learned so well. Fanon says that in that moment of racist objectification he became split into three, as 'the corporeal schema crumbled, its place taken by a racial epidermal schema' (BSWM, p. 79), relocated, or reallocated, to different disjunct spaces, that could not be reconciled: 'I was responsible for my body, for my race, for my ancestors' (BSWM, p. 79). The whole of his existence is invaded by what he interestingly calls 'historicity' (BSWM, p. 79).

The analysis of the reflections that Fanon develops from that encounter enables one to correlate the disjunctures of identity with temporal disjunctures, here those referring to the time of the body, of ancestors and of the race. Fanon is split between the historical-time of the race and ancestry, the memory-time of biographical experiences, and the body-time of his being-in-the world as a black, colonised man. The dislocations of his identity – as when he is at first unable to countenance the reality of blackness in the occidentalist discourse of otherness, and so wonders for a moment whether he is the one who is interpellated in the encounters he recounts – are lived directly by Fanon in his body 'given back to him sprawled out, distorted, recolored, clad in mourning...', no longer recognisable within the narratives of the good, respectful *nègre* (BSWM, p. 80). Blackness becomes the unsayable and unrepresentable, at least until he is able to find a counter-narrative to give voice to the existential reality of his difference. Today we recognise this mutism to be the effect of the absence of a language to speak difference (or its suppression or pathologisation). Feminist and 'postcolonial' analyses of this condition have shown it to be a form of ontological violence and an experience of abjection and trauma (see, for instance, Kristeva, 1982; Irigaray, 1985).

Fanon's account of the process he went through records several stages in the attempt to reconstitute a liveable subjectivity. The first reaction is anger, expressed in the determination to shock and provoke by performatively enacting the black stereotype imagined in racist discourse. There follows a painful search for the traces and the memory of the humiliations to which the colonised other has been subjected, and the dispossessions of power, agency, ontological security, culture which have accompanied subjugation. The process of disidentification and refiguration which Fanon relives for us then proceeds through the celebration of blackness, and the different narrativisations of African history and culture that the discourse of Negritude has constructed, in particular in the form of poetry (of Cesaire, Roumain, Senghor). He identifies with the heroic and mythical figures of Africa, finding in them and in the narratives of their deeds the support for disidentification and the instantiation of an alternative subjectivity. His body is no longer lived as the abject body, but the valued monument in which are inscribed and buried, that is, in which are inscrypted, the memory of the race and its deeds and its hopes. That shift is the prelude for a long search for an Other way of being, to be invented as part of the creative process of becoming otherwise, developed as a challenge to the objectifications of ontological violence (here racism) as well as the fixities of essentialism (here in elements of Negritude from which Fanon distances himself).

The refigurations of identity which Fanon undertakes display the effects of the application of the narratives that exist in discourses of the subject in philosophy, in colonialist and racist discourse and in the critical and dissident texts of resistance to colonial subject(ificat)ion. The rectifications of the self which he describes lead on to the hope that an unnamed and unnameable Other agent of history will emerge – though in Fanon's problematic of agency, still inflected by existentialism, it announces a rather tragic subject (BSWM, p. 98).[12] My analysis of his account indicates that the transformation of subjectivity involves a working through which relays the cognitive, the affective and the embodied dimensions of subjectivity in a complex, mobile and indeterminate process in which neither element is privileged. The mechanisms involved in this process of change clearly cannot be accounted for within the model of the self-steering mechanisms which the discourse of self-management describes, or within the model of social construction alone. The former, although it posits the folding of an outside within the subject – for instance, to constitute a 'soul', as in Nikolas Rose's (1989, 1996) work – does not make a place for the unaccountable, liminal element in the process of formation; the latter model does not deal well with the psychic dimension of subjectivity, thus with affect, nor, either, with the question of embodiment.

Furthermore, from my point of view, these models inadequately theorise the dimension of history or time in the process of constitution and reconstitution of identities. For instance, to return to the text of Fanon, we could say that time is truly out of joint for him, and for black identity, haunted by the history of colonialist violence and racist stereotypes that visit the living in the present, for nothing has been laid to rest yet, so long as it is still the case that 'the white man is not only the Other, but also the master, whether real or imaginary' (BSWM, p. 98 n.).[13] One can recognise in the reference to the Hegelian master–slave thematic of recognition the problematic of the constitution of subjects by reference to the other's gaze. This problematic, while it brings into view the centrality of the relation to the Other, and indeed shows that it is the recognition of the 'master' by the Other/the 'slave' which is essential for the identity of the master to be validated at all, does not clarify the question of the positioning of subjects in the economy of recognition. For one thing, the question of who occupies which place in this economy – here, the white man as both *Other* (in the Lacanian sense) and master – a matter to do with power, is not grounded in a genealogy of subjugation/subjectification, and the correlated history of resistance. For another, the mechanism of recognition in the formation of identity acquires its specific content from the historically produced and transmitted narrations of belonging and ancestry, 'roots' and 'routes', that have effects from birth. The functioning of all these narratives, together with the disjunctures in the lived experience of identity, need to be taken into account in the problem of transformation, related to a politics of transfiguration. In the case of Fanon, the critical elements in the discourse of modernity – the references to aspects of existentialism and of Enlightenment thought, or of psychoanalytic theory – as much as the counter-hegemonic and insurrectional texts of Negritude were necessary for disidentification.

I want to draw from the example some lessons for theorising subjective change. I will begin with a rather different analysis of the effects of historicity and of temporal disjunctures for the figuration and refiguration of subjectivity, drawing from Derrida's (1993) seemingly oblique questioning of who we are in the present, implicating an ethos, as Foucault did in his own refiguration of the Enlightenment and its legacy. The detour by way of spectres of Marx, added to the more general theory of identity in Ricoeur, will enable me to argue that the rewriting of the history of subaltern subjects and the reconstitution of their identities require a 'hauntology'. Derrida used the term to signal the extent to which the answer to the question of how to live, that is, the question of an ethos of being, triggers both ontological issues as well as issues to do with the historicity of being, thus with responsibility and justice. The point of view of responsibility and justice arises, firstly, because the foreknowledge of the consequences of our action in the present eliminates the excuse that we did not know what we were doing: it makes us accountable. Furthermore, as I pointed out in an earlier section, when we think of the present as a relation between the three modalities of time – the having-been, the to-come and the becoming-present – and if we have access to the reality of these moments in the form of narration, and thus in terms of the relation to the Other that gives social or intersubjective content to them and to the lifeworld, the question which is revealed is that of debt. For Derrida, this is a debt of justice and of dignity and a debt of an after-life (*sur-vie*), as he points out (1993, p. 15, 16, 17, and also in 1995). It is incalculable since it is owed especially to those who are no longer alive, victims of an injustice that cannot now be righted, and to those not yet alive for whom we must take responsibility in deciding upon one's action.[14] This aspect of historicity, as basis and trigger for responsibility, thus unfolds into the question of memory, which, in turn returns us to the dimension of affect.

I draw out these connections in order to propose that the changing of subjects, which correlates with a politics of identity, implicates a politics of memory to the extent that the process of (re)memorisation, via the idea of historicity as responsibility, is in solidarity with an idea of justice. The problematic of subjectivity that I am developing shows why the project of a new way of being for postcolonial and postmodern – thus transmodern – subjects, thought in terms of a new ethos, requires, additionally, a 'hauntology', that is to say, it requires a critical analysis which juxtaposes the kind of philosophical discourse of being which I am signalling with elements of the psychoanalytic discourse of subjectivity to bring to light the liminal and uncanny elements in the constitution of subjects. Such a deconstructive task deals with that which haunts being because of the trace of an immemorial loss, and that of countless other losses, and adds it to the effects of what human beings 'forget' in the course of their constitution. It therefore correlates the refiguration of a history of being, or, at the concrete level, the refiguration of particular identities, with the process of 'working through' in the psychoanalytic sense, as Lyotard (1988) and Ricoeur (1988) have established by reference to the process of the renarrativisation of subjectivity and the rememorisation of history respectively. Hauntology, therefore, suggests the combination of the questioning of our way of being, the questioning about who we are in the present, and the work of working through and mourning. The former questionings implicate an ethics and an aesthetics of being, as Foucault and others have argued, while the latter task, especially in view of the juxtapositions that I am proposing, implicates a work which draws from a non-egological psychoanalytic discourse of the subject.

The line of analysis of subjective transformation that I have been elaborating, while it makes visible notions of historicity, debt, ethical responsibility – especially in the sense of responsibility for the Other and of historical responsibility – has introduced an additional element. That element is the standpoint indicated by aesthetics, that is to say, the forms and the experience which express the un(re)presentable or unaccountable or sublime aspects of beingness which the problematic of subjectivity must recognise in order to encompass the complexity of the process of the constitution and reconstitution of subjectivity.[15] The implied inadequacy of one-dimensional approaches alone in addressing this complexity, for instance the reliance on the cognitive viewpoint in psychology or on an unreconstituted, egocentric psychoanalytic discourse, is revealed when one has to deal with cases that refer to people traumatised by a violence which strikes at the core of ontological security, for instance, concerning victims of ethnic cleansing, or working through the legacy of the Aboriginal 'stolen children', or that of the disappeared and tortured, or involving the consequences of modern forms of slavery in many industries and practices globally. In other words, the urge to rethink the theorisation of subjectivity is driven by the recognition that there are widespread problems today, affecting individuals and whole communities, that exhaust the resources of 'orthodox' theorisations of subjectivity.

Towards Transfiguration

In conclusion, let me summarise my analysis of subjective transfiguration in the form of a number of propositions deriving from the preceding arguments. It will be seen that the theorisation of change cannot be separated from the theorisation of the process of formation of subjects and selves. In my account, I have emphasised the compossibility and intertwining of self and Other (intimated in the notions of choreography and apprenticeship, and of being-with, which inscribe the primacy of the relation to the Other), the importance of language, particularly in the form of narrative, so that every 'self' is entangled with others in emplotments of lives that are open to rectifications. I have also emphasised the wider canvas, summarised in the concept of historicity, tied up with the claim that temporality is fundamental to human beings and to the existential meaning of being-in-the-world. This, in turn, introduced in one's understanding of subjectivity the point of view of its location in relation to a genealogy and to a concept of the lifeworld as host and as condition of possibility (to the extent that the subject belongs to it as 'flesh', understood in terms of a relation to the world that includes but exceeds the spatial dimension). I have drawn attention to a theorisation which makes visible the ethical and aesthetic dimension in the process of becoming of subjects.

So, concerning change, we must assume, to begin with, that some specific event initiates it, an event capable of triggering or disclosing the disjunctures which incite a particular self or group to question its way of being. Such disruptive events could cohere around a spatial and cultural disturbance, like migration, the translation across borders of identity, or a traumatic experience arising from political conflict and its consequences, like war, or the introduction of a counter-hegemonic account of the lifeworld, or an aesthetic experience that shakes being to its foundation, provoking the trembling of being in the face of the sublime or the ecstatic. Clearly, the experience of oppression and exploitation of whatever kind sensitises those who suffer from it for a discourse or a narrative that promises an emancipation from such conditions.

It is clear that critical and theoretical analysis, that is, the production of dissident or counter-hegemonic discourses, is necessary but not sufficient. We have known for a long time now that the existence of (counter)ideologies, for example to do with racism, does not by itself produce racists or persuade racists to change their values. The cognitive cannot by itself motivate the process of redirecting or recathecting affect which is central to the transfiguration of subjects.

What is therefore needed is something that works, additionally, at the level of affect, that is, a discursive practice that plugs into the economy of desire. It could be argued that this practice includes any work which attempts to disclose the sublime or unpresentable aspect of beingness. I have argued that such signifying practices, outside the scope of the problematic of representation, since they involve the domain of fantasy, bring into play the standpoints of aesthetics and of ethics and so direct attention to the work of *poiesis* and to a hermeneutics of desire. The central place of the writings of Negritude in Fanon's journey of self-transformation is an exemplary illustration of the need for works which not only refigure the experiential in a register which 'derealises' the seeming fixity of the world, but, equally, give voice to the yearning which drives the ethical and the aesthetic.[16] The importance of the imagination, and the register of the imaginary, is indicated by the fact that the poietic dimension in 'art' significantly includes a non-representational form like music. It is worth noting, as an extension of this point, that Toni Morrison, speaking about the functioning of music for psychic survival, has argued that on the American scene of the subjugation of the other, music inscribes that by which 'Black Americans were sustained and healed and nurtured' (Morrison, in Gilroy, 1993b, p. 181). Her novels, she claims, attempt to transcribe the 'texture' of that musical idiom.

Furthermore, the politics of transfiguration implicates practices that must be able to emplot the present within narratives that relate it to a past and to a future, putting into play both the historicity/temporality of being-in-the-world and a narrative of emancipation, that is to say, a narrative about the anticipation of a time to come that holds out the hope of the recovery of loss or the overcoming of insufficiency and lack, or the redress of some profound injustice, or indeed any promissory narrative, such as the 'promise of joy'. History and emancipatory narratives are intrinsic to the process.

We need a conceptualisation of the self which correlates mind and body according to a critical phenomenology, developing some elements from Merleau-Ponty's later work, bearing in mind too, the standpoint of differently gendered bodies, as in, say, Butler (1993), Grosz (1994), Irigaray (1984), and others. It is clear from what I have said that this theory of the subject is irreducible to any solipsistic or egological model of subjectivity, but promotes a profoundly social model.

In my analysis, two series of terms relay the subjective and intersubjective dimension. On the one side we find finitude, fragility, loss, the gaping of being, solitude, suffering, historicity. On the other side, we encounter being-with, being-in-the-world, hospitality, generosity, friendship, filiality, gift, Eros and its metonymies – caress, love, fecundity, voluptuosity (see Irigaray, 1984; Levinas, 1969), historicity. Historicity functions as 'point de capiton' (Lacan, 1977). But historicity implies a responsibility, argues Derrida (1995, pp. 5–8). And its principal modality is narrativity. We know from Ricoeur that narrative is beholden to the relation to the Other, both in the sense that the storied self is entangled with the narratives of significant Others and because it is the relation to particular Others that determines the choice of the emplotment of action that expresses the 'who' of agency in the narrative. Narration, therefore, draws into the analysis of subjectivity the relation to the Other, which in turn invokes concepts of debt and gift and, thus, of responsibility for the Other.

The relay between the different levels or dimensions of being-in-the-world is established through tropes, chains of signifiers, displacements, and so on, that is, through signifying practices that are the sites for the inscription of power and of affect. This means that choreography and apprenticeship relay each other, relaying the psychic and the social – and implicating their historicisation – producing paradoxes and ambivalences that are lived as disjunctures.

All of this means that changing the subject, or becoming – Otherwise, is not merely a technical or developmental problem: it is, equally, a fundamentally ethical and political issue. Hence the implications for a poetics and a politics of transfiguration. For the ethical standpoint obliges us to judge and to take sides, on the side of the oppressed everywhere.[17]

Notes

1. This is an extended version of the paper presented at the Millennium Critical Psychology Conference, UWS Sydney, May 1999. It is informed by the discussions I have had with V. Walkerdine, W. Hollway, several participants at the conference and colleagues at the Universities of East London and Nottingham Trent.
2. My understanding of occidentalism means that it cannot be reduced to either the West or modernity; it describes an imaginary and a conceptual space that inscribe several coarticulated elements, including phallogo-eurocentrism, and it refers to the historical process, complex and contingent, whereby that space has become hegemonic and global.
3. The basic reference here is to the work of Heidegger (1962), and Ricoeur's (1988) rephrasing of his ontological problematic in *Time and Narrative*.
4. I would argue that the consciousness of time, the consciousness of finitude, the emergence of language and the anticipation of death are correlated events or developments in the history of human beings. I would further relate these developments to that of representation and of what the inadequate term 'art' is supposed to designate. My argument is that the urge to express the intimation of an un(re)presentable dimension in human existence is the first sign distinguishing humans from other species. Human beings proper begin with the first musical instrument and song, the first time that they tried to carve or etch on the face of the earth the afterimage, the echo or murmur of the realisation that to know time is to experience loss as an intrinsic, inevitable condition, and that there may be ways of communicating this to one's others (and to the *Other*), so that this communication becomes a monument and memento that one bestows as redeeming gift. Furthermore – and this is another aspect of the temporality of being – I would argue that the space of the 'happening' of being should be conceptualised in terms of *epokhe*, if we understand this term to refer to trace and event, rather than *punctum* or *arche*, point or origin. My view is therefore different from Husserl's (1970) understanding of *epokhe* which sets the *epokhe* beyond or outside the space of becoming, thus in a transcendental, apodictic domain, as his discussion of Descartes and of the 'phenomenological-transcendental epoche' in *The Crisis of European Sciences* would indicate.
5. A long history of the subject within the western tradition from Augustine to Derrida leads us to the point where we can both assume and problematise this proposition: assume it in the sense of recognising that it directs attention to a basic element of what it means to be human at all, and problematise it in the sense that this recognition itself opens our questioning of being towards a view of the historicity of being and towards the standpoint of memory, of being-in-the-world which redoubles the who and the 'I think' with an Other within intersubjectivity. I develop this standpoint in *Occidentalism* (Venn, 2000).
6. The notions of lack and loss have references well beyond the more familiar terrain of psychoanalysis, namely, within philosophy, for instance in existentialist thought which itself elaborates the older theme of a fundamental insufficiency of being, or within theological and religious conceptualisations of being, both in Semitic (Judaic, Christian, Islamic) and non-Semitic discourses, according to which the human being is a fallen or imperfect or lesser being when measured against the idea of the infinite perfection of God.
7. Language also has a relation to death, to the extent that the anticipation of death, or the consciousness of finitude is bound up with the faculty of speech. See Heidegger in *Being and Time*, or Agamben (1991).

8. In saying this, I am taking into account arguments developed not only in Levinas (say, 1969), but in Derrida (1995), Lyotard (1993), and Ricoeur's grounding of responsibility in fragility, and thus in the future consequences as much as in the present effects of our actions: 'The appeal, the injunction, and also the trust which proceed from the fragile, result in its being always *another* who declares us responsible, or, as Levinas says, 'calls us to responsibility' (Ricoeur, 1996, p. 17; emphasis in original). Responsibility, in the sense I am using it, exceeds the discourse of law.

9. Several interesting themes emerge in this connection, such as the further elaboration of a socialised biology developing the point of view of the dynamic interpenetration of the biological–natural and the social–cultural, but avoiding the dogmas and simplifications associated with sociobiology and geneticism, that is, with strategies that reduce the one to the other.

10. The reference regarding the relevance of a concept like 'there is' is to Levinas generally, the later Derrida (say, 1992, 1995), Merleau-Ponty (1968), Ricoeur (1992). See also Lyotard's (1994) analysis of the sublime. The 'there is' stands for a number of recognitions: the always-already character of our beingness-in-the-world (and, thus, the refusal of originary narratives of being/of the subject), the 'thrownness' of being, the liminal aspect of the temporality of being as being-in-time, the intuition of the trace and difference of the other in the constitution of self. I have established elsewhere (Venn, 1999, 2000) the connections between notions of the sublime and the 'there is' sketched in this chapter.

11. A better translation would have been 'The Lived Experience of the Black man'.

12. I should point out that the existentialist narrative of being which informs Fanon cast a rather negative shadow on his analysis, since his discourse adds the nothingness of being in existentialism to the fact that racist discourse already reduces the racialised Other to nothing, a non-subject, which is why, I think, Fanon gives us a rather anguished vision of what is to come. For instance, we could make sense of the emphasis on the place of violence in his analysis of the decolonisation of mind if we add the thematic of violence in, say, Sartre's *Roads to Freedom* to the question of the functioning of catharthic violence in the process of liberation from the master–slave dynamic.

13. In postcolonial times concepts of modernisation, westernisation and development have displaced the trope of the white man in the economy of desire and recognition to signify the projected ideal in the imaginary becoming of the subject and the community.

14. Fanon says at one point: 'I am answerable in my body and in my heart for what was done to my brother' (1970, pp. 86, 87). For an elaboration, see Derrida's discussion of the secrets of European historical responsibility, namely that what Europe has 'forgotten' is 'the memory of its history *as* history of responsibility' (1995, p. 5; emphasis in original). His analysis is supported by the work of Levinas as a whole, Ricoeur on memory and indebtedness, and also Heidegger's (1962) notion of 'care'.

15. My elaboration of these issues appears in *Occidentalism*. See also Bowie (1990) and the work of Walter Benjamin generally, for example, the essay, 'The Storyteller' (1973).

16. Fanon's style and narrative deliberately break the codes of analytic discourse, giving substance to his claim to make himself 'the poet of the world' (BSWM, p. 91).

17. An implication is the development of a new ethics, post-Kantian and, in some sense, post-Levinasian, which I attempt to do in *Occidentalism*.

Bibliography

Agamben, G. *Language and Death* (Stanford University Press, 1991).
Benjamin, J. *Shadow of the Other* (New York and London: Routledge, 1998).
Benjamin, W. *Illuminations* (London: Fontana, 1973).
Bhabha, H. 'Cultures In-Between', in S. Hall and P. du Gay (eds), *Questions of Cultural Identity* (London: Sage, 1996).
Bowie, A. *Aesthetics and Subjectivity. From Kant to Nietzsche* (Manchester University Press, 1990).
Butler, J. *Bodies that Matter* (New York and London: Routledge, 1993).
Butler, J. *The Psychic Life of Power* (Stanford University Press, 1997).
Derrida, J. 'Some Statements and Truisms about Neo-logisms, Newisms, Postisms, Parasitisms, and Other Small Seismisms', in D. Carroll (ed.), *The States of Theory* (Stanford University Press, 1990).
Derrida, J. *Given Time: 1. Counterfeit Money*, tr. P. Kamuf (University of Chicago Press, 1992).
Derrida, J. *Les Spectres de Marx* (Paris: Editions Galilée, 1993).
Derrida, J. *The Gift of Death*, tr. D. Wills (University of Chicago Press, 1995).
Fanon, F. *Black Skin, White Masks* (London: Paladin, 1970).
Foucault, M. 'What is Enlightenment', in *The Foucault Reader*, P. Rabinow (ed.) (Harmondsworth: Penguin, 1984).
Gilroy, P. *The Black Atlantic* (London: Verso, 1993a).
Gilroy, P. (ed.), *Small Acts* (London and New York: Serpent's Tail, 1993b) 175–82.
Grosz, E. V*olatile Bodies. Towards a Corporeal Feminism* (Bloomington: Indiana University Press, 1994).
Hall, S. (1996a) 'Introduction. Who Needs Identity', in S. Hall and P. du Gay (eds) *Questions of Cultural Identity* (London: Sage, 1996).
Hall, S. (1996b) 'When was "the Post-colonial"? Thinking at the Limit', in I. Chambers and L. Curti (eds), *The Post-Colonial Question* (New York and London: Routledge, 1996).
Heidegger, M. *Being and Time*, tr. J. Macquarie and E. Robinson (Oxford: Basil Blackwell, 1962).
Husserl, E. *The Crisis of European Sciences and Transcendental Phenomenology*, tr. D. Carr (Evanston, Illinois: Northwestern University Press, 1970).
Irigaray, L. *Ethique de la différence sexuelle* (Paris: Les Editions de Minuit, 1984).
Irigaray, L. *Speculum: Of the Other Women*, tr. Gillian C. Gill (Ithaca and New York: Cornell University Press, 1985).
Kristeva, J. *Powers of Horror*, tr. L. Roudiez (New York: Columbia University Press, 1982).
Lacan, J. *Ecrits, a selection*, tr. A. Sheridan, (London: Tavistock, 1977).
Levinas, E. *Totality and Infinity*, tr. A. Lingis (Pittsburg: Duquesne University Press, 1969).
Lyotard, J. F. 'Reécrire la Modernité', in *Cahiers de Philosophie*, no. 5 (1988).
Lyotard, J. F. *Un Trait d'Union. Les éditions Le Griffon d'argile* (Quebec: Sainte-Foy, 1993).
Lyotard, J. F. *Lessons on the Analytique of the Sublime*, tr. E. Rottenberg (Stanford University Press, 1994).
Merleau-Ponty, M. *The Visible and the Invisible*, ed. C. Lefort, tr. A. Lingis (Evanston, Illinois: Northwestern University Press, 1968).

Ricoeur, P. *Time and Narrative*, vol. 3 (University of Chicago Press, 1988).
Ricoeur, P. *Oneself as Another*, tr. K. Blamey (University of Chicago Press, 1992).
Ricoeur, P. 'Fragility and Responsibility', in P. Ricoeur, *The Hermeneutics of Action*, ed. R. Kearney (London: Sage, 1996).
Rose, N. *Governing the Soul* (London: Routledge, 1989).
Rose, N. 'Identity, Genealogy, History', in S. Hall and P. du Gay (eds), *Questions of Cultural Identity* (London: Sage, 1996).
Venn, C. 'Beyond Enlightenment? After the Subject of Foucault, Who Comes?', *Theory, Culture & Society*, 14(3) (1997).
Venn, C. 'Narrating the Postcolonial', in M. Featherstone and S. Lash (eds), *Spaces of Culture* (London: Sage, 1999).
Venn, C. *Occidentalism. Modernity and Subjectivity* (London: Sage, 2000).

Part II

ETHNICITY, HYBRIDITY, TRAUMA

Introduction

VALERIE WALKERDINE

Couze Venn's Chapter 4 in the last section also serves as a fitting introduction to this one, by reminding us that we need to look both backwards and forwards to rethink the subject beyond the western modernist project. In this part, the chapters deal in several different ways with that subject encountered very differently in locations as diverse as India and Northern Ireland.

Erika Apfelbaum (Chapter 5) begins by an exploration of the ways in which we do indeed need to rememorialise the past in the face of the terror of loss of identity. However, in the examples of loss of identity that Apfelbaum poignantly presents for us – survivors of genocide or of torture, or refugees, for example – there is a desire for silence, for forgetting that which it is so very hard to say. However difficult it is, though, she makes clear that it is much easier for the children of 'survivors' if the parents make a discursive and emotional link between the past and the present. There can be no utopian looking forward without equally looking backward. She quotes the French version of the *Internationale* which states in verse 1: 'of the past let us make a tabula rasa' and look only forward. It is the failure to look backwards, as Venn also points out, that prevents the possibility of new forms of subjectivity.

John Cash (Chapter 6) examines the troubled times of Northern Ireland's attempts to end the very prolonged conflict. He argues that matters of discourse and subjectivity are absolutely central to an understanding both of the impasses and of the possibility of resolving them. He uses psychoanalytic theory to make a link between discursive positions and psychic mechanisms which he suggests accompany those positions. In particular, he examines what he describes as inclusivist and exclusivist positions. The exclusivist position is organised according to Melanie Klein's paranoid-schizoid position, while the inclusivist refers to the depressive position, both pre-Oedipal unconscious forms of defence in relation to the mother. He goes on to analyse the exclusivist stance taken by the unionist leader Ian Paisley and demonstrates how Paisley excludes other unionist leaders such as David Trimble who take a different and more inclusivist position. Cash's aim is to demonstrate the way in which any political negotiations, for example, those following on from the Good Friday Agreement, will stumble when they touch on differences in position which themselves bring up for negotiators and their supporters complex psychic defences. For Cash, then, the political negotiations cannot be understood or indeed be effective without an engagement with the unconscious emotional politics which are entwined within them. For change to occur, he argues, 'the unconscious rules that organise subjectivity and intersubjectivity' for the adherents of the exclusivist position also have to change for that political grouping. In other words, the exclusivist group has to shift its own group identity. What is most important for Cash is the ability of the exclusivist group leaders to deal with the unconscious anxieties of the group members. It is only when changes at the level of policy and political discourse are matched by emotional moves, that are also subjective shifts, that any lasting change can occur. If we are to take the lessons of other chapters seriously, this might mean, as for Apfelbaum, a reworking of the pain and losses of the past in order to look forward to a changed future.

Stephen Frosh (Chapter 7) also uses Kleinian and post-Kleinian psychoanalysis to make sense of the racism of white working-class schoolboys in London. In particular, he explores the way that some boys express confusions and contradictions around their own identity and their relations with black and Asian boys. He uses psychoanalysis to explore the way in which Otherness operates to contain split off and projected parts of the white boys' psyche – parts that it is hard to own. As Frosh puts it, 'those despairing fragilities and brutal violences which, if encountered directly as part of the subjects' own identity, might lead to self-hatred and dissolution'. The boys express deep ambivalence towards black boys often put forward as friends and to their own relation to aspects of black culture such as clothing and music for example. He uses Joel Kovel's work on racism and capitalism to explore the way in which multiplicity and sensuality have been projected onto the black Other as a counterpoint to a puritan capitalist asceticism. In this way it is possible to link the racisms enacted by these schoolboys with that contained within the west's anxiety about violence and sensuality and thus repudiation of its Other.

Swatija Manorama (Chapter 8), in keeping with the theme of multiplicity and the need to understand subjectivity in a manner which remembers but goes beyond the west, presents the necessity of moving towards a complex sense of multiplicity which recognises the complex and multiple history of subject forms within India itself. The Indian project of selfhood is a nationalistic one which forgets its fraught, plural and multiple history, she argues. She discusses the debates surrounding the idea of a Hindu mind and the way in which a supposed Indian identity is forged by producing a conservative narrative of Indian tradition by running roughshod over other possible narratives. For the Indian middle class, the loss of possible Indian subject positions is taken over by the trappings of western subjectivity under globalism, thus increasing the need to explore the possibility of counter-narratives of multiple Indian identities. Like other authors earlier in the volume, Manorama notes the difficulty of the coming to terms with multiplicity but the absolute necessity of it for the possibility of a different kind of (Indian) polity.

The four chapters in this section explore some of the ways in which political transformation necessarily involves a complex intertwining of the production of subjectivity. The need to look backwards both at the biographical past and at history in order to move forward politically is signalled in the chapters by Apfelbaum and Cash. The ways in which change is impossible without a consideration of the complex unconscious aspects is considered by Cash at the level of political change in Northern Ireland and by Frosh with respect to transformations of racism. Manorama presents similar issues of self and polity in a non-western context, the plural narratives of Indian history, being reworked by Hindu nationalism and globalisation into unitary narratives of self, which dangerously cover over a plurality which must be remembered, memorialised and worked through in order to face the possibility of a different future.

5

Uprooted Communities, Silenced Cultures and the Need for Legacy

ERIKA APFELBAUM[1]

In memoriam: **Maurice Halbwachs**[2]

On the Memory of a Wandering Child ...

A century and a half ago, a ten-year-old girl was found wandering through the woods near a small town in France. She could speak, but was unable to give any clear account of who she was and what had happened to her. She vaguely recalled having travelled across a wide expanse of water, and her story was eventually pieced together: she must have been a slave somewhere in the Caribbean colonies in the service of a woman whose husband later threw the girl out of the household. At an age when she normally should have had quite clear recollections of past events, this uprooted child was unable to distinctly remember her earlier life experiences. This puzzling anecdote of loss of memory provides the takeoff point for Maurice Halbwachs's extensive analysis of the social and collective groundings of individual memory and of what today we call identity. In the introduction to his 1924 book *The Social Framework for Memory*, he asks: 'What remains of the past when one is suddenly and/or brutally uprooted and transported to an unfamiliar setting, a new country or environment where one knows nothing of the customs, language, nor the people?'

Hannah Arendt's 1943 description of fleeing Nazi Germany and her experience of becoming a refugee almost seems to provide a direct response to Halbwachs's question concerning memory and uprootedness:

> We have lost our home, our hearth, that is to say the familiarity of our daily life. We have lost our profession, that is to say, the assurance of being of some service

in the world. We have lost our maternal language, that is to say, our natural reactions, the simplicity of gestures and the spontaneous expression of our feelings. (1943/1987, p. 58, my translation)

This description captures much of the disorienting and painful destructuring effects of uprootedness. Some thirty years afterwards, South American political exiles, forced into exile following political coups d'état, frequently reported, when reflecting about their daily lives: 'I have lost my identity.' Ana Vasquez, a Chilean refugee from the Pinochet dictatorship with whom I conducted research in Paris during the 1980s (Apfelbaum and Vasquez, 1983), had collected interviews with political refugees from various South American countries. Many of the men interviewed had been leading political activists, and we frequently heard the lament: 'I have lost my identity.' This expression in fact embodies a declaration of having become 'culturally orphaned'; it encapsulated all their pain and distress at having suddenly become politically impotent, and now having to face the failure of their long-standing commitment to struggles which had been the *raison d'être* of these men and which had provided them with the foundational social fabric of their identity 'back home'. In the uprooting, the exiles had in fact lost all their social references, lost what Norbert Elias (1950/87) called their habitus; that is their home place. Since the political context of the host country appeared to them as so different, foreign, or alien, they saw no possibility, nor perhaps retained the desire, to (re)elaborate a meaningful social project. (The feeling that one must be back on home soil to be effective and to have a social identity was also reflected among Spanish refugees in France after the Spanish civil war in the late 1930s, when the men often lived with a suitcase packed, ready to go home at any moment.)

Uprootings involve a separation, often irreversible as in the case of genocide, from the place of one's original social and historical linkages. Not only is one cut off from former family and social ties but the host social environment may pay little more than lip service to previous cultural life-experiences and identifications. How can one therefore exist on a day-to-day basis in any new space following an uprooting?

These questions have never been fully addressed by a social psychology whose epistemological focus has become increasingly narrowed to the point where much of its mainstream theorising is based on the fiction of an ahistorical, emotionless, decontextualised, subject/individual governed only by the rationality of 'Homo economicus'. For a long time, insufficient attention was paid by modern-day (experimental) social psychologists to the fact that we do not evolve in a sociocultural vacuum, but rather that we are inscribed in family and genealogical filiations as well as in world history, in a larger social environment with its changing representations of social categories over time which filter our life-experiences.

In this respect, Halbwachs's analysis in the 1930s is one of the rare inspiring attempts to theorize how the 'subject's identity', as modern social psychologists might label it, is closely linked to a person's broader framework of social experiences. Halbwachs analysed in depth the extent to which personal, private experience and recollections all needed to be couched in, or voiced within, a *collective, public* chronicle. The collectivity's historical accounts provided the foundational legitimacy for making sense of one's personal experiences and therefore for constructing one's identity. Halbwachs suggested in the 1920s, as if in a premonition of things to come, that, if we are haunted by some personal memories which cannot be shared because, for example, they are meaningless to others, we risk being seen as hallucinating. There is then no other alternative except to forget or, if this is impossible, to become silent and alienated from one's own society. There are ways to remain deaf-mute which impose a silence on those who try to speak, claims Foucault (1976).[3] In other words, censorship need not be officially imposed for it to operate.

For many decades, survivors of the Shoah or survivors of the earlier Armenian massacres have shared a similar experience of having to remain silent because they found no general public forum willing to hear of the traumatic events they had lived. This has been equally true for the victims of sexual abuse or the victims of torture. As long as the official accounts, such as history books or remembrance days, remain, at best elliptic, but more usually silent, about those events, there is no collective framework of intelligibility for the personal, privately lived experiences. The survivors exist in a wilderness of silence in which the memories of the past receive no legitimation from any sort of public recognition on the part of the immediate social entourage.

In those circumstances, recollecting, remembering and re-elaborating the memories concerning the personal traumatic history remains, at best, a family shared event, and more often the memories end up as a very private affair of individual silence and engender mutism. When in 1998 it seemed possible that Pinochet would be indicted for crimes against humanity, a number of former Chilean refugees started to speak up and bear witness about personal traumas they had kept to themselves all these years:

> 'Not that I wanted to forget, but I did not have the words to say this, neither in French, nor in Spanish, to recount the torture to my kids. It is difficult to explain, in France, that one has been tortured,' commented Luis Vargas, now a French citizen. (*Le Monde*, 11 December 1998)

This impossibility to speak and to be heard has psychological consequences for the person: Primo Levi claims that it increases the feeling of shame that one experiences as one witnesses the wrongdoing perpetrated by another; one is haunted by such wrongdoing, 'by the mere fact that it exists and has been irrevocably introduced into the realm of existing things, and that one's good will ... is insufficient and, worse, completely inefficient to hinder the perpetrator's acts (deeds)'(Levi, *La Trêve*).[4]

There are still other issues raised and existential difficulties to confront when we look at the next generation, the children of genocide survivors, or, more generally, at the children of collectively displaced and uprooted families.

'My parents tell me little about their pre-war life ... as if the war erased not only the literal world in which they lived but also its relevance to their new conditions' (Hoffman, 1989, p. 8). This quote is taken from Eva Hoffman's (1989) autobiographical account, *Lost in Translation*. Born in Poland of parents who survived the Nazi genocide of the Jews, she came with them to Canada when she was a teenager. Being disconnected from her historical roots by the silence of the family, she noted: 'I can't throw a bridge between the present and the past, and therefore [I] can't make time move' (pp. 116–17).

Obviously, withholding this information about their family's trajectory represented not only a strategy for the parents' own survival in a world that was deaf to their past, but also an attempt to protect their children and spare the transmission of the pain and anguish they had suffered. With hindsight, we know more now about the psychological burdens that such silence may produce. By not assuring the transmission of the family's chronicle, the genealogical continuity is broken, and because of this mutism there is an increasing rift between family generations. Jeanine Altounian, an Armenian psychoanalyst, claims that the reticence to transmit the family saga creates generations of children born outside any genealogy who can be considered as 'cultural orphans'. Such a child 'faces an eclipse of his/her origins ... [and becomes] a human being without "a shadow"' (Altounian, 1990, p. 204).

Although little research, to my knowledge, has systematically addressed such issues, several studies have looked at the difficulties of integration into the school system, as well as into adult professional life, faced by the children of migrant workers whose families came to France. These studies consistently indicate that the children of immigrants succeed better in their adult life in the *work-world* of the host country when the parents help maintain a continuity between past and present, between what was *then* and what is *now* (see Delcroix, 1998). On the other hand, children tend to do better *in school* whenever their teachers take an interest in the origins and cultural background of their students and express in a variety of ways their appreciation of the distinctive, culturally specific background of the children's parents. In Eva Hoffman's terms, the teachers are 'throw[ing] a bridge between the present and the past' for their students.

Not only is the possibility of a genealogical continuity most important for later life and identity, but so too is the need to find, in the collective discourses, the means to legitimate one's uprooted and disrupted existence. The degree of estrangement experienced by the second generation will depend upon (the host) society's official discourses and interpretations about the events surrounding their family's uprooting, with such representations of past history often subordinated to political and ideological purposes. Those differing official presentations of history all contribute to shaping what Halbwachs calls the 'social framework for memory' and consequently the construction of identity.

In this line of thought, one can better grasp the vital functions of trials concerning crimes against humanity or genocide, such as that in France of Maurice Papon or that proposed for General Pinochet. Such trials provide a space where the past crimes can be acknowledged and the official accounts of facts revisited and re-evaluated. But it is also a space open to the public for individual testimony and remembrance. While neither the trial nor the judgment can bring back the disappeared, it can break through personal and family mutism as well as through collective silences; it becomes the starting point for a redefinition of broken identities and for a delayed mourning. One can debate about the aim of for example the South African Truth and Reconciliation Commission. Recently, in Cambodia I met a young man orphaned by Pol Pot, who lost his parents and all brothers and sisters, and is part of a generation of similar survivors of this genocide. It was interesting to listen to his strong reticence toward an equivalent commission in Cambodia, claiming that there could be no forgiveness. How, indeed, could we the survivors substitute for those who are dead and who are the only ones entitled to forgive? The memories of those traumas will continue haunting generations after generations; Current life cannot be separated from past history, comments an Aboriginal respondent to a study led by Di Bretherton (1998); he says:

> My father and his father, his grandfather pass stories on ... they run in the family, old stories ... It still hurts mate, y'know? You can never take away the pain. Give us land, get our land back, whatever, still won't take away the pain.

I would however still argue that trials, reconciliation commissions and official acknowledgments of genocidal acts all tend to inaugurate a pathway by which institutional legitimation can be given to the individually remembered traumatic events that stamped a whole generation's identity.

A History of One's Own: Discourse on Origins and Group Identity

So far I have been mostly concerned with questions of identity at the individual level. What has been documented at the individual level may similarly apply for whole groups or communities whose very existence is affected by the public discourse concerning their origins. Revisiting one's collective history has consistently been the first step in the overturning of any society's regime; having 'a history of one's own', analogous to Virginia

Woolf's (1929/1991) asking for *A Room of One's Own*, is a vital step towards resistance and 'regrouping' (see Apfelbaum, 1979/1999) of any community which had been degrouped through the domination by another group. One of the very first tasks which feminists took up in academia was to unveil women's forgotten or denied contributions throughout history. The constitution of a history which showed the political role that women had played in various periods provided a radical shift in the social framework for memory, and offered a common 'social imaginary', so vital for building a positive, legitimating group reference. When I studied women in leadership positions and compared the narratives of Norwegian and French cabinet ministers (Apfelbaum, 1993), the Norwegian women, who now represent 40 per cent of each government's cabinet ministers, all consistently referred to the importance of the feminist movement to them, in explaining their own rise to power in political office. This was the case regardless of their political affiliation and of their own personal degree of involvement in the women's movement.

Another case in point is Alex Haley's novel *Roots: The Saga of an American Family*. Drawing partly on the history of his own family, Haley recounts the saga of a black American family retracing its history back to its African past. Published in 1976, *Roots* represented a major landmark in the reframing of the history of the black community,[5] providing an alternative view to the standard account of the place blacks occupy in American history. In bringing the African origins of the American black community into the foreground and into the open public arena, *Roots* contributed to a readjustment of the social framework of memory and the symbolic meaning of the slavery period. For millions of people, almost overnight – especially after the TV series – slavery had to be re-evaluated as an active enslavement of a people who then collectively suffered the consequences of white (economic) domination. *Roots* challenged as well the essentialistic view of 'natural' inequality, upon which had been built much of the racism and segregationist beliefs for over a century after the Civil War and the emancipation of slaves.

But for the black community *Roots* has also had healing consequences or at least some kind of reparation effect. The restoration of pride was the beginnings of a collective shift of identity. Slavery was now a historical marker, but being black and a descendent of slaves need no longer be a shameful individual stigma. In fact, one could now see that it was the white slave-traders and slave-owners who had been shameful in their actions. It may well be that the publication of *Roots* signalled a turning point from the ideology of the melting pot to the current ideology of multiculturalism, in its American version.

The reclaiming of a past legacy is an act of resistance, for example, against an attempt of cultural genocide. During the Nazi attempt to eradicate European Jewry, whole communities were decimated and as a result the eastern European cradle of Yiddish culture and language was effectively erased.

Yiddish had, in fact, become the 'language of no-one', as Rachel Ertel (1993) comments. For a couple of decades now, however, there has been a revival of interest in Yiddish among the younger generations who did not live through the war. 'Maintenance of language is of vital importance in avoiding cultural dispossession.' This is echoed in: 'Linguistic dispossession is ... close to the dispossession of one's self. Rage that has no words is helpless rage' notes Eva Hoffman (1989, p. 123), for as Hannah Arendt observed, 'In language, the past has its inalienable place, and it is in the face of language that all the attempts to rid oneself of the past finally fail' (Arendt, 1971, 1974).

But the reclaiming of legacy can also be a means of resistance when the past has been confiscated in the name of ideological and political purposes. The analysis which the Polish political scientist Bronislaw Baczko (1984) proposes of the trade union movement Solidarnosc (Solidarity) during the 1980s is here a case in point. Polish society had always had a strong sense of national identity with a consistent cultural heritage. The Catholic church played a determinant role providing the social values as well as the symbolism and the social Imaginary of the country and thus contributing to the cementing of national life. The installation of communist power after World War II imposed a radical break with the traditional social imaginary of Polish society in the name of revolutionary goals or of a better (collectivist) future. Baczko describes how much the social uprising successfully led by Solidarnosc had called upon the legacy and the historical memory of the nation. The references to the past, the traditional symbols, myths and imagination of the age-old Polish heritage played a central role in the upsurge of Solidarnosc's popularity and helped cement it as a resistance movement. Here memory and the legacy of cultural symbols explicitly played a role in the resistance to the domination of totalitarianism.

This last case particularly illustrates the fallacy of a commonly shared belief in leftist ideological traditions that the past is insignificant and can be fully dismissed, erased or ignored as long as one works toward the construction of a new, better world. The increasing number of nationalist movements which erupted after the decline and dissolution of the Soviet Union in the wake of the collapse of twentieth-century internationalist movements illustrate the failure of communist regimes to irrevocably uproot a community from its history and traditional Imaginary. These rising nationalisms illustrate the dark side of the obsession with the past but need to be examined.

The Return of Memory and Legacy: Why Now?

The end of the twentieth century seems to me to have been obsessed with the past both at the level of social policy and at an individual level. Was this just a simple expression of the nostalgia that normally appears in every epoch, but which takes on new urgency as the end of a century or of a millennium approaches? Or was it rather an indicator of a more profound disquietude – an index of a crisis in society and its values, those which had guided and constituted social and political life during the twentieth century?

Throughout the last century, there was a tendency to look into the future and away from the past, a tendency to contrast and oppose the traditionalness of memory to the hopefulness or progress of utopias, as if memory, in narrow retrograde fashion, was necessarily turned only towards the status quo (and its maintenance). Such a vision was, and still perhaps is, part and parcel of the leftist tradition of conceptualising (*traditionalisme de gauche*), of the certitude that social change and social progress go hand in hand, and that science, including the social sciences, entails working towards human welfare and betterment. This vision is anchored in the very discourse of the American and French Revolutions, which implied a radical shift, a rupture with the past towards the construction of a 'new man' (see Baczko, p. 232). In the nineteenth and twentieth centuries, the past was therefore often appropriated in the name of the promise of a happy future, if we reflect upon the words of the *Internationale*: 'Of the past, let us make a tabula rasa.' In this injunction for breaking away, for ideological uprooting, the subject's subjectivities and identity became subordinated to collective objectives, with the individual's pains and sufferings the price to pay for insuring the future collective happiness.

This urge not to look back has been operating broadly in all those societies which during the twentieth century came under some kind of influence from Marxist ideologies, in their various socialist and communist variants. For quite different reasons, the pursuit of the American dream of constructing a unified nation out of the melting pot of different immigrants *also* required a looking forward. Having fled various political and economic difficulties in the Old World, the immigrants and later generations had often themselves become active supporters of a state ideology which relied on forgetting the past and their original historical diversities. Thus, for various reasons in different places, western societies starting in the mid-nineteenth century began to be geared towards breaking their historical moorings and looking towards the future, rather than keeping alive any past legacy.

The social sciences have had their share of responsibility in the dehistoricisation and decontextualisation of the subject. They followed closely on society's ideological heels. In search of universal laws for its 'average' citizen or subject, the social sciences in their mainstream formulations portray us as belonging to a society of clones, where all subjects are alike, and seek social agents in their naked state, so to speak, stripped of their masks, costumes, dreams, representations, imagination, emotions and past. In the representation of psychology, we all become Peter Schlemihl, (Chamisso, 1827) Chamisso's tragic hero who sold his shadow to the devil in exchange for fortune, only to learn that his being shadowless has now alienated him from any possible social relations. This pure, abstract construction of the scientific subject, disconnected from their social fictions and affectivity, disembodied and represented by a statistic, fits the collective dream of a society which, like the panopticon, was transparent to those who had conceived it (see Baczko, 1984).

When the world 'discovered', at the end of World War II, 'what men had done to other men', there was a consensual cry that 'this would never happen again'. This is the explicitly stated goal for example in the extensive study by Adorno et al. (1950) on the *Authoritarian Personality*. There was also a consensual belief that this genocide had just been an accident in the path towards human progress and welfare. Thus social life, and business, went on as usual and the social sciences developed without ever questioning whether the massive atrocities which had just happened did not open up a major epistemological crisis, a crisis of human behaviour to borrow from Kren and Rappoport's (1980) title. The voices of those such as George Steiner, Hannah Arendt and Primo Levi, who have strongly argued that we need to confront squarely the meaning of this major event of the twentieth century, were long ignored.

In the light of the ongoing genocidal events which continued to occur through the second part of the twentieth century – and Kosovo is just the most recent one – can we still hold the belief that as social scientists we have contributed to enhancing human welfare? Remembrance is more than just our moral obligation; may it indeed also be a pathway for opening new channels of knowledge and understanding?

Notes

1. The author thanks Ian Lubek for his translation and editorial and substantive suggestions.
2. Maurice Halbwachs died of exhaustion in Buchenwald on a Sunday in 1944 in the presence of the writer Jorge Semprun, his former student in sociology, and later minister of culture in Spain (Semprun, 1994).
3. *'Mutismes des silences qui, à force de se taire imposent le silence. Censure.'*
4. *'Honte que le juste éprouve devant la faute commise par autrui, tenaillé par l'idée qu'elle existe, qu'elle ait etée introduite irrévocablement dans l'univers des choses existantes et que sa bonne volonté se soit montrée nulle ou insuffisante et totalement inefficace.'*
5. Even more so than the book itself, the subsequent eight-part television mini-series based on this story had a tremendous impact in the US when it was shown on TV in the last week of January 1977; its nightly episodes set historic records for television audiences. Its various episodes were each seen by over 30 million people,

setting all-time viewing records with from 43 to 51 per cent of all households watching. According to the Nielson television ratings (between 1961 and 1996) for sponsored programmes more than half an hour long, the last episode, broadcast on 30 January, still remains the third most watched programme in US history.

Bibliography

Adorno, T.W. Frenkel-Brunswick, E., Levinson, D.J., and Sanford, R.N. *The Authoritarian Personality* (New York: Harper, 1950).
Altounian, J. *Ouvrez-moi seulement les Chemins d'Arménie. Un Génocide aux déserts de l'inconscient* (Paris: Les Belles Lettres, 1990).
Apfelbaum, E. 'Relations of Domination and Movements of Liberation: An Analysis of Power Between Groups', in W. Austin and S. Worchel (eds), *The Social Psychology of Intergroup Relations* (Monterey, California: Cole, 1979), pp. 188–204. Republished in *Feminism and Psychology*, no. 3 (1999) 267–72.
Apfelbaum, E. and Vasquez, A. 'Les Réalités changeantes de l'identité', *Peuples Méditerranéens*, no. 24 (1983) 83–100.
Apfelbaum, E. 'Norwegian and French Women in High Leadership Positions: The Importance of Cultural Contexts upon Gendered Relations', *Psychology of Women Quarterly*, 17(4) (1993) 409–29.
Arendt, H. (1943/1987) *La Tradition cachée* (Paris: Bourgeois Trad Française, 1987).
Arendt, H. (1971/1974) 'Walter Benjamin', in H. Arendt (ed.), *Vies Politiques* (Paris: Gallimard, 1974).
Baczko, B. *Les Imaginaires Sociaux* (Paris: Payot, 1984).
Bretherton, D. and Mellor, D. 'Reconciliation between black and white Australians: The role of memory', Paper delivered to the International Congress of Applied Psychology, San Francisco, August 1998.
Chamisso, A. *Peter Schlemihl* (Nürnberg: Schrag, 1827).
Delcroix, C. 'Que Transmettent les Pères à leurs filles et à leur fils sur le travail? Journée sur 'Des Hommes et des femmes face à la précarisation. Quelles dynamiques biographiques?', Séminaire du GEDISST (Paris: Iresco, 6 April 1998).
Elias, N. (1950/1987) *La Société des individus* (Paris: Fayard, 1987).
Ertel, R. *Dans la langue de personne. Poésie yddish de l'anéantissement* (Paris: Seuil, 1993).
Foucault, M. *La Volonté de savoir* (Paris: Gallimard, 1976).
Halbwachs, M. (1924/1952) *Les Cadres sociaux de la Mémoire* (Paris: PUF, 1952).
Haley, A. *Roots: The Saga of an American Family* (Garden City, New York: Doubleday, 1976).
Hoffman, E. *Lost in Translation* (New York: Penguin, 1989).
Kren, G. and Rappoport, L. *The Holocaust and the Crisis of Human Behavior* (New York: Holmes & Meier, 1980).
Levi, P. *La Trêve* (Paris: Gasset, 1966/1936).
Levi, P. *The Reawakening* (New York: Collier Books, 1986).
Semptun, J. *L'écriture ou la vie. Souvenirs.* (Paris: Gallimard, 1994).
Woolf, V. (1929/1991) *A Room of One's Own* (London: Hogarth Press, 1991).

6

Troubled Times: Changing the Political Subject in Northern Ireland

JOHN CASH

I want to begin with a brief quote from Jacques Lacan, taken from his discussion of 'The Purloined Letter':

> Every human drama, every theatrical drama in particular, is founded on the existence of established bonds, ties, pacts. Human beings already have commitments which tie them together, commitments which have determined their places, names, their essences. Then along comes another discourse, other commitments, other speech. It is quite certain that there'll be some places where they'll have to come to blows. All treaties aren't signed simultaneously. Some are contradictory. If you go to war it is so as to know which treaty will be binding. (Lacan, 1988, p. 197)

This somewhat overlooked aspect of Lacan's theory of subjectivity – his emphasis upon the dynamic and disturbing implications of a conflict between discourses – is particularly apposite when set in the context of an analysis of conflict and change in Northern Ireland. By being very clear about the ways in which a new discourse can unsettle, as he puts it, established bonds, ties and pacts, Lacan brings the historical process of social and political change into connection with his account of the making and remaking of subjectivity. He extends this connection by being similarly clear about the way in which a new discourse, if it is able to establish a field of operations, will inevitably involve a new set of subjective orientations: new bonds, ties and pacts, indeed, new commitments. New discourses, if they achieve any degree of institutionalisation, will inevitably entail new subjectivities and new patterns of intersubjectivity. Finally, Lacan recognises the struggle and conflict that such a clash of discourses will inevitably produce. Commitments are conflicted. The struggle between discourses carries with it a struggle over subjectivity and intersubjectivity; a battle about which particular forms of subjectivity and intersubjectivity will come to count as the proper forms. In the process of change, violence and contradiction will expand. Eventually only some treaties, and only some readings of those treaties, will prevail. Such treaties, such *points de capiton* of institutional life, such discursive bindings of subjectivity lie at the very core of social and political relations. They, and especially the discourses that organise them, are both the medium and the outcome of social and political conflict and they touch, at once, whole societies and individual subjects. The political is profoundly personal; it is, at once, discursive, subjective and intersubjective.

The preceding commentary on this aspect of Lacanian theory has offered me a way of quickly highlighting certain features of social and political change that are tellingly exemplified in the current circumstances confronting Northern Ireland.[1] Since its inception in the 1920s, Northern Ireland has been, formally, a part of the much-celebrated civic culture of the United Kingdom. It has always constituted the other side of that civic culture, the blind-spot that has since come to light. Democracy has persistently met its nemesis in the political culture of Northern Ireland. However, over the past few years Northern Ireland has crept awkwardly and often perilously towards new political arrangements. Two major milestones along this troubled path are the signing of the Belfast Agreement on Good Friday of 1998 and the popular approval given in the referenda on new political arrangements, in both Northern Ireland and the Republic of Ireland, in late May of 1998. In Northern Ireland the referendum measured popular approval of the Good Friday Agreement at 71 per cent of the total Northern Irish population of voting age. However, to highlight the ongoing struggle within unionism over 'commitment', only 50 per cent of the unionist community voted in favour of this new 'treaty'.[2] Most recently, Senator George Mitchell's conclusion, in his review of the Good Friday Agreement, that 'a basis now exists for devolution to occur, for the institutions to be established and for decommissioning to take place as soon as possible' has created another milestone along the perilous path towards peace and democracy.[3] As the Northern Ireland Assembly and Executive are established and devolution of powers takes place, a new stage in the struggle for 'commitment' to one or another discourse has been reset in play.

I intend to develop in this chapter a brief analysis of Northern Ireland's current attempt to transform its political culture, in the belief that such an analysis can enhance our understanding of how Northern Ireland, and other divided societies, might move from a culture of enmity to an adversarial democratic culture. In attempting to catch the dynamics and tensions of such a potential transition, my analysis also addresses some major dilemmas and impediments that are likely to be encountered along the way to such a transformation.

First, I need to set out some markers regarding my particular approach. Along with the pressing substantive issues of life, liberty, equality, opportunity, democracy and national identity that have marked the conduct of everyday life in Northern Ireland, the very complexity of this society has also generated a series of social-theoretical conundrums. In short the complexities of Northern Ireland, and other 'divided societies', have confounded the prevalent theoretical approaches that have been relied upon to analyse the conduct of social and political life in such societies.

For instance, Northern Ireland is an anomaly when viewed from a perspective that highlights the transformative effects of modernity, or globalisation, whether these purported effects are construed in economic, social or political terms. In the face of the rapid industrialisation and modernisation since the inception of the industrial revolution, Northern Ireland has been re-produced as a society riven by sectarian difference. Northern Ireland has also proved anomalous for those pluralism theories, both implicit and explicit, that have taken this sectarian difference as an inherent, unchanging feature of social and political relations. Such a pluralism approach – a very common approach – has consistently missed the internal differentiation, and internal dynamism, of both the unionist and nationalist communities. Thereby, pluralism approaches have failed to take due notice of and apportion due weight to the inclusivist tendencies, present and active in both communities, favouring movement beyond the politics of sectarian difference. Finally, Northern Ireland has also confounded those theories and approaches that rely unduly on realist assumptions about self-interest and rationality. The complex array of forms of reasoning and feeling which together constitute Northern Ireland's political cultures are more central to the conduct of political life than those who make such realist assumptions about self-interest and rationality are able to comprehend.

In response to these anomalies I have developed an approach that attempts to take ideologies and identities, or discourses and the subjectivities they organise, more seriously (Cash, 1996). This approach attempts to hold together the social and psychic dimensions of ideologies and identities by exploring both their internal structure and their ongoing structuration. It attempts to address the intersecting psycho-cultural and socio-political processes that have been central to the re-production of sectarian difference as an institutionalised feature of the Northern Ireland state, and that are also central to the reimagining and reordering of political identities and political relations in Northern Ireland.

Simply put, my principal claim is that ideologies, or discourses, and the identities they organise, are central to the conduct of political life in Northern Ireland. The strengths of this claim are located in what is entailed. Ideologies are central to political life because they establish the range of common-sense understandings, the predominant reality principles, that are recursively drawn upon by politicians and other citizens to construe proper forms of identity, proper forms of political and social relations and proper forms of power, authority and violence. At the same time what counts as proper – the proper way of being, relating, feeling or construing – is recurrently fought over in the ongoing making and remaking of social and political relations.

To explore the implications of such claims, I have developed elsewhere a theory of the structuration of the unconscious as an ongoing social and psychic process and I have drawn on psychoanalytic theory to specify several sets of unconscious rules which structure particular forms of ideology. Regarding Northern Ireland, I have specified three 'positions' within unionist ideology (and observed three equivalent positions within nationalism/ republicanism) that are recurrently drawn upon in the making and remaking of identities and social relations. These are the dehumanising position, the persecutory position and the ambivalent position. The first two, which more generally can be termed exclusivist, are organised by psychic mechanisms characteristic of Melanie Klein's paranoid-schizoid position. The third position, the ambivalent, which can also be referred to as inclusivist, is organised by psychic mechanisms characteristic of Klein's depressive position.[4] For reasons of space I will provide brief descriptions of these positions and rely upon the examples I go on to discuss to illustrate, at least intuitively, their most salient features.[5]

Both the dehumanising and persecutory positions split the political and social order into 'good' and 'evil' categories and regard political interaction as a conflict between these two forces. Allegiance to group norms of an exclusivist kind becomes the criterion by which the proper position of political subjects within this split world is determined; simply put, you are either 'in' or 'out'. The *dehumanising* position establishes the emotional and conceptual boundary between 'us' and 'them' through the use of metaphors that construe the other as either a despised animal or a disgusting object. In this position violent aggressivity towards the other, allied with hateful contempt, constitutes the emotional climate of 'us–them' interactions.[6]

In the *persecutory* position others are construed as persecutory if, within the field of social and political relations, they adhere to, and act upon, values and beliefs that are different from those sanctioned by the subject's communal grouping. Merely acting differently is construed, within the persecutory position, as acting in a hostile and aggressive manner which must be opposed and defeated at all costs, in order to maintain the propriety and authority of the communal values, beliefs and interests of one's own grouping. This incapacity to tolerate difference is not restricted to the construction of members of the 'out-group'. The same intolerance is evident in the construction of members of the subject's own communal grouping who speak or act in ways that differ from those preferred ways that are sanctioned by communal norms. Another feature of the persecutory position is that the other, including the internal other adverted to above, rather than being graphically dehumanised, is construed in an iconic mode as a mere emblem or instance of the persecutory grouping itself. In this construction the other lacks complexity as he or she is reduced to a cipher of the persecutory design. Aggressivity and hateful contempt are present in the persecutory position, but these affects are alloyed with anxiety about the interests, welfare and future of one's own grouping. Moreover the persecutory position is capable of establishing a distinction between those others who 'know their place', as it were, and those who are construed as dangerous persecutors. It is only those who step out of place, by refusing to accept their allotted social position, who are construed as persecutory. Toleration, for the moment, is extended to those who accept their designated social place. In the case of any nominal members of the subject's own grouping, they are construed as proper members of the grouping for so long as they maintain their adherence to group norms and continue to draw upon the repertoire of exclusivist rules. To differ from group norms is to become an internal persecutory other deserving exclusion and retribution, usually, although not always, symbolic in kind.

Consider these recent statements by Ian Paisley, drawn from an interview with Mervyn Pauley published in the *Newsletter* about a week prior to the 1998 referendum. First, Paisley was asked his opinion about the fact that many local councils across Northern Ireland, including Belfast council and his own local council in Ballymena, had voted to endorse a 'Yes' vote at the referendum. It was put to Paisley that this might be regarded as a setback for the 'No' campaign:

> PAISLEY: No, because what it showed was that in every council unionists of all shades joined to vote but it was the nationalists in the councils that carried the day with other Official Unionists. If you look at all the voting *the majority of unionists, as such*, were voting for this particular proposition, so we had the majority of unionists in every council. (*Newsletter*, 16 May, 1998; my emphasis.)

Here Paisley's concern is to construct an account in which a majority of unionists, drawn principally from both major parties, is in favour of voting 'No'. Nationalists are symbolically disenfranchised in this construction. And already one wonders about the symbolic fate of the 'other Official Unionists' who sided with nationalists in supporting a 'Yes' vote. The interviewer then put the following proposition to Paisley:

> INTERVIEWER: But generally you would agree with the principle that each individual must vote according to conscience on this Agreement?

PAISLEY: No, I do not agree with that at all because you wouldn't have a unionist conscience if you voted Yes. I believe that any unionist that votes Yes is voting against the very basis of unionism and any unionist that votes Yes and claims to have a good conscience, he has a conscience seared with a hot iron, he should be in the pan-nationalist front and be honest, he's flying a pirate flag.

Here we see an exclusivist and persecutory construction that places unionists holding a political position different from Paisley is beyond the pale. Indeed they are cast into the pan-nationalist front, and construed as lacking the honesty to admit their betrayal of unionism. Later in the same interview Paisley comments:

> Now we are accused by Mr Trimble (leader of the Ulster Unionist Party) of running away. What Mr Trimble did was he ran away from the unionist family and joined Sinn Fein and sold his principles. That's what happened.

We now know where Paisley places those unionists who disagree with him. Trimble has become the latter-day Lundy who has 'joined' with the enemy.[7] The leader of the largest unionist party has been constructed as improper and thereby excluded from Paisley's construction of what is entailed in being unionist.

Addressing a political rally prior to the referendum, Paisley referred to Trimble and other pro-agreement unionists as traitors who had been suborned by the British government. He continued:

> They are liars. They have graduated from the devil's school. They have destroyed the act of the Union and given the title deeds of Ulster to Dublin on a plate. These people have sold out Ulster. As for me, I would rather starve than take filthy British money. (*Independent*, 12 May 1998)

It is worth noting that these examples highlight a striking feature of many divided societies: a great deal of political conflict is intragroup conflict within the nominal community. Of course such intragroup conflict is concerned, exactly, with the issue of which set of discursive rules should be drawn upon to think, feel, construe and act properly within the field of intergroup relations.

It is my claim that, within the unionist community, this exclusivist, persecutory form of unionist ideology is not peculiar to Paisley and his followers. Rather, it remains the predominant ideological form for the construction of political relations in Northern Ireland, although it is not always declared in such a forthright manner and with such reliance on religious symbolism. At the same time it is the ideological form whose predominance is being threatened by the current political and peace process. On all prior occasions when this exclusivist, persecutory form of being, relating, feeling and construing as a political subject has been seriously challenged, political groupings whose identity is strongly invested in its preservation have succeeded in recolonising the political space and reasserting the proper pre-eminence of such exclusivist rules. The political conflict within unionism has routinely taken this form, especially during the O'Neill premiership in 1969 and Faulkner's premiership of a power-sharing cabinet in 1974. It is clear that this battle within unionism over the proper place of exclusivism is being played out yet again, although not necessarily with the same outcome.

The *ambivalent* position of ideology is inclusivist. It construes individuals, groups and the whole political and social formation as complex and multifaceted. It is from this complex construction that the ambivalence arises. Rather than being split and projected in ways characteristic of the dehumanising and persecutory positions, Others and Other groupings, (including frustrating Others, distrusted Others and, even, despised Others) are construed as complex subjects with both positive and negative aspects. Thus, in contrast with the dehumanising and persecutory positions, the capacity for the handling of complexity, for the shifting of perspective and the enactment of bargaining and compromise, is greatly enhanced.

Consider these examples, again drawn from the unionist community. The deputy leader of the Ulster Unionist Party (UUP), John Taylor, speaking just after the announcement of the referendum result, predicted the end of the relationship between the Orange Order and the UUP. As he put it:

> You are going to find a more secular, modernised UUP. In particular, the link between the Orange Order is very questionable, especially since the Order jumped into the No camp. The time is now right to break the link. (*Electronic Telegraph*, 25 May 1998a)

The voicing of such an observation by a central unionist figure such as Taylor indicates a looming sea-change in the character of the UUP. Taylor was himself a victim of an IRA attack and has been a significant figure within the Orange Order for many years. For the past few years he, with others, has been engaged in an attempt to create what he here has termed 'a more secular, modernised UUP' – one that, in the terms already outlined, draws on inclusivist rules to construe its own identity, the identity of other groupings and its notions of the proper form of intergroup relations. Further, when speaking about the prospect of allocating preferences, under the proportional representation voting system used for the June elections to a Northern Ireland Assembly, Taylor entertained the prospect of UUP voters transferring their preferences to the nationalist SDLP. As he put it: 'It won't be simply a sectarian vote any more. It will be people deciding who are the positive candidates and who are the negative candidates' (*Electronic Telegraph*, 25 May 1998b). In his keynote address during the Northern

Ireland Assembly election campaign David Trimble drew on inclusivist rules when stating that '[w]e can now get down to the historic and honourable task of this generation: to raise up a Northern Ireland in which pluralist unionism and constitutional nationalism can speak to each other with the civility that is the foundation of freedom' (*Irish Times*, 23 June 1998). Whether this adoption of an inclusivist idiom can survive the tensions and dilemmas of political transformation is the issue upon which hangs the future of peace and democracy in Northern Ireland.

It is worth reporting that the UUP currently has 10 Westminster MPs, 6 of whom campaigned for a 'No' vote in the referendum. Several of these appeared with Paisley, Robinson and others from the Democratic Unionist Party (DUP), and McCartney from the UK Unionist Party, as part of the new 'united unionist' grouping which toured around Northern Ireland campaigning for the 'no' vote. The UUP, which is the major unionist party, is, then, entirely split between inclusivists and exclusivists. The split vote within the unionist community at the referendum, where approximately 50 per cent voted 'Yes' and 50 per cent voted 'No', suggests that a similar division exists within this broader community.[8]

Some clarification is called for here. Although, for shorthand, I have spoken of 'inclusivists' and 'exclusivists' it is critical to recognise that political actors and other citizens can move between these positions. Of course, someone like Paisley is highly unlikely to move. In part this has to do with his own psychological disposition, no doubt. More significantly, it has to do with the character of the party he created. The DUP, unlike the UUP, has never tolerated, and hence has never institutionalised, any rules of an inclusivist type. However, this is not the case with the UUP, which has always contained both inclusivist and exclusivist scripts, so to speak. Less than twelve months before the Good Friday Agreement the UUP leader David Trimble drew regularly on exclusivist scripts and rules to construe, evaluate and act. He is, after all, notorious in many circles for the role he has played at Drumcree over the past few years, when Orangemen have demanded the right to march down the Garvaghy Road, passing close to a nationalist housing estate. On such occasions he has drawn entirely on exclusivist rules when acting as a leading spokesperson for both Orangeism and unionism. This same David Trimble is, today, lionised on most sides (we have seen one exception in Paisley's evaluation of him) as the champion of a 'new deal' in Ulster. As leader of the largest unionist party Trimble is caught between two conflicting requirements of the situation he finds himself in. On the one hand, in many circumstances he needs to draw upon exclusivist scripts for internal unionist consumption. On the other hand, as the principal unionist negotiator in a setting where new rules have been demanded by some of the principal actors, he needs to draw on these inclusivist rules in order to continue as a viable political actor within the new setting. These principal actors who have insisted on the propriety of inclusivist rules include the two sovereign governments of the UK and the Republic of Ireland, along with the United States president and government and the European Community. Their capacity to act, cooperatively, as powerful carriers of the new discursive rules of inclusivism has reinforced an internal political process moving in the same direction. In this coincidence of internal and external forces, battling to establish the hegemony of an inclusivist political discourse, lie the conditions favouring a successful political transformation in Northern Ireland.

So far I have illustrated the claim that unionist ideology contains both exclusivist and inclusivist forms for the construction of subjectivity and intersubjectivity. I have also made the empirical claim that, on all prior occasions, any movement towards the institutionalisation of inclusivism has immediately called forth a strong exclusivist reaction – most tellingly in the defeat of O'Neill and in the overthrow of the power-sharing executive by the Ulster Workers' Council strike. I have also suggested that the role played by several principal actors, including the two sovereign governments, along with the United States and the European Union, has created the possibility of a different outcome on this occasion. But to achieve this different outcome new institutions, such as the Northern Ireland Assembly, will need to institutionalise inclusivist rules as the proper mode of being and relating. These inclusivist rules will need to achieve a new legitimacy. In turn, this would amount to a profound transformation of Northern Ireland's political culture. Inevitably, such a transformation must confront and, eventually, displace a dilemma inherent in the current situation.

The new Northern Ireland Assembly will need to institutionalise what we might term an inclusivist lingua franca, or common sense. For many unionists, even pragmatic acceptance of such a lingua franca will produce critical questions of legitimacy – questions regarding the proper forms of subjectivity and intersubjectivity. Such a situation contains a dilemma for many of the principal political actors. To achieve authority and legitimacy as a political actor in the intergroup context, for instance in the Assembly, it will be necessary to play by the inclusivist rules. However, for some of the principal political leaders, especially on certain highly sensitive issues such as decommissioning, prisoner release and the perennial issue of parades, intragroup legitimacy may require adherence to an exclusivist script. The dilemma is that the intergroup setting now requires adherence, pragmatic or otherwise, to inclusivist rules. However, for many, in many circumstances, successful and proper intragroup communication, and the legitimacy it confers, will require continued reliance on the well-entrenched exclusivist rules. The problem of distorted communication arises in this context. It is the effect of the deeply entrenched institutionalisation of exclusivist rules within the cultures of Northern Irish institutions along with the copresence, now with a new legitimacy, of inclusivist rules that are attempting to displace these entrenched ways of being and relating. The very prospect of substantive change challenges the forms of thinking, feeling and reasoning which characterise the exclusivist position. This is the case because substantive change itself must always move beyond the merely tactical or pragmatic. Substantive change, involves, eventually, a transformation of the predominant set of unconscious rules that organise subjectivity and intersubjectivity. Along the way the dilemma of distorted communication will have to be resolved.

The dilemma for some central political leaders is that any movement on their part towards enhancing the scope and propriety of inclusivist rules risks throwing into dispute their own authority to speak and act for the group. Such a move is likely to generate internal conflict which, if settled through the reassertion of exclusivism within the group, will immediately rebound with perverse effects in the intergroup context. As a consequence, distortions of communication between groupings will expand as the pragmatic acceptance of an inclusivist lingua franca is radically undercut. At this point the new political structures themselves would be thrown into crisis. On the other hand, if elite members of the various groups participating in the new political structures can hold to a pragmatic acceptance of the inclusivist lingua franca, eventually they will have to carry this inclusivist set of rules back into their own grouping. In so doing they, again, risk the emergence of distorted communication within the group and, potentially, the loss of their own authority. However, should they succeed in gaining, at least, a pragmatic acceptance of inclusivism by the members of their grouping, they will, thereby, have initiated or reinforced a process of cultural change within that grouping. David Trimble's success in gaining 58 per cent interim support, from the members of the Ulster Unionist Council, for entering a power-sharing executive with, among others, members of Sinn Fein, holds out the promise of such a beginning to cultural change within key unionist institutions (*Irish Times*, 29 November, 1999). This process, if it succeeds, will involve movement from pragmatics to a new ethics: a lived ethics of political being and doing that now is structured by an inclusivist imaginary in which adversarial democracy has displaced violence and exclusion as the leading form for governance, dispute resolution and intergroup relations.

The new assembly and power-sharing executive, then, could be described as a kind of testbed for the capacity of leadership to rework the predominant set of unconscious rules that organise a grouping's identity. Moreover, the further political cooperation across the sectarian divide proceeds, the more testing circumstances will become. As particular proposals, constructed according to inclusivist rules, take on specific definition, the challenge to exclusivism will become more pronounced. A predominant form of thinking, feeling and reasoning about social and political relations will be threatened with imminent displacement. And the agents of this displacement may include a grouping's own leadership. At such moments, the potential breakdown of political cooperation and negotiation, due to the emergence of distorted patterns of communication both within and between groupings, is heightened. It follows that the potential for the recolonisation of the political field by exclusivism is enhanced at such moments. It is important to note that this 'danger' is the other side of the political advances towards establishing the legitimacy of inclusivism. As inclusivism begins to effectively establish its legitimacy it powerfully challenges the old, entrenched exclusivism and triggers, as it were, a sharp battle for ideological hegemony.

How can we best analyse the characteristics of such a battle for hegemony? I have argued that this battle entails an ongoing conflict within the process of structuration, a conflict over which discourse – and hence which forms of common sense, identity and intersubjectivity, and which constructions of power, authority and violence – should come to organise the political and social field. As at many previous critical moments in the history of Northern Ireland, the hegemony of exclusivist rules has been fundamentally challenged. These apparently 'primordial' rules – replete as they are with persecutory anxieties, mechanisms of splitting and projection, dehumanisations or iconic representations of the other and replete also with constructions of what is proper that are regulated by reference to conformity with group norms – offer certainty and reassurance regarding questions of identity. Therefore they are particularly difficult to dislodge, not just because they are currently in place but also because attempts to displace them threaten already established forms of identity and relatedness and set in train the dilemma of addressing intragroup and intergroup concerns, at once. This attempt to look both ways opens up in turn the conflict between different rules for the organisation of subjectivity and intersubjectivity. Characteristically, but not inevitably, in such a conflict exclusivism has tended to re-produce itself. Certainly this has been the empirical outcome in Northern Ireland. However, as exclusivism cannot resolve the problems it creates within the political and social field – unless unacceptable 'solutions' such as partition are resorted to – the persistence of civil conflict provides the basis for further attempts to reconcile the differences.

The current situation has, again, reset the conflict between inclusivism and exclusivism. My analysis, while highlighting the dilemma and related difficulties attending substantive change, points to the discursive, social and psychic processes that such a change would involve. It further indicates that such a transformation will require, within a broad range of social and political institutions, a type of leadership that can resist the emergence of distorted patterns of communication and address the anxieties of those groupings that construe change through an exclusivist lens. Such leadership will need to address and displace the predominance of exclusivist rules for the construction of identities and social relations. It will need to displace a predominant, although in no way necessary or inevitable, form of thinking, feeling and reasoning about the self and the group within the field of social and political relations. As I suggested at the outset, it will need to move Northern Ireland's political culture from one marked predominantly by enmity to one organised by the inclusivist rules of adversarial democracy. The very dynamism of discourse – of identities, boundaries, desires, rules and rewards – becomes the ground upon which such leadership can act.

Notes

1. This chapter was written in April 1999. It contains some minor additions made in November 1999.
2. See note 7 below for more detail regarding these figures.
3. See 'Mitchell Issues his Concluding Report', *Irish Times*, Friday, 19 November 1999.
4. See, for instance, Mitchell (1986).
5. Elsewhere I have specified the characteristics of these positions in considerable detail. See Cash (1996), ch. 4.
6. Currently in Northern Ireland, in distinction from earlier periods, the dehumanising position is seldom drawn upon in public discourse. The displacement of a reliance on this position within public discourse is itself a major indicator of the significant change already achieved in Northern Ireland. The role of the paramilitary groups and their political 'wings' has been crucial in this regard.
7. The term 'Lundy' has become the ultimate term of abuse within the unionist lexicon, signifying, as it does, treachery and betrayal by a member of one's own community. It derives from the name of the Governor of Derry in 1689, Robert Lundy, who proposed to surrender Derry to the Jacobite forces in order to forestall the siege and attempted starvation of Derry, which at that time was offering protection to 30 000 Protestant refugees. His attempted surrender was stopped by a group of apprentices, whose actions are celebrated by unionists to this day. The distinguished historian, A.T.Q. Stewart, has written of this incident: 'The unfortunate Governor of Derry whose notoriety is so preserved in Protestant mythology was in no sense a traitor, but simply a prudent soldier acting in the interests of the preservation of the people under his care. He has become the archetype of those who truck with the enemy; therefore each crisis inevitably produces a new Lundy. It is not an archaic survival but a recurrent nightmare. If Lundy had not existed, it would have been necessary to invent him' (Stewart, 1977). This analysis nicely states aspects of my own argument.
8. The weight of evidence suggests that slightly more than 50 per cent of unionist voters voted 'yes' at the referendum. The percentage seems to lie somewhere between 51 per cent and 53 per cent. For an informative discussion of the level

of unionist support for the referendum see 'Gloves Off as Unionists Square Up for Poll' by Martina Purdy, *Belfast Telegraph*, Monday, 25 May 1998. Purdy concludes her discussion by noting that what 'is clear is that unionists are divided and the vote was close'.

Bibliography

Cash, J.D. *Identity, Ideology and Conflict: The Structuration of Politics in Northern Ireland* (Cambridge University Press, 1996).
de Bréadún, D. 'Trimble Commits Himself to Era of Change in North', *Irish Times*, Tuesday, 23 June 1998.
Harnden, T. 'Trimble Faces Tough Fight to Heal the Rifts' *Electronic Telegraph*, no. 1095, Monday, 25 May 1998.
Harnden, T. 'Trimble Attacks Adams in Arms Row' *Electronic Telegraph*, no. 1095, Monday, 25 May 1998.
Lacan, J. *The Seminar of Jacques Lacan, Book II* (New York: Norton, 1988).
Mitchell, J. (ed.), *The Selected Melanie Klein* (London: Penguin, 1986).
'New Deal Interview – Ian Paisley – Fighting Battle to Defend Union', *Newsletter*, 16 May 1998.
Sengupta, K. 'Paisley's Fire and Brimstone Gospel', *Independent*, 12 May 1998.
Stewart, A.T.Q. *The Narrow Ground* (London: Faber & Faber, 1977) 48.
'The Courage of Mr Trimble', *Irish Times*, Monday, 29 November 1999.

7

Racism, Racialised Identities and the Psychoanalytic Other[1]

STEPHEN FROSH

ALAN: *Seems to be all black boys have a chip on their shoulder. Er, you do get white bullies – I'm not sayin' that, but half of the school here, erm, half the black boys – all of them walk around walkin' like that, brand names, lookin' down at people, like Year seven's, the little girls. They look at you and stare at you as if you're lower than them. (.)[2] And the worst bit is and then they say, 'What you doin' ruckin' up my clothes?' And you're like, 'Pardon? Ruckin up your clothes – what's that?' And they say, 'You're juggin' my clothes, you're ripping them, you're touchin' them', and you're like, 'Sorry, we're in a corridor', and you're bound to bump into them, especially when they're walkin' in a line. And they're lookin' at you as if to say, 'What you doin' here? Why are you here?'*

INT.: *Mmm.*

ALAN: *Not being racist, but they come over here. Mean I have no problem with black people. Most of my friends are coloured and foreign but sometimes it really annoys me especially when they say, 'What are you doin' – why are you here? Go home,' and all of this. I'm like, I am home, this is England. And I say in my mind, why have I got to go home – I live here. This is my home. Sometimes I feel like sayin' 'Go back to your home, Jamaica' – somewhere like that and then think about sayin' most of my friends are coloured, be upsettin' them as well.*

INT.: *Most of your friends are black are they – or?*

ALAN: *They're black and white, like Indian.*

INT.: *Right.*

ALAN: *Have some friends who are white as well.*

INT.: *Yeah.*

ALAN: *I think about what my friends would feel. I mean the amount of trouble I'd get in.*

INT.: *Mmm.*

ALAN: *And I realise it would be out of order to say that anyway – it would be racist.*

INT.: *Mmm.*
ALAN: *And that's the last thing I want to be called – racist.*
INT.: *Right, ok.*
ALAN: *Cos I probably would of said it if I hadn't thought that and then lookin' back on it, got in so much trouble, probably wouldn't be here – be eatin' hospital food or somethin'.*
INT.: *Right.*
ALAN: *There'd be so many people gangin' up on you, carryin' knives and pointin' them at you and you're like, 'OK, sorry'.*
(White twelve-year-old boy)

Racism seems to stay with us all the time, only its manifestations shifting; these manifestations infiltrate most aspects of contemporary society and represent some of its most dangerous destructive impulses. If we are to create a truly 'critical' critical psychology, it must take the threat of racism seriously and engage with it, at a variety of levels: theoretical, offering some understanding of the intertwining of personal racist consciousness and social forces; empirical, grounding this in evidence about racist activity; and practical, in suggestions for, and attempts at, anti-racist work. This chapter tries to do something at least with the first two strands, offering a theoretical account, inflected by psychoanalysis, of the construction of racist identities, using material that shows how young masculinities are 'racialised' as part of the process through which they are created.

The London boy quoted above, speaking in an interview study of young masculinities, tells us that the 'last thing' that he wants to be called is 'racist'. In fact, if anyone found out what he was thinking, it would indeed be the 'last thing' for him: *'There'd be so many people gangin' up on you, carryin' knives and pointin' them at you'*; he'd be *'eatin' hospital food or somethin'*. Anyway, he knows that the thoughts he has are wrong: *'I realise it would be out of order to say that anyway – it would be racist.'* He thinks of the friends he has, black, white, Indian; 'coloured', he calls them. He thinks they would be upset if he gave voice to his feelings and then he would get into trouble. He knows from this that it would be 'out of order'. Wrong, that is, not in itself, not solely (but, to give a sympathetic reading, perhaps *partially*) because he would be upsetting them, but because of the consequences, the trouble.

What is the nature of the racism in this passage? Partly it lies in the dynamic of Alan's response to what he recognises as racist thoughts (*'it would be racist'* to give voice to them). The reason he censors himself is not the upset these thoughts would cause, if spoken aloud, but because of the trouble they would cause *him*; that is, he fears a violent response. From whom does he fear this and why? From the black boys, who *'all... have a chip on their shoulder'*. These black boys would get him with their knives, make him say sorry, send him to hospital. So part of the workings of racism here lies in the assertion that what's wrong is the *articulation* of racist thoughts, not the thoughts themselves, and that they are wrong because they produce troublesome effects. Alan polices his racism in order to keep out of trouble; he does it too in the interview, in a time-honoured way: as soon as the racist cat is out of the bag, it is put back in again: *'Most of my friends are coloured'*.

Alan sees the black boys in his school swaggering and looking down on him, as if to say to him, *'What you doin' here? Why are you here?'* They take up all the space, deny him his rightful place; after all, these boys are *'coloured and foreign'* but *they* tell *him* to go home. This is most of all what he hates in them, their superiority, the way they treat the place as home, when it is *his* home, *'I live here. This is my home.'* His feeling sometimes is, all of them, from wherever they might have come, they should go back to *their* home, *'Jamaica'*.

This 'Jamaica' is an important place in British racism's psychic geography. It is one of the places from which all these 'coloured and foreign' others come to invade and take up all the space. In Alan's mind, it is the immediate association: *'my* home England, *their* home Jamaica'. Many of the boys (black and white) we have interviewed see African-Caribbean boys as 'hard', possibly stylish and admired, but carrying an image of aggression and disdain for others. In Alan's mind, *all* black boys are of this kind, all the same, all other. Importantly for understanding contemporary racism, they are not *inferior*; rather, they belong elsewhere, so their airs – their superiority and disdain, their *'lookin' down at people'*, their *'[staring] at you as if you are lower than them'* – are intolerable; *they have no right*. For Alan, it is as if his home has been invaded and taken from him, and he can do nothing about it because, in his imagination at least, the knives would then be out.

The white London boys we have interviewed commonly complain about the assumption of *superiority* on the part of the outsider. Here is a passage from an interview with another white boy, this time fourteen years old, where the anger is directed at Asians (that is, people from the Indian subcontinent):

PETE: *In England I think the Asian people er think that they're higher than the black and the white people.*
INT.: *Do they?*
PETE: *Well they don't like show that, they just go around in their groups and terrorise people, like I heard that there were these little kids that go and rape this lady from Holland or something, who just came over to see the country and then she's like walking down an alley one day and then there's little kids about twelve who go and rape her, I think that's disgraceful really, I mean if that's what's going to happen.*
INT.: *Are there any boys like that here in this school?*

PETE: *No really no, no, because they've been well educated, they're not like those kind of people, they've got these stupid schools where they do nothing, and you don't get an education and you don't get taught to be polite and stuff like that.*

The 'Asian' (that is Indian, Pakistani, Bengali) boys see themselves as *'higher than the black and the white people'*; the way Pete knows this is because *'they just go around in their groups and terrorise people'*. As it happens, he does not actually know any boys like those he imagines to have raped the *'lady from Holland'*, but he assumes that they are the products of *'stupid schools'*, ill-educated. So Pete's version of things is that the Asian boys see themselves as superior ('higher'), but in fact it is their ignorance that sustains this belief: in reality, they are ill-educated, impolite. The fantasy is that they are rapists and terrorisers. Interestingly, many of the boys we have interviewed see black and white boys as being more like one another than they are like Asians, whose difference is marked out by their tight culture, strong family ties, and – particularly – their language:

INT.: *Yeah what about the, the language cos you have mentioned in the group interview that one of the things that the boys don't like is* (2) *that the Bengali people speak in their own language.*
ANGUS: *That's what most people don't like about* (3) *the Bengali people cos they speak in their own language and you can't really understand what they are saying but when you are speaking in English you can you can understand what they are saying* [INT.: *Yeah*] *right and ...*
INT.: *Is that something you don't like about them?*
ANGUS: *Yeah cos you don't even have to say anything about you* [Int.: Right] (2)
INT.: *Do you think they might be saying things about you then?*
ANGUS: *I don't know.*
(White fourteen-year-old)

Once again, the theme here seems to be the way the white boy feels excluded, with this exclusion carrying a paranoid charge.

Let us try to think what psychoanalysis might have to say about some of this. What is most noticeable about contemporary racism is its remarkable sinuousness, its capacity to appear as something else, for instance nationalism or liberationism, and its power to catalyse fantasy and imagination in such a way as to set neighbours against one another and propel nations into civil war. Nation-states are explicitly feeding on racist sensitivities in order to mark out their own boundaries; indeed, the postmodern polyphony of voices and cultures in this arena seems not to be resulting in celebratory enjoyment, but rather to be provoking a counterrevolution in which what is sought is safety in mythical but nonetheless concrete boundaries from which otherness can be excluded and denounced. Cartographies, 'England versus

Jamaica' in the relatively anodyne formulation of twelve-year-old Alan, are central to this exclusionary dynamic. *They* belong elsewhere; *this* is ours.

In this minefield, what psychoanalysis might be called upon to offer is an account of how Otherness operates in the subjective geography of the racist psyche. What is the dynamic at work here, fuelling the map-drawing, the search for an other-free, dark-continent-free 'whiteness', that 'purity' which seems so desirable to the racist consciousness? How is it that 'all' black people can represent so powerfully the Other in the white subject's struggle for identity? Traditionally, psychoanalysis has argued that predictable, albeit irrational, defensive processes are at work here, for example (or particularly) those projective processes which Kleinians identify as linked with the preservation of the self – that is, defences against paranoid or even 'psychotic' disturbances of emotion and the personality. The paranoid nature of racist thinking is apparent in conspiracy theories and fantasies of being flooded by waves of immigration, or of being infected by immigrant-borne diseases, or poisoned by alien foods, smells and culture – fantasies present only just below the surface in the discourse of many of the boys we have interviewed. In Kleinian (or, more precisely, Bionian) terms, this pattern of what one might call projective evacuation is an anti-thought process, a defence against thinking in the constructive sense of making meaningful links between aspects of the world. As Michael Rustin (1991) points out, racial categories are particularly useful repositories for such anti- or pseudo-thinking not just because they are socially valorised for political purposes (such as colonialism and economic exploitation), but because they are fundamentally 'empty' categories, with very little externally grounded, 'objective' meaning. Rustin comments that

> virtually no differences are caught by 'black' or 'white' ... This is paradoxically the source of racism's power. It is the fact that this category means nothing in itself that makes it able to bear so much meaning – mostly psychologically primitive in character – with so little innate resistance from the conscious mind. (p. 63)

The process of racist ideation is therefore one in which unwanted or feared aspects of the self are experienced as having the power to disturb the personality in so damaging a way that they have to be repudiated and evacuated or projected into the racialised other, chosen for this purpose both because of pre-existing social prejudices and because, as a fantasy category, racial Otherness can be employed to mean virtually anything. Moreover, once the projective impulse takes hold, it feeds on itself, creating a lie at the centre of the personality, something destructive and damaged, which must be endlessly defended against, poisoning the world around. Rustin comments, 'The "lie" in this system of personality organisation becomes positively valued, as carrying for the self an important aspect of its defence against weakness, loss or negative judgement' (*ibid.*, p. 69). The more strongly it is held, the more it is needed; the subject comes to be in love with the lie and fearful of anything that challenges it. Racism, socially originated though it may be, is consequently deeply invested in by the individual, distorting and disturbing her or his relations with reality and with truth.

Close contact with the racialised other is not, therefore, likely in itself to contest racism – as all the many examples of the 'most of my friends are coloured' variety testify. The lie is loved because it contains within it hated aspects of the subject, those despairing fragilities and brutal violences which, if encountered directly as part of the subject's own identity, might lead to self-hatred and dissolution. Alan's imagination about the knives of the black boys expresses this powerfully: his own hatred turned outwards, it would seem. In the racist psyche, it is always the other at fault, the cause of the racist dynamic. John, another white boy of thirteen, who also claims to 'hate' racism yet goes around with a racist gang attacking Asian shopkeepers, gives his own version of what happens here:

> INT.: *... you said that you didn't like the policeman because you felt you got picked upon by the police and er, one of the occasions was when you'd been cussing Asian people and they phoned up the police to come along.*
>
> JOHN: *What really bugs me is they can pull me over when it wasn't even me. And that really bugs me then I go around to the shop or wherever it was and then I can have a go at them.*
>
> INT.: *The Asian people? I see, yeah.*
>
> JOHN: *And say why, why you saying, giving my description and stuff and start cussing them.*
>
> INT.: *But presumably it's because you hang around with other boys who were doing it.*
>
> JOHN: *Yeah and that, looking up and then I get pulled over while I was walking down the street. I can get searched as well most the time and get asked questions. I just don't like it. I really hate it, I hate getting pulled over cos it (3) cos it just really pees me off and they just accuse you of doing it when you hardly, didn't even do anything.*

The 'hateful' state of mind here is one of being rubbished, picked on, abused, interrogated. In John's psychic world, it is 'them' again, those others – the Asians, the police – who pick on him '*when you hardly, didn't even do anything*'; the violence which erupts is not, therefore, his violence, but theirs.

Again, why should this be so racialised? Here is Joel Kovel (1995), linking anti-black racism with the advance of capitalism in the west:

> A persistent shadow had dogged puritanism, the dominant cultural type of the early capitalist order – a spectre of renunciation and rationalisation, of the loss of sensuousness and the deadening of existence. In this context the animality

projected onto the black by virtue of his or her role in slavery became suitable to represent the vitality split away from the world in Puritan capitalist asceticism. Sensuousness that had been filtered out of the universe in capitalist exchange was to reappear in those who had been denied human status by the emergent capitalist order. Blacks, who had been treated as animals when enslaved, became animals in their essence, while the darkness of their skin became suitable to represent the dark side of the body, embodying the excremental vision that has played so central a role in the development of western consciousness. In this way blacks were seen as beneath whites in reasoning power and above whites in sexuality and the capacity for violence. (p. 217)

Kovel is arguing here that a set of social circumstances, economically motivated, with slavery and capitalist accumulation at their centre, produced in the west a psychological imperative to disown multiplicity and sensuality and to project it into the black Other. The power of this psychosocial organisation is so great that it can 'enter into the evolution of the psyche' (ibid., p. 212), closing down the possibility of openness to any new experience which is not in the interests of accumulation. Instead, the repressed sensuousness, preserved unconsciously because otherwise the psyche dries up completely and is 'deadened', is experienced as threatening and subversive, as well as exciting. It is bestial, animal, fit for projection onto those human subjects designated by the complex social drive of capitalist imperialism as non-human – the slaves. Their physical blackness, marking them as distinct, is merged together with already-existing psychic defences against what Norman Brown (1959) has called the 'excremental vision' (see Kovel, above) to create the ideal object of repudiation. Excrement, mess, animality, anality, polycentric enjoyment, the 'primitive': all these are denounced by capitalist accumulation, and their psychic representation is blackness.

Kovel proposes that the turn of capitalism to western-style racism is driven by its own power to disrupt the personality, to place selfhood and identity under threat. Again linking with Rustin's analysis and with the wider critique of modernity as exciting and annihilating at one and the same time (for example, Berman, 1983), Kovel argues that it is at those moments and in those spaces where identity is up against the dissolution of itself by the logic of modernity's brute force that it most needs the extreme defence against Otherness provided by racist ideology. Recognising its own terror it converts it into loathing, thus feeling it and extruding it in the same gesture. Racism consequently, totally regressive though it is, also expresses the contradiction of modernity and the desperation of the racist as she or he experiences the threat of loss of self. The racist needs the hated other as a repository of all that she or he has lost and fears losing further: 'Without the spectacle of lost nature to hate and be fascinated by, it is doubtful whether the reduction of the psyche to a homogeneous personality could be sustained' (p. 218). Just as, in the basic scheme of domination, master needs slave for his mastery to be recognised, so the denuded, alienated and split-off racist consciousness needs its denigrated object for it to feel alive.

Here again is John, working on the fragility of his white identity:

> INT.: *How would you, how would you identify your own ethnic background. What would you say you were?*
>
> JOHN: (4) *(I dunno) I'm* (2) *just English. Um* (1) *My ancestors could be* (2) *German for all I know but I am English. I'm* (1) *I'm all English. My mum, my dad's English. My nan an' granddad are English. And so basically I'm English.*
>
> INT.: *Do you think of yourself as white? Is that* … ?
>
> JOHN: *Yeah, but um I don't try and mix in with the blacks. I don't start listening to the* (1) *like, swing. I like a bit of swing, yeah, but I don't try and fit in with the like, the backwards hat, the baggy trousers an' stuff like that. I just wear what I wanna wear. [*INT.: *Right] Rather than trying to fit in. I just wanna wear what I think looks good on me.*
>
> INT.: *Yeah. Do, do some white boys, do they try and be like blacks then, or* … ?
>
> JOHN: *Not that I know of. But I mean, maybe in different schools, boys could be doing that. But I haven't really noticed that.*
>
> INT.: *No I was just interested in why, why you were saying that you don't* (1) *try and* =
>
> JOHN: *Because then I'd be saying* (1) *I'd be told that I would be a black wannabe. [*INT.: *OK, yeah] Which I'm not. [*INT.: *Yeah] An' I don't wanna be a black person. [*INT.: *Yeah] I'm perfectly, I'm perfectly happy with being white.*
>
> INT.: *Yeah. But there are some black wannabes are there?*
>
> JOHN: *Mmm. Yeah. There's* (3) *there's one boy round my area that* (2) *that sorta acts like that. He wants to be* (.) *like, he tries to bowl. He tries to walk like a black person, like, being stylish an' stuff like that. But* (1) *I don't really try and do that. Just wear* (2) *normal trainers, jogging pants an' T-shirt an' then I'm done. That's what looks good on me an'* (1) *that's fine. I don't try an' fit in.*
>
> INT.: *Well why d'you think some, some white boys do try to be black wannabes?*
>
> JOHN: *Because maybe they just don't wanna be white. P'raps they'd prefer to be black.*
>
> INT.: *Yeah why?*
>
> JOHN: *Maybe they like black race better than white* (.) *um the white race. [*INT.: *Yeah] You know.*
>
> INT.: *I was just wondering, you know, whether* (2) *some white boys think of it as being* (1) *tougher and harder being black at all.*
>
> JOHN: *Some of the hardest boys I know in the school are white. [*INT.: *Mmm] An' some of 'em are black. [*INT.: *Mmm] You know I don't think that's got to do with it really. I dunno why people want to be a different colour than they are. They should just be happy for what colour they are an'. I am. I'm perfectly happy being English. I'm perfectly happy being white. [*INT.: *Right]*

It seems easily apparent that John is trying to find something concrete here in regard to his own ethnic identity. This comes through most clearly in the section where he tries to establish that he is 'English' through and through and 'basically', something he achieves only with considerable effort, by means of a mounting yet hesitant series of clauses about his parentage which seem to have the function of drawing up the evidence or perhaps naming something for himself:

> *(I dunno) I'm (2) just English. Um (1) My ancestors could be (2) German for all I know but I am English. I'm (1) I'm all English. My mum, my dad's English. My nan an' granddad are English. And so basically I'm English.*

The impact of this is to raise a question about the security of this identity judgement, especially as it is followed immediately by a 'but' which has a defensive rather than a logical function:

> INT.: *Do you think of yourself as white? Is that ... ?*
> JOHN: *Yeah, but um I don't try and mix in with the blacks.*

The construction of himself as white English seems immediately to call into existence the spectre of the Other, a concern over whether somewhere lurking inside him is the wish to be black. It is as if John has an awareness, perhaps not quite conscious, that identity is built on the basis of an occluded Otherness, perhaps the mixture of desired sensuality and dangerous hatred described by Rustin and Kovel. In John's case, the energy which he puts into defending himself against the imagined accusation that he might be a '*black wannabe*' is very striking, suggesting that an important piece of emotional work is taking place here, keeping something troublesome at bay. What this interview raises for John is an uncertainty over the security of his 'hard, white, English' identity, so the interviewer comes to represent a slightly persecutory, questioning voice. Hence, without the interviewer raising the issue, John launches into a denial that he has any aspiration to be like the black youngsters; no-one has challenged him on this, rather the doubt about what he really wants has come from within himself. His further strategy, having slipped into this defensive arrangement, is to claim that everything he does he does because he wants to, not in order to fulfil anyone's expectations. He likes the way he is ('*I'm perfectly happy being English. I'm perfectly happy being white.*') and everyone should be happy with what they are.

But is he happy? Taking into account the exclusionary fantasies described earlier, the Jamaica and Asia of the British racist imagination, what seems to come across is that the fragility of the racialised (and in this instance, masculinised) identity is one which produces a desperate and at times vicious projection which requires an other to make it viable. This other is the active repository of split-off hatred; without it, identity formation fails. Yet the other is also imbued with desire, is admired (the striking physical superiority of the black is the most obvious fantasy here) as well as rejected. To use a parallel from Judith Butler's (1995) formulation of gender identity, it is the '"acting out" of unresolved grief'; the ' "never" loved and "never" grieved' (pp. 32, 34); that is, these racialised identities enact their own precarious foundations, which contain within them a hidden and denied series of repudiations and wishes. Psychoanalysis suggests, therefore, that the boundaries both contain and exclude, that the petty racisms we see in our young interviewees link with the gross racisms brutally enacted around the world through sharing an anxiety about enfeeblement and dissolution at the hands of a violent and sensual other. What is this other, then, if not the disowned but projectively identified terroristic self? And what does it say about us all, and the societies in which we live, that this terroristic self is so much part of us, in the schoolboys of London and in all the places where the unspeakable 'real' of racism breaks through?

Notes

1. This study, funded by the British Economic and Social Research Council, is called 'Emergent Identities: Masculinities and 11–14 Year Old Boys'. It is jointly directed by myself and Ann Phoenix; Rob Pattman is the interviewer and research officer on the project. Names of all participants have been changed.
2. (.) indicates a brief pause; longer pauses are timed, for example (2) means 'two-second pause'; = signifies overlapping speech.

Bibliography

Berman, M. *All That is Solid Melts into Air* (London: Verso, 1983).
Brown, N. *Life Against Death* (Middletown, Connecticut: Wesleyan University Press, 1959).
Butler, J. 'Melancholy Gender/Refused Identification', in M. Berger, B. Wallis and S. Watson (eds), *Constructing Masculinity* (London: Routledge, 1995).
Kovel, J. 'On Racism and Psychoanalysis', in A. Elliott and S. Frosh (eds), *Psychoanalysis in Contexts* (London: Routledge, 1995).
Rustin, M. *The Good Society and the Inner World* (London: Verso, 1991).

8

Coping with Plural Identities

SWATIJA MANORAMA

Cause and effect: such a duality probably never exists; in truth we are confronted by a continuum out of which we isolate a couple of pieces, just as we perceive motion only as isolated points and then infer it without ever actually seeing it. The suddenness with which many effects stand out misleads us; actually, it is sudden only for us. In this moment of suddenness there are an infinite number of processes which elude us. (Nietzsche, 1974, p. 112)

Experiencing Plural Identities

'I want to live. I do not want to die.' She held my hand in a tight grip and said these words to me while I collected her burn wound swab. Those words still haunt me. I was then a postgraduate researcher, recently graduated, working for my master's degree in microbiology and burn wounds was my topic. I was stunned by her gesture and by my helplessness. Her destiny was obvious – she had 90 per cent burns.

Another patient was a fond mother of a very young child. Clinically she was out of burn shock. I had begun to feel hopeful. The next day I went for my bacteriological reports and learnt that she was dead. I could not even weep. I learnt that the patient in the bed next to her had succumbed to her burn wounds. The body was quickly removed, but the young daughter of the first patient could not be stopped from her outburst. By all accounts, her cries and her grief, longing for her mother, played a crucial role and this woman patient, who was otherwise recovering rapidly, had died within the next two or three hours. I stood there thinking of what must have happened inside her. Did she as mother realise the pain and sorrow of her offspring? Did the death of a fellow patient bring home the eventual meaninglessness of her struggle with death? What was it that shocked her so badly?

I found that the burn patients were invariably women. And that among them an overwhelming majority were dowry-related deaths often masquerading as accidents. Nationally in India, the issue was beginning to surface in a big way and the women's movement was demanding that exemplary punishment should be meted out to people who lead women to their deaths. This was related to the incident which finally laid to rest my identity as a researcher of the bacteriology of burn wounds.

For a few days I had begun very few samples since very few patients were being admitted. I learnt that I was not getting cases because of an acute shortage of kerosene caused by a failure of the public distribution system. I realised with horror that what I was finally doing as researcher was simply to wait for enough women to be burnt so that I would complete my study of the bacteriology of burn wounds. When the supply of kerosene eased the shortage would be over and women would be burnt again. That was the last day of my research and the dreams of acquiring that particular degree. But it left behind a host of questions. What anyway was a degree? What for that matter was science, and why should I pursue it?[1]

These concerns forced me to look beyond my discipline, and my own experience. Some questions kept bothering me throughout. Why do women opt for such drastic measures? Why do women see death as positive? Such questions did not sit well with my ideas of women's worldview and behaviour as constructive. This contrast took me to an exploration of the concept of self, and the self of women in oppressive and subjugated settings. It did not simplify matters for me. In the Indian context, the millennia-old pluralism of cultures and practices and consequently hierarchies and identities cuts across the fabric of daily life and all civil society. There are no clear lines separating the oppressed from the oppressors; there is a continuum, not a divide.

The entire experience of those days came back to me as I began work on this chapter. I realised the necessity of theorising multiple identities, their interaction, the clash between them. I went into that experience as much a young woman coming of age as a postgraduate research student. And it is the experiences and conflicts that confronted me which helped form a feminist and 'people's science movement' activist.

It was obvious that I needed an open mind and a different framework to answer such questions. It also strengthened my own understanding that in the Indian context the western model and framework based on sharp breaks may not be sufficient, and may not be able to explore truly the subversive acts of individuals not adhering to their norms or categories. The Indian context does not fit well into a class ideology, nor into a caste ideology. Gender, region, hierarchy, sect, ritual – these form part of a kaleidescope in which multiple identities are constructed. This chapter is part of a larger attempt to evolve a framework appropriate for the Indian context.

My experience led me to feminist ideas and opened up a new vision. It also taught me that a rigid categorisation of identity in terms of norms and behaviour limits understanding and masks the complexity of the situation. It emphasised for me the need for a critical psychology in the Indian context. What I refer to as a kaleidoscopic vision is the ability to see complex interweaving and flexible interconnectedness of each facet of our subjectivity – a critical analysis that rebuilds rather than diminishes plurality as complexity.

Nationality and Diversity

Women are constructed at the intersection of a large number of multiple identities, situated as they are within the matrix of every kind of social grouping. Throughout history women have had to engage with these multiple identities at different levels, to find ways of coping with them. It needs to be understood that they have not done this passively but have engaged with these identities in a dynamics of struggle, compromise and also a search for a constructive way of combining them.

In order to do this, I felt I needed to go beyond mainstream, western psychology. In the Indian context, as we are going to see, the multiple aspects of subjectivity are dependent on and interwoven into each other. For example, while a lower-caste dalit (an ex-untouchable) is dalit or poor in all aspects of life, the way in which being a dalit is regulated is complex, contradictory and multiple.

In the Indian context, over millennia, at least from Mesolithic times, our history is a history of migrants coming and settling in the land, making it their own. It is this diverse mosaic which underlies Indianness.

Today, at the turn of the century, the so-called religious conversions and reconversions of the adivasis (tribal peoples) and the dalits (the ex-untouchable castes) are being resisted by killings and violence. Those who have not responded to their plight for centuries but are now arguing against their conversion implicitly treat them as Hindu and impose on them their majoritarian norms and identity. Tribal traditions, customs and identities are not uniform even among and across tribal groups and represent a special case which brings out the problem. The personal laws governing different social groups in India are based on religion. But strictly speaking, tribal societies are structured in a way where the religion of tribal peoples does not have a codified legal system the way other religions have. So far as personal laws are concerned, traditional Hindu codes consider tribal peoples to be outside the bounds of majority Hindu caste law and consider them to be regulated by their own customary law. However, the judicial system has taken customary law to mean not that customarily observed by these tribes but unreformed Hindu law, which is often worse in many respects. This has created enormous difficulties because tribal clans have so many different patriarchal and matriarchal, patrilocal and matrilocal as well as patrilineal and matrilineal practices. The identities of the tribal peoples are divided in different ways within the polity and in civil society.

Masculinity and the Imposition of Uniformity

When we are talking about how multiple identities are lived by women it is important to recognise that the notion of unitary identity that is promoted is masculine, Hindu and nationalist. Hinduism and nationalism are presented as synonymous with masculine virility. Militarism, aggressive majoritarianism (in India, the Hindu extremists or the Sangh Parivar) and male, macho idiom have gone hand in hand. Perhaps the most blatant example of this is the remark by the outspoken Hindutva exponent Bal Thackeray who exclaimed about nuclear weapon tests carried out recently by the Indian government that 'We had to prove that we are not eunuchs'!

The nuclear tests are for Thackeray a proof of the national virility. This is not an accident; the idiom of virility, of manhood, of male honour pervades all his speech and his writings and is an essential vehicle in garnering support for his project of aggressive imposition of Hindutva on the minorities. There is also most often an equation of women and nation as motherland. Women, helpless and pitiable, in danger of violation, need to be protected by men. So, also the motherland. Aggression becomes a necessary virtue and any means of overpowering others an essential proof of one's virility.

For the Hindutva exponent, masculinity and patriotic feelings go hand in hand. To show true patriotic feeling is to be hostile to minorities – tribal peoples, Christians, dalits, especially Muslims. So, the nuclear tests are for them a means of overpowering Pakistan, a Muslim nation. The remark about eunuchs is also double-edged; it utilises the traditional derogatory status of eunuchs (transsexual) as castrated men to label those who oppose the nuclear testing as castrated men, men without testicles.

The recent nuclear tests we had to witness in India have had their repercussions in the way many people see themselves. Public opinion polls conducted just after the nuclear explosions showed that 91 per cent of adults in six cities in India supported nuclear testing. Equipping the 'nation' with nuclear arms has become an issue for the expression of nationalist feeling for the ruling political party and represents a new attempt to bolster its falling popularity. Secular and women's groups responded to the nuclear testing by highlighting the violence of nuclear armament and the politics of aggression.

This sense of an increased capacity of violence against so-called enemies translates into and justifies everyday aggression against women, minorities and other under privileged sections. Consequently, women's fear of sexual violence, used even otherwise as a form of contentment, increases with the celebration of masculinist violence. Such a milieu can impede women's struggle for personal independence and safe society, and trap them into either accepting greater containment of their activity and mobility or militarising themselves, into either retreating from public spaces or allowing themselves to be pulled into the language of violence against 'others' (Sangari, 1998, pp. 52–5).

Hindu Identity: Contextualised and Decontextualised

Nationalism presents an Indian identity as a unitary category which covers over the multiple nations which compose India and therefore elides the complex struggle between them. Nationalism in the Indian context has been a complicated issue because during the last fifty years many nations have emerged in the subcontinent.

In fact, as Tharu puts it:

> [Nationalism] is not the awakening to self consciousness of a nation and a tradition that already exist at some deep level. Nations, like traditions and work of art, are *made* – built, created imagined. These discourses of nationalism and its cultural languages suture over gaps and create what might be called social Imaginary. They draw on the past, and indeed might use ancient and 'ethnic' or 'indigenous' materials, but the structure and the politics of these traditions are contemporary. (Tharu and Talitha, 1993, p. 52)

History and tradition have therefore become a surrogate battlefield for fighting contemporary battles. Shorn of their historical moorings and contexts, meanings are often deceptive and multiple readings are often needed to bring to light their different perspectives, to properly contextualise and situate these traditions. An illuminating example is that of dharma, a word that translates as easily into duty as into religion and is the source of their endless conflation and confusion in any consideration of Hindu concepts.

We can see in the following quote how the traditional concept of dharma, while retaining space for multiplicity, omits key caste dimensions which make the takeup of dharma more unitary than it is for lower castes. In the words of Sudhir Kakar:

> Though a person is enjoined to base his actions on the precepts of *Dharmashastras*, on the lives of men who have attained self realisation, and on his own understanding, the final answer is that no one can really in an absolute

sense, know what his *dharma* is. This is due to the fact that man's *dharma* is always considered with regard to four factors: 1) *desha* (country) which I would call the culture to which he belongs, 2) *kala* (time) the period of history in which he lives, 3) *shrama* (work) which takes into account his stage of life, 4) *guna* (attribute), which refers to ... inherent psycho-biological traits. (Kakar, 1982a, p. 5)

In contrast, Dr Babasaheb R. Ambedkar, who was champion of our secular constitution and dalit leader by birth, refuses to decontextualise the concept of dharma and draws radically different conclusions. He concludes that the dharma of a Hindu person has no meaning in an individual context, but is best described as the following of caste rules and prescriptions. The contextualising term is what appears as shrama (work) in Kakar, but which in reality is severely, and in the case of the lower castes entirely, constrained by caste. It is the decontextualisation which allows Kakar, who otherwise takes account of multiple identities very effectively, to simply dissolve the dimension of caste, a simple but merely ideological removal.

The 'Hindu Mind' and the *Bhakti* Movement – Making Space for Multiplicity

The question does not remain confined to the issue of nationality but is also deeply psychological. Kakar's work *Shamans, Mystics and Doctors* is quite important in this respect. He brings out forcefully the limitations of western psychological theories in handling psychological complaints of a people steeped in an entirely different tradition. As he says, '[I]f your world view is demonological ... then any task of buried feelings towards father is irrelevant and certainly very irreverent.' (Kakar, 1982b)

In India, mental illness is a much larger problem than is realised, and even the WHO has now recognised this. The difficulties of practising an essentially alien science steeped in equally alien traditions in the Indian context are immense. When solutions and therapies presuppose traditions, activities and practices which are non-existent, it should not be surprising that psychiatry and psychoanalysis lose many of their potential clientele to so-called quacks, shamans and religious movements where they find a greater solace and peace of mind which may be as temporary, but which may for them turn out to be much more fulfilling.[2] As the head of a psychiatric hospital expressed it in conversation:

I feel sad about my inability to reach out to my inmates even while I know the course I have taken will not help me to reach out to them. I would much rather talk to them about the philosophy and the understanding of human nature of saints from the *Bhakti* movement who have, in my opinion, given us the best possible perspective to understand human nature.[3]

In the same vein, Professor Max Mueller in his introductory piece in the book titled *Six Systems of Indian Philosophy* gives an illustration of the commonality of some views in all the branches of Hindu philosophy. He likens the Indian 'mind' to a lake and the philosophies to rivers with different identities going to north, south, east and west, yet he contends that the Hindu 'mind' is the same from the Himalayas to the Arabian Sea (Dandekar, 1986, p. 80).

This amounts to an elimination of multiple identity or at least a denial of its significance. There is thus taking much invariance for granted in these perspectives, especially in their Sanskrit expression. And there is also no doubt that they are related to the psychology or 'mind' of the superior, oppressor castes being taken for granted. This is essentially what Ambedkar does when he contextualises the abstract dharma as duty, and shows it to be mainly, if not solely, duty as a member of a caste.

The Unity of Multiple Identities in the *Bhakti* Movement

We need to refrain from a polarising reductionism which would reduce everything to caste, and portray everything through the overriding identity as caste identity. This can best be illustrated by what formed the oppositional current to the vedic, brahminical traditions – the folk tradition of the *bhakti* movement, a movement that emphasised personal devotion irrespective of caste, which swept the country from about AD 1000 onwards. In Maharashtra it took the form of the *varkari* movement, a *varkari* being an ordinary householder or housewife who vowed to be a devotee, and who plied his or her trade but lived by saintly precepts of good behaviour and undertook an annual pilgrimage on foot to Pandharpur, the seat of the central deity Vithoba. *Varkari* saints were all poets and they composed their work not in high Sanskrit (like high Latin, the language of courts and scriptures) but in the spoken, vernacular languages of the common folk, in Maharashtra, in Marathi. They came from all castes and walks of life. As a later woman poet Bahinabai puts it, Dnyaneshwar (a brahmin poet-saint) laid the foundation of the movement and Tukaram (a low-caste, shudra poet-saint) became its pinnacle. It is the relationship between these two that interests us here.

There is a tendency either to contrast the relationship between them as one of difference and opposition because of their caste backgrounds or to conflate them as nothing but part of the *bhakti* movement. What is important is to realise how these two identities are essential to each other, how both of them contribute to the unique experience and philosophy they reflect and preach. The *bhakti* movement redefined the relation between this-worldliness and Other-worldliness. Mainstream vedic tradition orients a person away from daily life, the search for selfhood often leading the person to become an ascetic or a mendicant, to *tapas* (self-torture or extreme self-abnegation). In effect, this meant that simple folk plying their daily trades could not keep on doing so and attain knowledge of selfhood, achieve peace and nirvana or *moksha*. One of the most important elements of the *bhakti* movement, which set itself apart from the mainstream vedic tradition, was its view that one could do so even as one plied one's trade and performed consciously all the duties and fulfilled all the obligations that daily life placed on people. For this, Dnyaneshwar, considered to have laid the foundation of the *bhakti* movement in Maharashtra, appealed to the Geeta. His first work, now called *Dnyaneshwari*, is a flowing Marathi commentary on the Geeta. The concept which united the this-worldliness and the other-worldliness is a concept that can be roughly translated as 'performing one's duties with no expectation of reward'. The radical implication of this is that one's identity as householder or housewife is no longer in conflict with one's identity as 'seeker'. In fact, in contrast to the mainstream vedic tradition which necessitated an ascetic rejection of daily life, the *bhakti* tradition goes on to assert daily life as natural and necessary.[4] His explanation not only preserves daily life but strengthens it, and expresses its devotion and its philosophy in day-to-day symbols in the vernacular, making devotion accessible to people at large. This positive content is what made it so important. Dnyaneshwar (in Dandekar, 1986) calls his commentary a critical understanding of Geeta. Yet it is clearly not the same Hindu 'mind', as Mueller might have it. Though the concepts of Brahman and atman are all there, the relations have undergone a radical change. The identity of 'seeker' and 'householder' are no longer at loggerheads but have formed now a unity. *The merging of these identities without submerging either is a major achievement of the* bhakti *movement, the emergence of a new 'mind'*.

From Expanded Access to Revolt

The *bhakti* movement brought about a radical expansion of access to legitimate devotion and spirituality for the common people. In the hierarchical, caste-based Hindu society it was difficult to keep and implement all these without democratic values or a universal perspective. But the enhanced meaning of these universal principles and opening of the road to salvation was not so smooth and not so clear, as is illustrated by the lives of the *bhakti* movement saints, all of whom had invariably to face opposition from the brahminical, orthodox and priestly elites. The *bhakti* movement was also a revolt. If in Dnyaneshwar this revolt was at best a muted subcurrent, it was a raging torrent in sixteenth-century Tukaram, who is considered the pinnacle of the *bhakti* movement in Maharashtra. His *bhakti* is as much as anything a revolt to overcome the oppressive pressures of the caste system and the denial of knowledge to lower-caste people. His poetry is the most rooted in the Marathi of the common people, his preaching is strong and direct and based on the experience of life. His brevity and expressiveness is phenomenal and has a direct influence on his verse. It is true that Dnyaneshwar and his writings do reflect day-to-day experiences, but they concentrate much more on the philosophical explanation of principles and are an instrument for explaining that which still remains beyond or behind experience.

In one of his verses Tukaram thanks God for his having been born a *kunbi* (a farming caste) and not, by implication, as every commentator agrees, a brahmin. His verses are a scathing indictment of brahminhood, something entirely lacking in Dnyaneshwar:

> Well it is, O God, that you made me a *kunbi*
> Or else I would have died of hypocrisy and pride
> Well it is, O God
> That I now dance at your feet
> Had I but (been brahmin and) acquired some learning
> ...
> With pride (in my caste and in learning) I would have become unbending and ended in hell[5]

And it extends to royalty as well. On an invitation from the great King Shivaji, he is said to have even told the king:

> What is gained by my coming
> Except the pointless fatigue of walking?
> ...
> At the king's palace the favoured earn honour
> The common people none[6]

But that does not diminish the contribution of the *bhakti* movement as a whole. Had Tukaram not been a seeker he could hardly have been the rebel that he was. The *bhakti* movement in Maharashtra included in its fold poet-saints from every walk of life and every caste, including women saints. Tukaram's identity as seeker, and the prior expansion of access brought about by the unity between 'householder' and 'seeker', allowing common folk to be 'seekers', was as important as his own caste identity. It would be wrong to reduce these multiple identities to any single dimension. The special position that Tukaram has occupied in this galaxy is a result of the multiple identities which are united in him – that he is a true seeker in the tradition of the *bhakti* movement and also a rebel against the caste system. It is these two poles and the tension they create which define his uniqueness.

Reappropriation: Coming to Terms with Plural Identities

Reappropriation of such traditions and their redefinition is an ongoing and significant task which is being carried out today. In this context it is also important to note stories and legends in which supposedly subordinate positions have been turned into instruments of acquiring strength, of creating space. There are subthemes which when highlighted can transform the meaning of these stories. As Tharu and Lalitha (1993) put it, it involves

> learning to read (them) in a new way, to read them not for the moments in which they collude with or reinforce the dominant ideology of gender, class, nation, or empire, but for the gesture of defiance or subversion implicit in them'. (p. 35)

One example of this is the way Tara Bhawlakar, a scholar of Marathi women's literature, interprets the story of Savitri. Tradition portrays Savitri as a model *pativrata* – a woman loyal and faithful to her husband – who argues with Death and the gods for the life of her husband and succeeds in bringing him back to life. The story is generally told as a lesson in loyalty for women and the lesson is that women are expected to observe a fast on that particular full moon and pray so that they may have the same husband for seven births. When the story is reinterpreted, however, according due importance to the individuality and identity of Savitri, she comes out not merely as a loyal and devoted wife but even more so as a human being fighting for justice and equality. Until this reinterpretation of Savitri's story, its subversive potential remained hidden.

Tradition and Modernity

Ignoring traditions, it can be argued, serves only to strengthen them. Dhere (1998), while talking about the places connected with mythology and goddess worship, points out the need to take these into account and how

> for centuries these places have stored within them the source of strength to individuals as well as to the masses. That means we must be able to gather the energies from these places to deal with our problems bravely and in a meaningful way. (Dhere, 1998, p. 8)

But it has never been easy for those demanding total change to be comfortable with traditions. In this context it is interesting to see how Sonal Shukla, a women's activist, writer and columnist, and who now heads Vacha, a women's resource centre, unreservedly accepts tradition:

> I am traditional but not conservative. Tradition is not ritual alone but tradition comprises creative expression of women and those creative expressions too I consider as traditions. I believe in colourful life and also believe that the Indian climate is bright and colourful. It is not monotonous. I also believe that I am traditional and modern at the same time. I believed in education and also learnt ballroom dancing then when I was young and it was considered British. I eat pizza too. But I also prefer *Jawar roti* because I am concerned about environmental politics and believe that traditional Indian food is special and unique to our environment.[7]

She writes a column for a paper on a wide range of subjects not restricted to women's issues *per se*. She has written about national politics, about inheritance rights, about international politics as well as about French and British culture. Many people who have liked her writing because it is well studied and well argued have also tended to think that she is a man! Men are allowed that multiplicity, women are not. Sonal has brought to the movement her traditions of Gandhi's nationalism and visions of independent India and her views reflect the engagement between feminist concerns and Gandhi's ideas of truth and non-violence:

> As I started looking into his writings anew I realised the problems I have with his philosophy and that I also have faith in his education method. I also feel that in the coming millennium the principle of non-violent struggle and his method of education will have to be adopted by the feminists.
> [But] in his early writings ... the implicit understanding involved a separation of spheres one for men and one for women ... Of course in his later writings and his practice he looked at men and women as equal because it was the need of the hour (if women were to participate in the independence struggle) and also his realisation. Yet the strong upholder of truth could not accept his mistake of his earlier days ... I think this also applies to his earlier writings which identify urban and rural as separate spheres ...
> This I never could agree with, this implicit ideology, but as I see it today with my feminist perspective of personal is political and of pluralism in cultures, I feel feminism which cuts across class and caste and the barriers of rural and urban, without undermining any given identity, it would do well to absorb Gandhi's creative ways of learning and balancing between tradition and modern. That is the only methodology which will be work in our society. And Gandhi's principle of non-violence can be the only way in the context of today's globalisation.[8]

The Aggressive Imposition of Hindutva and Plural Identities

Today, at the beginning of the new millennium, we may be facing that choice much faster and much more urgently than we would have thought.

Sonal hails from Gujarat, the same state that Gandhi came from. And in Gujarat itself, Gandhi's traditions are fast being undermined. In the communal frenzy that followed in the wake of the demolition of the Babri Masjid in 1992, Muslim women were raped, and the incident videotaped. During 1998–9, Gujarat was in the limelight for the persecution of not only Muslims but Christian tribal peoples as well, with the passive if not active connivance of the state.

There is not much point in singling out Gujarat. All this is being done all over India by the Hindu extremists, in the name of Indian tradition, Indian values and so on. The latest and the one most directly aimed at the women's movement is the virtual ban enforced on the screening of the film *Fire*. This deals with a developing lesbian relationship between two women in a household they enter through marriage. Many organisations from the Hindu extremists, with the Shiv Sena in the forefront, have vowed not to allow any screening of the film to take place and have burnt cinema halls in a couple of cities and have had a virtual ban imposed on the film's screening in most cities in western and northern India. In spite of the fact that many Indian erotic sculptures show lesbians making love, in spite of the fact that the *Kamasutra* too deals with it, the ban has been imposed in the name of an Indian tradition:

> The discourse of 'Indian tradition' currently being touted by the Sangh Parivar ... which is built upon such tropes as Indian 'values', 'Indian family system' and 'Indian Culture' has became central to the construction of the Indian identity among the urban middle classes. It is also found in the reconstruction and reification of 'Indian Culture' by the wealthy NRI set, as reflected in films depicting ideal family life such as *Hum Aap Ke Hai Kaun*. In this discourse, Indian society and its 'values' are always counterpoised to the decadent west. (Upadhya, 1998, pp. 3176–7).

Plural Identities Must Interact

The problem is deeply connected with the process of globalisation and the effect it is having on the global middle class. This class is fast losing its connection with the living pluralist traditions in this country and is in no way integrated into the traditions of the west except for superficial trappings. The Sangh Parivar homilies, offensive as they are, are nevertheless beginning to serve as useful cutouts to be placed in the gaping holes that have opened up in middle-class identities. Multiple identities, multiple cultural expressions are common. But they cannot just exist side by side. They must interact, mutually act on one other change, so that there is a harmonious whole, even if it is not a monolithic entity. This is in fact the balance between traditional and modern that Sonal had talked about, which Gandhi was so adept at striking. Globalisation has increased the urgency of this task many times. Plural identities cannot always be denied and done away with individually, because we acquire many of them through others, through what others think we are. Traditions and identities we may have denied, or may have let lapse, rear their heads at the most unexpected moments, forcing us to re-engage with them. This is what had happened with Bina Fernandez, the editor of *Hum Jinsi*, the first resource book on lesbian, gay and bisexual rights in India.

> It was December [1998]: most hard realisation came to me about my specific identity in Indian society. My problems had started the year before when I came out on a joint platform at the press conference to report about the Proceedings of the workshop on Strategies for furthering Lesbian Gay and Bisexual Rights in India, Mumbai 7–9 November 1997. I took them in my stride but this December it really made me aware and acutely conscious about the peculiarity of my identity. First, the outburst against *Fire* which was violent and ugly enough and later what was worse, the brutal attacks and massacre of Christians. I never felt till then my Christian and lesbian identity but suddenly I became conscious and my need to identify my roots and multiple aspects of my identity became important to me.[9]

The women's movement has been in the forefront of this process in India as much as elsewhere:

> We believe that as women each of us has multiple identities, which affect the way in which we experience the patriarchal structures in society. Hence, we believe that the women's movements must provide autonomous spaces for women from specific groups to organise under the large umbrella of the women's movement. These spaces are very important for all women to be able to identify the paths and ways in which their specific struggle can move ahead. While also having some shared vision of the society as a whole.
>
> Further we believe that the women's movements with other people's movements like *dalits*, tribals, workers and other minorities can create a society in which there will be equality between different classes castes, religious communities and also across gender and sexual orientation...[10]
>
> We seek the right to make choices about our lives, our bodies, our sexuality and our relationships. Some of us are single; some of us are married. Some of us have our primary emotional/sexual/physical/intimate relationships with men, others with women, some with both. Some of us do not have sexual relationships. We feel that we must evolve the supportive structures that can make all of these choices a meaningful reality.[11]

Not Counter-Stereotypes But a Kaleidoscopic, Synthetic Vision

It is important to see this because the problem of allowing a harmonious coexistence of multiple identities is not restricted to India, or to any one country, alone. The Hindu extremists in India is part of a worldwide phenomenon. All over the world, there are a growing number of people who are preaching one form or other of imposing, by violence if necessary, their ideas and ideals on others. What disturbs me is that I find the same kind of thing reappearing in some of the currents who are fighting *against* such trends. This is especially true about the counter-stereotypes which are being set up.

Over the few millennia of our existence as civilised beings, we have paid a heavy price for having seen what separates us much more clearly than what binds us together. Perhaps the need of the hour is to have some kind of kaleidoscopic vision.

None of this is easy. But it is necessary. The need for a kaleidoscopic, synthetic vision is vital to a constructive resolution of the conflicts and strains which plural identities place on us. And it must also partake of both sides of the divide between emotion and rational thinking which is so common. It is only such a viewpoint which will allow true egalitarianism, knowledge which will become an instrument of harmonious coexistence rather than an instrument of domination.

Acknowledgements

I wish to acknowledge the invaluable support and help provided by Suhas Paranjape in writing and editing this paper. My special thanks go to my friends Sonal Shukla and Bina Fernandez. I also thank all my friends who have helped me shape these ideas and enrich them.

Notes

1. From my diaries and memories of the years 1973–6.
2. Similar points have been made in Kakar (1982b) and Fox (1984).
3. Personal communication by the head of a mental hospital where the husband of a friend was to be admitted after being diagnosed as schizophrenic.
4. According to Dnyaneshwar:

    Would a pot reject the earth (it is made of)?
    Would a cloth separate itself from thread?
    Can fire ever tire of heat?
    Can a lamp be jealous of its light?
    Can asoefetida tire of its pungency and smell suddenly sweet?
    Can water be anything but wet?
    So long as you live in the form of a body, what madness then to reject its duties? – Dandekar (1986, ch. 18, verses 219–21; translation mine)

5. Translated from Neurgaonkar (1982, p. 66; translation mine).
6. Translated from the *abhang* quoted in *Asud* (1999, p. 6; translation mine).
7. Interview with Sonal Shukla.
8. *Ibid.*
9. Interview with Bina Fernandez. Bina is active in the Forum against Oppression of Women and Stree Sangam (a les–bi women's group) and works for the Human Rights Law Network.
10. Excerpts from FAOW (1999, pp. 109–13). Forum Against Oppression of Women (FAOW) came into existence in 1979–80 as a platform for all women irrespective of their affiliation or non-affiliation to different political parties in Bombay. It has remained unregistered and without any formal hierarchy during all these years. It is voluntary and functions mainly as a campaign group. I have been an active member since 1984.
11. A Declaration by the Sixth Nari Mukti Sangharsh Sammelan (National Conference of Women's Movements), Ranchi, December 1997. The history of these conferences is interesting in the sense that each succeeding one has incorporated new ideas and new methods. There are no paper presentations at these conferences, the organisation of each conference is handled by a collective body which comes together at each conference. The conference brings together autonomous women's groups (which are mainly urban, middle-class-based groups), rural and urban non-governmental organisations and far-left women's wings and individuals who are committed to the declarations of the conference.

Bibliography

Asud Shraminkancha Asud (Mumbai: Shramik Mukti Dal, March 1999).
Dandekar, S.V. alias Mamasaheb (ed.) *Sarth Dnyaneshwari* (Pune: Swan & Prakashan, 1986).
Dhere, R.C. 'Adishakti cha Vikas', in *Padmagandha*, Divali issue (Mumbai, 1998).
Forum Against Oppression of Women (FAOW) 'Another Challenge to Patriarchy', in B. Fernandez (ed.), *Hum Jinsi: A Resource Book on Lesbian, Gay and Bisexual Rights in India* (Mumbai: India Centre for Human Rights and Law, 1999).
Fox, D.R. *Psychology and Controversy: Points for Discussion*, unpublished (1984), www.uis.edu/~fox/papers/points.html
Kakar, S. (1982a) *Identity and Adulthood* (Mumbai: Oxford University Press, 1982).
Kakar, S. (1982b) *Shamans, Mystics and Doctors* (Mumbai: Oxford University Press, 1982).
Neurgaonkar, S.K. (ed.) *Shri Tukaram Maharajanchi Sarth Gatha*, Pracharya Dandekar Dharmik (Pune: Shaikshanik va Sansritik Vangmay Prakashan Mandal, 1982).
Nietzsche, F. *The Gay Science*, tr. W. Kaufmann (New York: Vintage Books, 1974).
Paranjape, S. 'Restructuring the Evolutionary Paradigm: From Scarcity and Competition to Co-operation and Plenitude', paper published in the three-volume proceedings and presented at the Golden Jubilee celebration National Seminar on 'Rediscovering Co-operation' held at the Institute of Rural Management (Anand, Gujarat, India, November 1996).

Sangari, K., Malik, N., Chhachhi, S. and Sarkar, T. 'Why Women Must Reject Nuclearisation', in *Out of Nuclear Darkness: The Indian Case for Disarmament* (Delhi: MIND, 1998).

Tharu, S. and Lalitha, K. (eds) 'Twentieth Century: Women Writing the Nation', in *Women Writing in India: 600 B.C. to the Present* (Delhi: Oxford India Paperbacks, 1993).

Upadhya, C. 'Set This House on Fire', *Economic and Political Weekly* (Mumbai: 12–18 December 1998).

Part III

SPIRITUALITY, EMBODIMENT AND POLITICS

Introduction

VALERIE WALKERDINE

Interest in spiritual and occult phenomena grew enormously during the later decades of the twentieth century. To traditional left thinkers any interest in matters spiritual might be understood as part of the opium of the people, as Marx described religion. To many psychologists such an interest would be understood as delusional. On the one hand we need to understand therefore what kind of social and cultural phenomenon the interest in the spiritual is, but on the other we need to address the understanding of the spiritual and the occult that exists within psychology in order to cast a critical eye upon it. In fact, many of those who have an interest in critical psychology also are interested in or practice some kind of alternative health or spiritual regime, such as yoga or meditation. All of these forms operate with a concept of unseen energies and spirituality which often sits badly against the rationalist and material positions taken in much critical academic work. Indeed, when critical academics turn to such practices and start to find out about their theoretical assumptions they often feel profoundly uneasy. Yet, they also recognise the value and power of these alternative practices. All of the writers in this section recognise that tension and turn their attention to exploring spirituality from a more critical perspective.

If we examine the history of psychology, it becomes obvious that an interest in matters spiritual and unseen was present from its very inception. There was a veritable explosion of interest in occult phenomena towards the end of the nineteenth century and well into the twentieth. All of the early psychologists make some reference to such phenomena and struggle with grounds on which they can accept or reject the evidence for their existence. For the most part, even the most agnostic bow to the rules of evidence that matter must be visible. However, from the standpoint of another conjuncture, we can appreciate that the laws of physics as they are taken to operate now have an entirely different relation to the occulted or unseen. Indeed, subatomic physics positively depends upon an understanding of matter not visible to the naked eye. We have long understood that academic psychology tended to depend upon Newtonian physics: we can therefore legitimately ask what a different physics might actually mean for psychology.

Ephemeral experiences outside the rational cogito have been largely ignored by critical psychology – is there another way in which we could approach what has been widely understood as irrationalism? How might we approach the political potential of the interest in spirituality? The chapters in this part address such questions in a number of ways. Lisa Blackman (Chapter 9) examines the practice of hearing voices, exploring those discourses which seek to explain the 'problem of hallucination'. She is particularly interested in the way in which hearing voices is understood as a sign of disease and illness and the embodied cultural and discursive strategies and practices employed by voice-hearers to engage with particular kinds of somatic and neurological experience. In order to do this she compares the practices at the Retreat, a Quaker asylum at York, during the 18th century and the practices of the Hearing Voices Network (HVN), an international network of voice-hearers who attempt to understand, manage and experience their voices outside of frameworks of the psy disciplines. Rather than understanding their voices as signs of disease, the members of the HVN use various techniques to understand their voices through spiritual discourses and practices, as 'soul support', enabling them to develop and manage their voice-hearing as a gift rather than as an illness. The York Retreat attempted to understand hallucinations as alternative forms of sensibility and did not automatically categorise hallucinations as signs of disease. In the present, both the practices of the York Retreat and the HVN point towards the possibility of different practices of self which are not based on mastery and control of rationality but on an 'ethics of expansion'. This work suggests therefore that in understanding practices such as hearing voices and their relation to spirituality, we would need to examine the place of psychology's claims to know about the body and mind and the place of unreason and the way in which alternative practices challenge the concepts of human subject upon which those knowledges depend.

Helen Lee and Harriette Marshall (Chapter 10) examine constructions of spirituality which challenge its conception of being individually bound. In particular, they are interested in the forms of socially embodied spirituality which refer to notions of 'oneness' or 'connectedness' between people as in rave or DIY culture. They argue that such forms of spirituality not only challenge psychological constructions of spirituality, such as transpersonal psychology, but also open up a space for spirituality and politics. They discuss the way in which the body becomes central within practices such as meditation, requiring a certain kind of posture and a general sense that the body can become a source of knowledge (intuition, gut feeling) that challenges rational forms of understanding. Although these forms of knowledge are themselves radical, they remain contained within conceptions of the subject which understand spirituality as a form of personal development. They argue that the forms of spirituality contained within rave and DIY culture challenge the boundaries of the individual body and present the possibility of a different conception of the relation between spirituality and politics.

Benjamin Sylvester Bradley (Chapter 11) examines debates about synchronicity, challenging the primacy of the diachronic over the synchronic within psychology. He points to the importance of the shift from Newtonian to post-Einsteinian physics and the move away from a concept of absolute time. Of course, as Bradley makes clear, the idea of synchronicity, 'the temporal coincidence of the same or closely related pieces of mental content in two different people', is impossible to explain from a diachronic scientific perspective and has often been understood as an aspect of the paranormal which at best must be viewed with deep suspicion. He considers the work of the linguist Saussure and the importance of his distinctions between synchrony and diachrony in language as a way of understanding synchronicity. American physicists, he says, have discovered a weightless pulse that exceeds the speed of light, 'leaving the accelerator before it enters'. This overturning of Victorian physics sits alongside the attempts by Saussure to think about the synchronous, of Freud's suggestion that there is no time within the unconscious and James's assertion that the stream of consciousness always mixes the past, present and future. Bradley argues that this allows us to understand mind as collective, spreading out from notions of intersubjectivity towards theories within physics of a global 'morphic resonance'. Within this framework, it is possible to rework and rethink the relation between psychology and occulted phenomena and their relation to unreason and therefore pathology or impossibility.

Kathleen McPhillips (Chapter 12) examines the place of enchantment in the postmodern world. In particular, she is interested in ways in which the cultural desire for re-enchantment relate to the emergence of new forms of religious imagination. She argues that late modernity demands a self-regulating subject, as discussed in several chapters in Part I. However, this is cross-cut and challenged by the practices which place the body as a site for spiritual revelation and can therefore be understood as the site for social and cultural change, precisely because they unsettle those other practices of the self. The desire to experience a form of subjectivity not so tightly bound by the need for rational control is very potent. She cites Weber's notion of instrumental rationality as central in the rise of capitalism, itself accompanied by a necessary disenchantment, a move away from religion. It can be argued therefore that the crisis in cultural and individual meaning predicted by Weber, a crisis brought on by the loss of other meanings of self and social in favour of competitive individualism, produces re-enchantment as an obvious resistance. New practices of spirituality can be understood in these terms, but of course we can also recognise that such practices can be coopted by capitalism as their softer face. One can also understand enchantment as an alternative cultural logic as in the global mourning of the death of Princess Diana. McPhillips gives a number of examples of ways in which we might understand re-enchantment in the current context, from environmental movements to indigenous struggles. However, re-enchantment brings with it the hope for something different and the possibility of imagining different kinds of 'significant and embedded connections between self–body–other'.

Here we are back at the book's first part. In their very different ways, each of the authors in this part bring us towards issues of a different conception of subjectivity, in this case one which is lived outside the limits of the cogito, outside the limits of the individual subject. The new practices of subjectivity do not take us simply and directly back to the pre-capitalist communities that Kathleen McPhillips writes of. As stressed in Part I, they take us beyond globalism, economic rationalism, towards new and multiple forms of subjectivity which look both backward and forward, towards a mobile future, new forms of politics and possibilities of being. This complex process places an understanding and working with subjectivity centre stage within any understanding of political change. Critical psychology is one site for the development of this work – never has it been more urgently needed.

9

A Psychophysics of the Imagination

LISA BLACKMAN

This chapter examines how particular phenomena, such as the hearing of voices, are made intelligible through the discourses of psychology and psychiatry. Many discursive psychologies argue that those concepts and explanatory structures which define and articulate, in this case, the 'problem of hallucination', do not map or describe human subjectivity in anyway (Parker, 1989; Potter and Wetherell, 1986). There is a refusal to engage with the psychological other than through its location within language. The human subject becomes a discourse-user creating meanings of the social formation in their local, specific accounting practices (Nightingale, 1999). If we were to follow these moves, one implication would be that we would no longer be interested in mapping underlying internal psychological or neurological mechanisms, and would instead concentrate on the different ways in which the voice-hearing experience is mediated through culturally available narratives. This would be a useful strategy, and would indeed bring to light the different narratives or texts, which construct the meaning of hallucination in markedly different ways. However, this chapter will draw out some of the problems with moving to this linguistic constructionist position, as a general strategy for critical psychological practice.

The Old, Tired Theme of Social Constructionism

The move from essentialism to constructionism characteristic of discursive psychology leaves us with two unhappy alternatives (Riley, 1983). On one side we have essentialist views where social and psychological life are easily reduced to biological and neurological referents. On the other side we have perspectives which appeal to the social, where most human behaviour, thought and action is viewed as a social construction produced by the workings of language, discourse, ideology and so forth. Within these views biological explanations are rejected, but no radical rethinking of this area is offered. What this does is effectively leave the biological–social dualism intact, and to simply move from one side of the dichotomy to the other (Fuss, 1989). This chapter will begin to consider the ways in which the biological needs radical revision if we wish to enter into a dialogue with the human and life sciences. To do this effectively we need to be able to engage with the ways in which the biological, social and psychological are combined and articulated, within these disciplines, in particular kinds of ways. This needs urgent attention if we want our work to have an impact on those who suffer and struggle with the very real realities of these issues (see Blackman, 2001).

This chapter will outline one move which signals an important new direction within critical psychology: the issue of embodiment. This term draws attention to the ways in which phenomena, such as hearing voices, which are traditionally viewed as 'biological' (signs of disease and illness) are never lived out by the individual in a pure and unmediated form. Attention to 'embodiment' entails a consideration of those cultural and discursive strategies and practices that voice-hearers have developed to engage with particular kinds of somatic and neurological experience. The chapter will focus upon a set of understandings and techniques central to the practices of the York Retreat (an English Quaker asylum) in the eighteenth century. These practices formed part of an understanding and reformulation of the meanings and therefore potential cure of madness, prior to the emergence of clinical medicine in the early nineteenth century. I want to make a point of comparison between these practices – practices that are often referred to as 'moral therapy' – with the practices of the Hearing Voices Network (HVN). The HVN is an international group of voice-hearers who are attempting to understand, manage and experience their voices outside of the frameworks of the psy disciplines (particularly the medical model central to the practice of clinical psychiatry). I want to stress that by comparing the practice of 'moral therapy' with the practices of the HVN I do not simply want to suggest that there is a historical continuity between the two. Rather I want to examine how both practices create a radical discontinuity with psy techniques of self- understanding and production, especially in relation to how one may embody psychological phenomena and the kinds of emotional experiences or 'emotional economy' created through their embodiment.

Discourses of the Interior

The rise of discursive psychologies over the past two decades, characterised by their focus on the subjectifying force of language, has led to a reluctance to engage with the psychological, other than through its narrativisation (Potter and Wetherell, 1986; see Blackman and Walkerdine, 2001; Henriques *et al.*, 1984). The once 'interior' realm of the psychological – the subject matter of the psy disciplines – has been enfolded and located in the very languages we use to speak about selfhood. This move from essentialism to constructionism – from a belief in the fixed and quantifiable nature of selfhood to a view that experience of selfhood(s) is the end point of a complex process of discursive production – creates a problem when we wish to address the bodily experiences we all have of distress, anxiety, fear, pain and so forth. These recalcitrant experiences are often viewed as the residue body lying beyond discourse – the 'outside', resistant materials from which to critique the regulatory functioning of the practices attempting to discipline and objectify the human subject. These bodily, sensuous experiences have become a figurative model in many of the philosophical perspectives attempting to deploy particular bodily experiences to create a 'non-rationalist' philosophy. Merleau-Ponty (1962) offered a 'phenomenology of the body' which used a language of sensation to describe the encounter of the individual with the world in which they live. Ponty drew on metaphors of touch where the world is brought into being through the way it impinges on the body through a series of glances, blows and strikes. William James (1985) developed a hallucinatory model, which drew on the idea of a 'stream of consciousness', a world of sensation and experience beyond rationality. Clement (1994) uses the notion of syncope to describe those fractures or ruptures in experience which defy linear space and time, while Deleuze and Guattari (1988) draw on an energetic model of subjectivity, both having much in common with ecstatic modes of being developed in other cultures.

There is an inherent romanticism in some of these perspectives, taking acts, gestures, states of mind and bodily experiences which in western cultures repeated signify as Other – as irrational and pathological – and instead investing them with an insurgent and revolutionary potential. What has had less attention paid to it is the way that particular experiences such as the act of hearing voices, seeing visions or spectres, the experience of pre-cognition, clairaudience, ESP and healing practices, ecstasy, trance, hypnosis and allied states of consciousness are lived or embodied by actual subjects. These ephemeral experiences, those seen to lie outside the rational cogito, have been ignored by critical psychologists. They raise problems, I would argue, for critical psychology because the experience and embodiment of these states undermines the very rational model of subjectivity which implicitly and often explicitly underpins the approach to subjectivity within many discursive psychologies – the rational 'discourse-user' making sense of the world through the discourses on offer or available to him or her.

'You Have the Power to Change!'

To elucidate and highlight the importance of this argument I want to think about the cultural significance of the rise of practices of self-help currently circulating in many cultural spaces, such as the chat show, women's magazines and so forth. Media scholars have been quick to comment on their social significance, arguing that they reproduce sexist and oppressive fictions of femininity. McRobbie (1996), for example, argues that these practices align women's fears and desires with a consumer culture offered to them as a compensatory device for their bodily and emotional dissatisfactions and inadequacies. What is given less attention is the role these practices may play at an emotional and psychological level. This psychological realm and emotional economy is neither interior, if that implies outside discourse, nor private, if that implies it is not socially shared. It is a view of emotional experience which must be analysed in relation to the difficulties of living the psy image of personhood, what Rose (1990) terms the 'fiction of the autonomous self'. We must begin to recognise how an economy of pain, fear, anxiety and distress is part of the apparatus through which this fictional identity is produced, lived and kept in place (see Blackman, 1999a, 1999b).

For example, practices of self-help identify particular experiences – the mundane psychopathology of everyday life – as potential transformative experiences. We are probably all familiar with the incitement and injunction of change constantly beckoning us from adverts, holiday brochures, New Age practices, chat shows and so forth – 'You have the Power to Change'. Conflicts and problems in relationships, the world of work, health, beauty and friendships are offered as the site or stimulus for change and self-improvement. In relation to this injunction to change a certain emotional economy is promoted as a powerful chain of signifiers of failure – lack of confidence, unhappiness, unease, distress, lack of control, anxiety, guilt and frustration for example. The first step in change or transformation is recognising or identifying these experiences as signifiers of personal failure and inadequacy and believing that you can be in control, you can choose, you can be independent, you can be autonomous. Ironically, then, the psy image of selfhood – the freely independent, choosing individual – is maintained as normative through the way the very difficulties of living this fictional identity are contained within these practices as evidence of personal failure and provide the site of change or transformation. The psy image of personhood is the ideal, aspirational image within these practices, producing the very psychopathology created through its impossibility, in the form of signs of pathology and inadequacy – as Other – exceptional, regrettable phenomena.

Let us compare these common practices of self-help with some of the practices of self-help advocated by the HVN. The phenomenon of hearing voices is most often associated with illness and disease. In the psychiatric manual the DSM IV – the bible of American and British psychiatrists – hearing voices is a first-rank indicator of schizophrenia. Voice-hearing signifies disease and danger, to be suppressed or denied through dangerous psychotropic drugs. The supposed healing practices of the psychiatric regime (healing in that they are based on a curative process) work by encouraging the voice-hearer to recognise their voices as signs of ill-health and disease – as 'not-me'. The concept of insight is viewed as a measure of psychological health and normality: when a person can recognise the voices as disease, can suppress and deny them, – then they are on the road to recovery.

The practices of the HVN start from an entirely different premise. Voices are not a problem in and of themselves and indeed may have something to say about the person's life, their present and past and even about levels of existence above and beyond the corporeal, material world. One of the main contentions underpinning the coping practices advocated by the HVN is that voices are not simply meaningless epiphenomena of disease. Unlike the psy disciplines, talking to the voice-hearers about their voices is not seen to merely reinforce and reproduce an already confused reality. Indeed, acknowledging and attending to the voices is seen as crucial in the transformative relations one may construct with the voices allowing the possibility of very different emotional experiences. For example, if a voice-hearer believes their voices are signs of disease and illness it is likely that they will have a particular emotional response – fear, confusion, paranoia, dread, anxiety, shame and so forth. However, if one believes that the voices are messages from the dead for example, then one is likely to have a very different emotional response – joy and revelation perhaps. This is not to say that these very different embodied experiences of voices are simply achieved by a leap of cognition or faith – a view entrenched within cognitive psychology.[1] Rather, we need to pay attention to the various practices, techniques, sets of understandings and 'soul support' which enable voice-hearers to enact their identities in very different ways: that is, as telepathists having a special gift or sensitivity, rather than as psychiatric patients suffering a biochemical imbalance. In my work with the HVN, I sat in on self-help meetings, met voice-hearers in their homes, talked with them about their lives and how the voices were integrated into their lives. I was much more interested in analysing their texts, their narratives or words, which I subjected to a form of discourse analysis more inspired by the later works of Michel Foucault (1979, 1987, 1990) than by some of the microanalysis conducted by many discursive psychologies (see Blackman, 1994a, 1994b).

This is where I want to raise the problems and possibilities for this work into the new millennium, especially in considering and analysing new forms of spirituality. What I did not do adequately in this work was consider the role the emotional or psychological plays in the transformative practices of the HVN. As an example, practices of telepathy are one of the most popular and successful ways of managing voices within the groups. Those who through hard work, effort and struggle have come to embody their voices as a key site for spiritual development and transformation have much more positive experiences of their voices than those who believe they are signs of repressed trauma, for example. I argued at the time that this was because the spiritual church, as an authoritative institution, not only offered guidance, compassion and understanding but actual techniques and practices, such as development circles, where voice-hearers could attend to and transform their relations to their voices. I would also argue that what the spiritual church does is engage with an emotional economy itself produced through psy relations to the voices – fear, distress, dread, terror, shame, confusion and anxiety. Disintegration and states of mind not usually associated with waking rationality are viewed as conducive to a state of psychic mindfulness. Relaxation and reverie worked on through active and expectant attention and focusing achieve this state. Thus those very bodily experiences of distress and anxiety that are viewed as symptoms of psychopathology within the psy disciplines become sites of transformation and change through sets of practices which attempt to achieve relaxation through more meditative and visualisation techniques. In other words, they are worked on and transformed at the level of sensuous, bodily awareness, where the mind is active and expectant in this process. Thus, bodily distress is identified not as failure but as the very potential for psychic reverie.

What I am attempting to address in my argument is that we must be wary of the determinism and reductionism of talking about experience at the level of the discursive. The discursive as an apparatus must consist not only of all those practices, knowledges, theories, problems and concepts which Foucault (1973) so cogently described and analysed in his archaeologies of the human sciences. It must also explore the emotional and psychological economies – themselves discursively produced – which are engendered through our complex and often contradictory positionings as human subjects. These I would argue are the link points which enable subjects to invest themselves in certain ways of understanding their own and others' selfhoods. This argument may not signal a retreat to psychoanalysis (although this is one avenue) as the only means of explaining these forms of identification, but perhaps a very different way of approaching the very embodied natures of distress and suffering. The field of discursive relations constructing the meaning and embodied experiences of a phenomenon such as voice hearing are made up of very different ways of specifying the mind, body, will, imagination and the relations between them. These are not simply different meaning systems or symbolic representations, but have very real and material consequences for the ways in which we imagine and experience our own subjectivities.

The History of Voices

Many historical accounts of the shift of voice-hearing from religious to more moral frameworks conceptualise it as a one-way directional movement. Once voices were considered as signs of a divine entity speaking through particular people and as having some religious or prophetic significance (Carpenter, 1805). They then, within more moral frameworks, came to be seen as errors or signs of the excess of the mind shocked from its habitual paths of association. However, it is important to state that these arguments existed alongside one another and exist in the present in different spaces and places. I will start my narrative in the early part of the nineteenth century when the voice-hearing experience was still discussed alongside altered states of consciousness such as dreaming, somnambulism, trance, hypnosis and ecstasy. Madness was viewed as a form of error, a way that the mind could trick or deceive itself when it was not kept in check by habit. The mind as a reasoning apparatus was precarious and could often fail or err. This moral view of insanity, as Porter (1987b) cogently argues, was very influenced by the philosophies of Locke and his conception of the mind as a reasoning apparatus. Moral insanity was viewed as a (mis)association of ideas, accidental connections and unnatural associations. The mind was delirious and if left in this imaginary realm might 'go off the track' (Donnelly, 1983, p. 111). The key determinant of the mind's ability to keep on track was the will, which was viewed as the censor that allowed the mind to maintain external relations with the outside world. The mind's ability to actively reflect upon and restructure ideas was part of its creative process. This process was linked to the imagination, which was viewed as a fantastical space of 'vacant reverie' (Maudsley, 1879, p. 9). The suspension of the will and the action of the imagination would allow not only the grotesque associations of the mind in error but also the creative associations which linked, within this discursive configuration, the mad with the genius. The mind, will and imagination were linked within a triad which created a reverence for the imagination – the 'condition of poetic fire' (Porter, 1879, p. 99). There was also a fascination with those twilight states such as trance, hypnotism, ecstasy, somnambulism and dreaming which were linked to the action of the imagination and the suspension of the will.

This image and spirit of 'moral man' was central to the practices of the York Retreat prior to the emergence of clinical medicine (1792). The York Retreat aimed to rehumanise persons who had become estranged from their surroundings and were at the mercy of the excesses and errors of the creative associations of the mind and the excitable imagination. This 'moral insanity', unlike twentieth-century disease-models was, curable and the purpose of the Retreat was to provide a space where the will could be strengthened and restored through habit. Quakers ran the Retreat and according to Foucault (1971) in *Madness and Civilisation*, religion was central to the spirit of benevolence and affection, which characterised the relations between the physicians and their patients. Much has been written about the asylum and its transformation of the image of asylums as places of contagion to rational, ordered spaces promoting the health rather than the illness of its habitants. I want to focus here on the writings of Hack Tuke, the son of Samuel Tuke, the founder of the York Retreat, as they provide an illuminating account of the image of the human subject which underpinned the principles central to the practice of moral therapy.

Tuke published two books in the late nineteenth century, in the midst of theories of degeneracy, which recount the 'psycho-physical principles' (1892, p. x) which he argued should be part of clinical practice. His book was not simply an account of the virtues of moral therapy, but a thorough elucidation of the principle and basis of the imagination that he suggested was the pivot through which moral therapy had its effects. The two books, I will argue, show not merely the place of religious beliefs within the therapeutic context but also the radically different way of specifying humanness which made possible both the discourse of moral therapy, and, more speculatively, the actual experience of the process. Tuke (1872, p. ix) aimed his earlier book specifically at the medical profession, which had outlawed in the early 1800s the practice of hypnosis which shared similarities with his conception of the 'psycho-physical'. Revisiting the Retreat in his writings, he wanted to subject the underlying principles of moral therapy to systematic, medical analysis to remove it from its enduring legacy of quackery:

> There are two classes of readers to whom I wish more especially to address myself. The medical reader who, I hope, may be induced to employ Psycho-therapeutics in a more methodical way than heretofore, and thus copy nature in those interesting instances, occasionally occurring, of sudden recovery from the spontaneous action of some powerful moral cause, by employing the same force designedly, instead of leaving it to mere chance.

Tuke's advocacy of 'psycho-physical' principles was a critique of clinical psychiatry and the supposed symptoms, treatment and pathology of insanity. The problem of insanity was a 'problem of will' and the concomitant errors of the mind that ensued. Tuke argued that 'man' can only ever be understood in relation to 'his' environment (both physical and psychical), and the problem of will was one whereby, under certain conditions, the mind would lose its sympathy with its surroundings. The concept of 'habit' was the principle seen to strengthen the will and was realised through the monotony of work and the rational ordering of the asylum at the Retreat (cf. Rose, 1985). However, the notion of 'sympathy' was also the nodal point for a radically different discursive configuration, made up of differentiations made between the imagination, the body, the mind and the will. Tuke (1872, p. 82) argued that the mind and body were in an 'inseparable union', and could affect each other through the sympathetic action of one with the other. In the contents pages of his first manual entitled *The Influence of the Mind upon the Body* he outlines the 'action of the imagination' upon voluntary and involuntary organs, upon the organic and vegetative functions to include the blood, sweat, bile, skin, hair, urine and gastric juice, the action of the emotions upon the body, and then a second section outlining the influence of the will within this process. The focusing of the will was due to what Tuke termed 'expectant attention', which is aptly summed up in the following claim by him: 'I am confident that I can fix my attention to any part until I have a sensation in that part' (1872, p. 5).

Tuke develops this notion of sympathetic action through drawing parallels with spiritual phenomena and the importance of mesmerism in relation to the idea of 'expectant attention'. With the suspension of the will, the imagination could be focused upon particular locations bringing about effects in the voluntary and involuntary organs, the blood and so on, and, in relation to mesmerism, the mind's ability to create phantasms which have no basis in external reality. Tuke (1872, p. 82) discusses the 'psycho-physical' principles of the stigmata and the healing properties of prayer, linking the relations between the imagination, will and the mind without recourse to the action of a divine entity. In the following quote we can see the reconceptualisation of spiritual phenomena, through the union of the mind with the body, that Tuke seeks to instigate as the basis of a materialist psycho-medical practice:

> The periodicity of Stigmata is a further interesting example of the influence of attention and Imagination upon the direction and localisation of the cutaneous circulation. On saints' days and on Fridays, the seat of the marks become more painful, and a brighter colour indicating a fresh influx of blood to the part – the mystics' thoughts being specially concentrated upon the Passion.

The 'suffering of Christ' invoked by the idea of passion is central to the psychical process, according to Tuke (1872, p. 22), through which an idea becomes represented or experienced physically in the body. Thus, the action of the imagination and the invoking of particular emotional states, such as fear, hope and agitation, are central to the process through which ideas or concepts induce sensations or changes in the body. It is this principle which

Tuke argued was central to the doctor–patient relationship within the York Retreat which was founded upon the subtle process of persuasion. As well as the *habit*-forming effects of work and monotony which were seen to strengthen the will (by making the action of the will involuntary rather than voluntary), the doctor's imagination was practically utilised to appeal to the imagination of the patient by gently arousing their will and inducing expectation or hope. This was seen to be especially important where patients were suffering mental shocks sending the mind away from its habitual paths of association. Again Tuke (1972, p. 375) draws parallels with the healing properties of prayer and the inducing of hope with its sympathetic effects of mind with body – through agitation and calm – in the cure of mental and physical disease:

> Those who have visited the continental churches will remember the large number of crutches, sticks, splints, etc. which have been left by those who have been cured or relieved of contracted joints, rheumatism, and palsy, by prayers offered up to some saints, or by the supposed efficacy of their relics.

Tuke saw the basis of a 'New Science' in his explanation of the 'principle of the imagination' which he used to explain mesmerism, hypnotism, the effects of the emotion in producing disease, the effect of the intellect on the health of the body, to induce anaesthesia and so forth, which were all linked through a notion of *sympathy* – the organising structure through which the mind, body, will and imagination were linked. This was not simply the championing of the 'moral' over the physical, nor the reflection of the impart of religious beliefs in the practice of medicine, but an *art* of existence (or practice of sociality) based upon a radically different way of conceptualising 'what it means to be human'. The underlying basis of 'moral therapy' as practised at The Retreat was, for Tuke, an exemplar of the effective development of this art through its methodical application in the restoration of health. Interestingly, the 'insanity' of the patients made them more amenable to this process because of the 'suggestibility' produced through the suspension of the will. This state Tuke viewed as being akin to a dream state, where the mind would lose its anchoring with external relations and create its own representations, feelings, perceptions, images and emotions (1892, p. 35). This dream state was allied to ecstatic states, hallucinatory states and trance where the body would undergo physiological changes, the will would become suspended and the mind would become more 'automatic' and receptive to the commands of others. This was the ideal state for hypnosis to successfully occur and was also integral to the inducing of anaesthesia with an associated loss of bodily and psychic sensation.

It was this 'ecstatic state' through which Tuke also discussed the status and significance of hallucinations. A hallucinator was literally somebody who 'wandered in mind' and who created images and sensations without accompanying perception of any external stimuli. Tuke drew similarities with states of religious exaltation where through the focusing and absorption of the mind upon an idea, fantastic images and voices were credited with divine illumination or supernatural character. Tuke (1892, p. 565) defined hallucination as 'a sensation perceived by the mind, whether through the sense of sight, hearing, smell, taste, or feeling, without any external cause capable of producing it'. He was clear that hallucinations *per se* were not signs of insanity; the problem was when under certain conditions, voices or visions were credited with the status of reality and would therefore have a dictating force on subsequent action. In line with the emerging shifts occurring in clinical medicine in the late nineteenth century, voices and visions were a 'risk' because of the threat of irresponsible behaviour that may ensue. Tuke (1892, p. 566) begins to make this differentiation of the state of hallucination from other ecstatic states of consciousness in the following quote: 'Voices are the most common, and when they assume the character of a mandate they become exceedingly serious. They are a fruitful source of homicidal and suicidal acts.' Tuke was writing at a time when significant shifts were occurring in the discipline of psychiatry and where the 'problem of will' was shifting to a governmental concern with criminal behaviour and how one was to adjudicate the culpability of the 'dangerous individual' (Maudsley, 1874). Esquirol (1845) writing in the mid-nineteenth century characterised some of the hesitation and uncertainty which underpinned the formation of hallucination as a discursive object and how it was to be differentiated from other states of consciousness such as trance, ecstasy, somnambulism and so on. Esquirol similarly championed the moral over the physical in his explanations of madness, but as will become clear 'moral' was part of a configuration and set of associated meanings very different from Tuke's 'psycho-physical' framework of explanation. It was also dependent upon a very different way of specifying subjectivity made possible by the emergence of evolutionary theory and the image of the human subject at its heart.

At the time of Esquirol's writing organic or physical explanations of insanity coexisted with the moral. All insanities were disorders of sensibility and will – the mind losing its anchoring or sympathy with external relations. However, some disorders were viewed as cerebral phenomena, evidence of a mind which was deranged owing to the effects of mental disease. These constitutional disorders were more *simple* forms of insanity due to the deficiency or abolition of an essential property of the human mind (1845, p. 149). Others were more *complex* and linked to the familiar notion of the mind in error associating ideas in absurd and strange combinations. This was an example of reasoning from false principles (error) and was the consequence of a perverted form of reasoning rather than the *lack* of the mind's ability to feel (sensibility), where 'man' was unable to reason and connect ideas. This simple–complex dichotomy structured the way that insanities were represented in the nosographical tables at this time. Monomania was representative of a complex form of insanity and became the object of discussions surrounding the difficulties of adjudicating criminal actions. These persons were seen to have a kernel of reason through which they could be restored to sympathetic relations with the world. However, the simple to complex insanities were linked developmentally and as we can see in the following quote were linked by degree rather than kind:

> The different forms of insanity terminate in each other. Thus, mania terminates in dementia, or lypemania; and mania with fury, terminates critically by dementia, when the latter is the product of too active medication, at the commencement of mania or monomania. All forms of insanity degenerate into dementia, after a more or less brief period of time. (Esquirol, 1845, p. 59)

The simple–complex dichotomy structuring the administration of insanity along its axis also provided one of the key conditions for the aligning of hallucination with the physical and organic rather than the moral. Esquirol began to differentiate delusions from hallucinations that prior to this shift had been discussed synonymously as part of the workings of the erroneous imagination. Rather than being a deceptive state due to the mind's ability to deceive itself and reason from false principles, hallucinations had become located within a convulsive condition of the brain, prior to and independent of the mind. Rather than being in a hallucinated state, the hearing of voices and seeing of visions was to become evidence of a somatic disorder. Hallucinations were not so much disturbing as evidence of a disturbed life. Esquirol (1845, p. 109) transforms the object hallucination, from the mind in error to a pseudosensory product of the mental disturbance itself in the following sentences describing the hallucinator: 'He sees and hears, but these impressions do not reach the centre of sensibility. The mind does not react upon them.'

Although in Tuke's writings we can also see similar debates about the seat of hallucination, and whether they should be regarded as cerebral phenomena, the concepts and terms within which these divisions are made are radically different from the concepts structuring the debates being made in the psychiatric texts of the time. Tuke expressed confusion over whether hallucinations should be regarded simply as evidence of a diseased brain. He argued that hallucinations were psycho-sensorial phenomena, possibly linked to the combined action of the imagination with the sense organs. Hallucinations were considered an 'exaggerated degree of imagination' (1878, p. 18) and not simply reflex phenomena of a brute brain. The key concept underpinning Tuke's claim was the idea of 'intensity' and of the possibility that the imagination could *a*ffect the ganglia of the senses, producing sensorial phenomena, such as visions and voices *as if* they were real. The idea of intensity aptly described Tuke's conception of the imagination, which through its 'exciting' action could affect the body and mind sympathetically, producing a 'psychical representation' in the affected location. The notion of 'sympathy', central to Tuke's configuration of the relations between the mind, body, will and imagination, had mutated in the nineteenth century to a notion of sympathy which was the hinge through which a person's level of involvement with external reality, and hence their responsibility to themselves and others, was judged. Sympathy had moved beyond suggestibility to a concern with how persons developed a sense of responsibility and were able (conceived of biologically) to maintain contact with the world in which they live(d). The meaning of sympathy had shifted, owing to the place the sign now occupied in a number of connected terms and meanings, which were reliant upon terms and concepts which were in discord with Tuke's 'psycho-physical' principles.

I think there are several pertinent points we can take from this discussion which are developed in Blackman (2001). The first shows that our current conceptions of hallucination, of the mind and of the body are rooted in a particular discourse of the individual, primarily evolutionary theory which became central to the articulation of the 'problem of insanity' in the nineteenth and twentieth centuries. This configuration of the body and its matter is a recent historical phenomenon bound up with shifting patterns in the classification, regulation and management of the population (see Rose, 1985). Descartes' mind–body dualism and its inscription within specific discursive practices, such as the psy disciplines, is less a philosophy of mind, more an emerging technique of self and social formation. I think perhaps what is more pertinent for this discussion is the increasing failure of those knowledges that 'claim to know', such as psychology and psychiatry, in providing the means to live a 'good life'. We have seen in my discussion of practices of self-help (which promote the psy image of life and morality as normative) that they engage with the very gaps and contradictions created through the difficulty of living the psy image of autonomous selfhood. As we have seen, particular resolutions are set up to conflicts and problems within these practices where they signify as signs of personal pathology and failure. Perhaps what we are witnessing, and will continue to witness, is the rise of other practices (based on an ethic of expansion rather than an ethic of mastery and control over lack), such as healing, yoga, meditation and so forth, which may engage with the difficulties of living in a more harmonious way. They may be effective means of transforming the ways people live in their worlds and deal with the difficulties, pain and oppression produced through a regulatory image, which recognises contradiction as lack.

This work suggests a particular route in understanding and analysing the social and psychical significance of emerging forms of new spirituality. These forms of spirituality are often thought of as evidence of increasing individualism in modern western societies (Ross, 1992). However, I would suggest that this makes sense only if we locate them within the practices of self-help which have emerged in the last two decades as we witness the 'psychologisation of everyday life'. We must approach them as embodied phenomena, exploring the new forms of subjectivity (in terms both of the body and of how it is understood and acted upon) which they make possible in their practices. These forms of subjectivity are not simply about the 'power of the mind' to transcend its material conditions, but also create radically different ways of specifying, relating to and acting upon selfhood. They include different ways of signifying and mediating the body which has gone beyond the raw material of its biology and become an energetic body capable of experiences some can only ever imagine. These forms of 'bodywork' are crucial for the development of a 'critical psychological practice' which is embodied, situated and able to intervene in the difficulties of living modern forms of subjectification. Discursive psychologies, in the retreat from Cartesian models of selfhood, have left the body behind, overlooking that the body is always an 'already signified body' mediated through cultural signs and discursive activity. The disembodied voice of many discursive psychologies, with its focus upon text and narrative, must begin the project of mapping the many different kinds of body (and the allied field of discursive relations) currently existing in the heterogeneous practices making up the social and psychic spaces which we inhabit.

Note

1. Cognitive behavioural techniques (CBT) are now being advocated for the management of psychoses as well as neuroses (Haddock and Slade, 1996; Jones et al., 1998).

Bibliography

Blackman, L. 'What Is Doing History? The Use of History to Understand the Constitution of Contemporary Psychological Objects', *Theory and Psychology*, 4(4) (1994a) 485–504.

Blackman, L. *Contesting the Voice of Reason: An Archaeology of Hallucinations from the 18th Century to the Present*, unpublished doctoral dissertation, University of London (1994b).

Blackman, L. 'An Extraordinary Life: The Legacy of an Ambivalence', *New Formations* 'Diana and Democracy' (special issue), no. 36, August (1999a) 111–24.

Blackman, L. 'Beyond the Fragile Chains We Call Autonomy: Ethics, Embodiment and Experience', in W. Maiers, B. Bayer, B.D. Esgalhado, R. Jorna and E. Schraube (eds), *Challenges to Theoretical Psychology* (Toronto: Captus Press, 1999b).

Blackman, L. *Hearing Voices: Embodiment and Experience* (London: Free Association Press, 2001).

Blackman, L. and Walkerdine, V. *Mass Hysteria: Critical Psychology and Media Studies* (Basingstoke and New York: Palgrave, 2001).

Carpenter, E. *Who Are the Deluded?* (London: W. Marchmont, 1805).

Clement, C. *Syncope. The Philosophy of Rapture* (Minneapolis: University of Minnesota Press, 1994).

Donnelly, M. *Managing the Mind* (London: Tavistock, 1983).

Deleuze, G. and Guattari, F. *A Thousand Plateaus* (London: Atholone, 1988).

Esquirol, J.E. *Mental Maladies: A Treatise on Insanity* (Philadelphia: Lea & Blanechard, 1845).

Foucault, M. *Madness and Civilization. A History of Insanity in the Age of Reason* (London: Tavistock, 1971).

Foucault, M. *The Birth of the Clinic* (London: Tavistock, 1973).

Foucault, M. *The History of Sexuality. Volume 1. An Introduction* (London: Allen Lane, 1979).

Foucault, M. *The History of Sexuality. Volume 2. The Use of Pleasure* (Harmondsworth: Penguin, 1987).

Foucault, M. 'Technologies of the Self', in L.H. Martin, H. Gutman and R.H. Hutton (eds), *Technologies of the Self* (London: Tavistock,1990).

Fuss, D. *Essentially Speaking: Femininity, Nature and Difference* (London and New York: Routledge, 1989).

Haddock, G. and Slade, P. *Cognitive Behavioural Interventions and Psychotic Disorders* (London and New York: Routledge, 1996).

Henriques, J., Hollway, W., Urwin, C., Venn, C. and Walkerdine, V. *Changing the Subject: Psychology, Social Regulation and Subjectivity* (London: Methuen, 1984).

James, W. *The Varieties of Religious Experience* (Cambridge, Massachusetts: Harvard University Press, 1985).

Jones, C., Cormac, I., Mota, J. and Campbell, C. (1998) 'Cognitive Behaviour Therapy for Schizophrenics', *The Cochrane Library*, no. 4 (1998) 1–21.

McRobbie, A. (ed.) *Back to Reality. Social Experience and Cultural Studies* (Manchester, New York: Manchester University Press, 1996).

Maudsley, H. *Responsibility in Mental Disease* (London: Harry S. King, 1874).

Maudsley, H. *Pathology of the Mind* (London: Macmillan – now Palgrave, 1879).

Merleau-Ponty, M. *The Phenomenology of Perception* (London: Routledge & Kegan Paul, 1962).

Nightingale, D. '(Re)Theorising Constructionism', in W. Maiers, B. Bayer, B.D. Esgalhado, R. Jorna and E. Schraube (eds), *Challenges to Theoretical Psychology* (Toronto: Captus Press, 1999).

Porter, R. *A Social History of Madness. Stories of the Insane* (London: Weidenfeld & Nicholson, 1987a).

Porter, R. *Mind-Forg'd Manacles: A History of Madness in England from the Restoration to the Regency* (London: Athlone Press, 1987b).

Potter, J. and Wetherell, M. *Discourse and Social Psychology. Beyond Attitudes and Behaviour* (London, Newbury Park, Beverly Hills and New Delhi: Sage, 1986).

Parker, I. *The Crisis in Social Psychology and How To End It* (London and New York: Routledge, 1989).

Riley, D. *War in the Nursery* (London: Virago Press, 1983).
Rose, N. *The Psychological Complex. Psychology, Politics and Society in England 1869–1939* (London, Boston, Melbourne and Henley: Routledge & Kegan Paul, 1985).
Rose, N. *Governing the Soul* (London and New York: Routledge & Kegan Paul, 1990).
Ross, A. 'New Age Technoculture', in L. Grossberg, C. Nelson and P. Treichler (ed.), *Cultural Studies* (London and New York: Routledge, 1992).
Tuke, D.H. *Illustrations of Influence of the Mind Upon the Body: In Health and Disease* (London: Churchill, 1872).
Tuke, D.H. *Insanity in Ancient and Modern Life with Chapters on its Prevention* (London: Macmillan – now Palgrave, 1878).
Tuke, D.H. (ed.) *Dictionary of Psychological Medicine*, vol.1 (London: Churchill, 1892).

10

Embodying the Spirit in Psychology: Questioning the Politics of Psychology and Spirituality

HELEN LEE AND HARRIETTE MARSHALL

In late twentieth-century western culture, 'spirituality', indicative of a plethora of understandings, meanings and practices, has become increasingly prevalent in certain domains (Bruce, 1995; Heelas, 1993). This chapter centralises spirituality and explicates its juncture with notions of embodiment. It is written on the basis of the first author's PhD research and the second author's supervision of this work. In order to locate this work, it seems important to note that the first author's initial interest in this area was informed by her involvement with various forms of spirituality which predate her study and research within psychology. The first author's engagement with aspects of spirituality has combined with her work as a postgraduate student in shaping her critical questioning of the understandings, meanings and practices that circulate in the domain of spirituality.

In this chapter, first we are concerned with the ways in which spirituality is constructed both within psychological knowledge and in a wider cultural context. Second, we aim to explore certain links between these domains. Subsequently, we are interested in thinking around the social and political implications of such knowledge. As such, in this chapter, we are less concerned with the details of talk and text and have chosen instead to focus on the somewhat broader-based psychological and sociocultural constructions of spirituality.

Transpersonal psychology (a subsection of the British Psychological Society set up in 1996) includes the study of eastern spiritualities and has in many ways been instrumental in informing more popular, cultural understandings (Daniels and McNutt, 1997; Vitz and Modesti, 1993). Therefore it seems imperative that a critical psychology engages with spirituality. Moreover, embodiment and the body has become of increasing importance in social-scientific theory (see for instance, Bayer and Shotter, 1998; Featherstone *et al.*, 1991; Shilling, 1993) as well as within popular understandings of spirituality (the latter is indicated through allusions to 'mind, body and spirit'). In this accord, it is notions of 'the body' and 'embodiment' that shape the focus of inquiry into spirituality that follows. We refer in particular to the ways in which 'spirit' or 'god' with a small 'g' is constructed as residing or embodied within the individual and/or the material world.

As such, we are concerned with the ways in which transpersonal psychological knowledge works through certain constructions of the body to constitute spirituality in particularly individualistic, self-orientated ways. The chapter is structured in such a way that we outline first a 'vehicular body', and second 'embodied knowledge'. The latter part of the chapter moves to examine constructions of spirituality that pose challenges to and open up such transpersonal and individually bounded conceptions. Accordingly, we discuss certain socially embodied notions of spirituality, whereby what are referred to as spiritual notions of 'oneness' or 'connectedness' are located within specific social contexts. In particular, we refer to 'embodying "oneness" in rave and DIY culture'. It can be argued that such socially embodied constructions of spirituality provide a challenge to psychological constructions while at the same time opening a *space* for a spirituality and politics. The arguments that follow do not attempt to account for spirituality as a whole but instead work from specific examples and speak from a particular and partial, critically informed perspective.

The 'Vehicular' Body

In this section we refer to particular practices in which the body and bodily posture are rendered pivotal. One example is 'sitting meditation', a practice which in 1990s Britain is frequently used by people outside any particular tradition, for instance specific forms of Buddhism. Transpersonal psychologists have been highly influential in this formulation of spirituality. David Fontana for instance, as joint founder of the transpersonal section of the British Psychological Society in 1996, publishes both academically as well as in a more 'public' realm. His book *Meditation* (1992) talks the reader through the practice of meditation and in so doing includes a section that emphasises the importance of bodily posture.

The 'correct' bodily posture espoused involves keeping the spine straight and it is in this sense that a sitting posture is most often preferred. This is because in sitting upright the spine becomes straight. In addition, correct posture requires the feet or knees to touch the floor and the arms to be relaxed. This posture is viewed as allowing a 'free flow' of energy through the body, that is, down the spine and circulating throughout the relaxed limbs. Such a posture as an integral part of meditation is then practised regularly with the aim of transcending the rational mind, stopping 'streams of consciousness', the endless 'chatter' that passes through our minds every minute of the day.

The body as it appears in this context is viewed as helping a person to *transcend* the mind; it is instrumental in the attainment of something that the mind alone cannot obtain. As such, the body is granted importance, but is not of itself central. To an extent this conception of the body recalls the reported experiences of medieval mystics who displayed manifestations such as 'stigmata' and 'lactation'. Such experiences, depicted in terms of being 'at once beyond yet rooted in bodies', were viewed as signifying a union with God (Bayer and Malone, 1996, p. 674). These mystics are referenced as producing a challenge to early Christian conceptions, which denigrated the body as it was considered to be a barrier to transcendence and the soul. In contrast, in meditation the body takes centre stage, *enabling* transcendence. However, at the same time, the body defies a clear-cut understanding, as paradoxically it is important for establishing a union with god/spirit or universal energy, yet is not in itself first and foremost of importance. Hence, the body is viewed as a vehicle to achieving something other in a manner that resembles the Gnostics' dissociation from corporeality and sense of being 'in but not of the body' (Frank, 1991).

'Embodied Knowledge'

The influence of transpersonal psychology can, to some extent, be seen also in the construction of embodied knowledge. Mary Ballou's writings (although not from a transpersonal perspective) are useful here as they refer to embodied knowledge as 'a body sense inclusive of emotional and physical responses as arbitrators of knowledge' (1995, p. 13). This resembles a Jungian sense of a 'voice within' or 'intuition', terms that often frequent transpersonal writings (Heery, 1989). In this sense, the body is construed as providing a material basis, a 'real', concrete foundation for 'spiritual' knowledge that is set out as a different kind of knowing from that of the rational mind. This is illustrated in the two extracts below. The first is taken from the popular author Shakti Gawain who writes in the 'mind, body, spirit' genre. The second is taken from an interview study which forms part of the first author's PhD research and seeks to explore diversity in the ways in which people constitute and utilise 'spirituality'.

1. Most of us have programmed our intellect to doubt our intuition. When an intuitive
2. feeling arises, our rational minds immediately say, 'I don't think that will work,'
3. 'nobody else is doing it that way,' or 'what a foolish idea,' and the intuition is
4. disregarded...[1] As we move into the new world, it is time to re-educate our intellect to
5. recognize the intuition as a valid source of information and guidance... It means
6. tuning in to your 'gut feelings' about things – that deepest inner sense of personal
7. truth. Shakti Gawain (1993, p. 66)

1. INT.: What sorts of things are important to you?
2. R. ...knowing that everything is within me that I wa' (.) that I need ... that all the
3. answers are here (.) they're within me ... I'll feel the answer (.) I can feel what's
4. right (.) it's like I suppose (.) I don't know (.) I feel it physically (.) mm how it feels
5. in my body and I can feel it in parts of my body (.) whether it's good or bad I feel (.)
6. sometimes I feel tense and (.) and that to me means that something isn't right and I
7. shouldn't be doing it or sometimes I feel relaxed and I'll go with it and for me (.) it's
8. about trusting myself and trusting my intuition and my feelings and like (.) my gut
9. feeling more and more ... – SUSANNA

These extracts are illustrative of the way in which the body is constructed as being able to provide a form of knowledge. In the first extract, Gawain stresses the importance of acknowledging 'intuition' as 'a valid source of information and guidance' (line 5) and alludes explicitly to the body through her reference to 'gut feelings' (line 6). In like manner, Susanna in the second extract subscribes to embodied knowledge as she states 'all the answers are here, they're within me' (lines 2–3). Further, she explicitly refers to her body as she asserts 'how it feels in my body' in 'parts of my body' (lines 4–5) and, as with Gawain, Susanna specifies her 'gut feelings' (lines 8–9) as the corporeal site for knowledge.

The body is made central in this construal of personal knowing. As a taken-for-granted 'real,' 'physical', 'entity', the body provides a 'foundation', which is taken as 'evidence' for what, is then rendered 'real'. That is, the body is viewed as providing 'actual' evidence for the existence of knowledge, it works to construct the existence of such knowledge, and in so doing constitutes such knowledge as 'real'.

It seems important to examine some assumptions about the form of spirituality implicated in these constructions. Here we argue that transpersonal psychology's influence is evident in these two constructions of spirituality, the 'vehicular body' and the body in 'embodied knowledge'. These work to maintain a taken-for-granted, individually bounded body and an individualistic notion of 'selfhood'. (Although at this point it seems important to reiterate that we are not claiming to speak for everyone who has ever meditated or engaged with notions of 'embodied knowledge'.) Frequently, such understandings are produced within a discourse of self-development or personal growth. Indeed David Fontana outlines the benefits of meditation to include a decrease in tension, anxiety and stress as well as an increase in self-worth, independence, self-discipline and sense of identity (paraphrased from Fontana, 1992, p. 8). That is, Fontana frames the benefits of meditation in 'self-orientated' terms.

Our argument, then, is that these forms of embodied knowledge serve to restrict spirituality within the bounds of a 'self-contained' selfhood. First, this is achieved through the construction of the individually bounded body, a body which is constituted, on the one hand, as a 'vehicle' for the attainment of transcendence in sitting meditation, and on the other, as a 'foundation' for the realisation of spiritual knowledge. Second, this self-contained body within which spirituality is located is itself embedded within the intertextual layering of a culturally pervasive discourse of therapeutic, self-development. Both work to construct a spirituality that centres on the individual, the individual body, and the self. Consequently, intrapersonal boundaries of mind, body and spirit are transgressed while interpersonal, individual–society, self–other divisions are maintained.

Challenges to self-contained notions of self have been posed from a critical psychology perspective. For example, the work of Isaac Prilleltensky, Ed Sampson and Nikolas Rose that questions the politics of self is of relevance here. In particular they question the role of psychological knowledge in constituting the 'individual'. Psychology's focus on the individual has been cast as anti-social in its rendering of the individual as a self-contained, bounded and masterful entity separable from others, from society, as well as responsible for and capable of bringing about change (Rose, 1990). Indeed, the centrality of the individual is stressed to such an extent that other forces – for example, social and political – are ignored and as such are not called upon to instil change. The point to be made is that these charges can also be brought to these individually bounded notions of spirituality. That is to say, that psychology's infamous production of the individual is alive and well but, moreover, is being created as divine within these embodied constructions of spirituality.

Social Embodiment: Embodying 'Oneness' in Rave and DIY Culture

In the rest of this chapter we aim to outline some examples of embodied spirituality that stand outside psychological knowledge and work to challenge the boundaries of the individual body. We refer to what has become termed a spiritual notion of 'oneness' or 'connectedness', that is, the idea that everyone or every living thing is connected in some way or is part of some greater whole (Anthony and Robbins, 1990). More specifically, we are concerned with how this 'oneness' is being constructed in regard to rave events and aspects of DIY culture in Britain in the late 1980s and 1990s.

At this point we draw on the work of Anna King (1996) who refers to contemporary spirituality within eco-movements; Dorothy Riddle (1994) who argues for a spirituality and politics; and L. Gregory Jones (1996) who acknowledges a socially embodied sense of spirituality. Their conceptualisations of spirituality extend beyond the boundaries of the individual body towards notions of social embodiment, which we argue are applicable to the contexts of rave events and DIY culture. Moreover, these socially embodied notions of spirituality provide a space which moves beyond a distinctly individual focus and the limits of personal change, towards an engagement with social change and a political agenda.

In talking about rave events and DIY culture, we refer to areas that are not exclusively distinct from one another. As such, the initial definitions of rave and DIY that follow take each of these areas in turn, yet 'spirituality' within these contexts is somewhat similar. In terms of rave, we refer to events that grew out of the 1980s parties, in the UK, which were often located in squatted industrial warehouses. These are events that became politicised after the Criminal Justice Act 1994 which served to prohibit large gatherings of people listening to the kind of repetitive-beat music frequently played at raves (McKay, 1988). Furthermore, we refer to the Free Party scene (depicted as having emerged to challenge the commercialisation of rave with its high ticket prices). There is of course diversity within this scene, and again we present only a partial perspective.

A link between rave and spirituality has been made elsewhere. For example, Ben Malbon (1999) and Nicholas Saunders (1995) have written about rave and mystical–transcendent experiences. In addition, within a more commercial arena, CD covers display spiritual insignia. *Return to the Source*, a group which organises rave events, provides one such example. Its CD is entitled 'Sacred Sites' and refers to the group's claim that the music was inspired by its visits to various sacred sites around the world. In addition, the cover displays a prominent Buddha's head, illustrating quite clearly the link they make between spirituality and rave.

In terms of DIY culture we allude to what in the UK has come to be known as 'Do-It-Yourself culture: party and protest'. George Monbiot states that, 'The whole business of DIY culture is that you get together and you say 'This is an issue that affects the people in this room, and we want to do something about it' (1994, p. 8). DIY culture is said to encompass a multiplicity of issues including the Free Party movement, environmental groups, road protest and action at local grassroots level. The emphasis is placed on 'coming together with others to do it', and it is in this sense that some people refer to 'Do-It-Ourselves' instead of 'Do-It-Yourself'. Further, as the slogan 'party and protest' implies, rave-style events are central, referring to the partying before and/or while protesting (McKay, 1998).

In terms of spirituality we highlight the ways in which a spiritual notion of 'oneness' is embodied within these social contexts. In talking about rave events similar links have been made, for instance, by Maria Pini's (1997) 'texts of sameness' and Philip Tagg's (1994) reference to 'collective consciousness'. In the context of rave, this sense of 'oneness' is constructed as working to break down both intrapersonal and interpersonal boundaries between self and others, such that one is able to feel part of something bigger than oneself, part of the whole crowd. As Gilbert argues, 'The very idea that human beings are hermetically sealed units, irreducible and unitary individuals, rational agents, is challenged by the ecstasy and collectivity of the dance' (1997, p. 14). Indeed, such 'oneness' can be viewed as embodied in the smiles to one another, the respect for people's space, even on a crowded dancefloor, along with the sharing of drinks, cigarettes and conversation with relative strangers, all of which are aspects of rave events that people talk about frequently. In addition, this notion of spiritual 'oneness' is constructed in other ways and for some it is reproduced through the construction of particular values. The term 'PLUR' is relevant here, standing for peace, love, unity and respect, used both on the internet to depict the 'spirit of rave' and also within talk about DIY culture (McKay, 1998).

To illustrate this spiritual notion of 'oneness', the extract below is taken from a interview with a young man who defines himself as a resident member of a 'Collective of people'.[1] This 'Collective' has over the last six years renovated derelict buildings, one into a community farm and another into a hostel. They also organise free parties within their local community, as such, bringing together rave and DIY culture:

1. R.: ... now I'm part of something erm something that's (.) dedicated to making things
2. better for ourselves and for everyone around us (.) [INT.: aha] before we were all
3. derelict people I was derelict (.) you know (.) I ain't looking to do the same thing with
4. my whole life (.) it's just stagnant (.) demoralising (.) I mean it's not spiritually
5. fulfilling (.) but coming to the Collective when you're doing things for like not just
6. yourself (.) and not to just to make someone else rich (.) you're doing it to make all
7. these people soulfully and spiritually rich (.) you're doing it to make all these people

8. smile and help them feel happy in all this despair (.) there's so much despair out there
9. (.) but here (.) here we're building a future together (.) for everyone erm and I'm part
10. of that (.) making that happen (.) doing something for everybody for all brothers and
11. sisters.
12. INT.: So would you say that being part of the Collective is spiritually fulfilling?
13. R.: Nowhere else gives me as much satisfaction and love (.) there's nowhere else that I
14. want to be (.) this kinda life is the most unlonely life you can imagine we live
15. together (.) love together and play together and we're working together to do
16. something for everyone (.) that's fulfilling (.) I'm working here (.) I'm like building up
17. and running the farm a place for the community (.) communal is the key word around
18. here (.) we all get better together (.) that's what makes this difference between this
19. kinda life and that kinda life (.) [*INT*.: aha] the alternative is the rat race (.) sort of roll
20. your sleeves up get your guns out and fight it's being part of something that powerful
21. (.) power to make an effect (.) take direct action and that's what we're doing together
22. we're a group of people that is dedicated enough spiritual enough if you like to reject
23. personal gain and to work for making the world a better place for everyone (.) we're
24. angry enough to be passionate and spiritual enough to be non-violent ...
25. INT.: And when you say everyone ...
26. R.: Everyone (.) anyone who wants to come down here is welcome (.) anyone there's
27. people here that are what I call from excluded groups (.) excluded because of colour
28. (.) criminal record (.) style (.) attitude (.) whatever (.) people coming together and
29. thrashing out their differences sexual (.) spiritual (.) racial (.) and all these barriers
30. mm all these barriers that society has put up we're breaking down (.) ... – Jason.

This extract is particularly rich in the constructions of spirituality, collectivity and direct action by means of metaphor, use of pronouns and contrasts. However, for the purpose of this chapter and as a means of illustrating the ways spirituality can be constructed through social embodiment, we want to highlight the ways in which Jason, the speaker, constructs the 'Collective' in relation to spirituality. Accordingly we outline (1) a counter-culture construction of spirituality; (2) the reference to non-violence and (3) an allusion to oneness, or unity.

First, Jason's understanding of spirituality portrays a 'counter-culture' notion. He sets up a contrast, which he reiterates at several points, between life and work in the 'Collective' and mainstream living. As he talks about 'this kinda life and that kinda life' (line 19), Jason polarises the two lifestyles and in so doing reveres the 'Collective' while denigrating mainstream living. More specifically, he contrasts 'making other people rich' (line 6) that is, working within a capitalistic context, to provide financial wealth for someone else, with working as part of the 'Collective' 'to make all these people soulfully and spiritually rich' (lines 6–7). In addition, in lines 19–20 he adds 'the alternative is the rat race (.) sort of roll your sleeves up get your guns out and fight'. In this accord, mainstream society is rendered a lifestyle rife with exploitation, competition and war, whereas life in the 'Collective' is constructed in positive terms, as fulfilment. Furthermore, Jason refers to the 'Collective' as a group of people that are 'spiritual enough ... to reject personal gain' (lines 22–23). Consequently, the use of polarisation, whereby the productivity of life in the 'Collective' is to make people 'spiritually rich', instils a sense of shared gain which is set against capitalism, competition and personal gain. These work to produce a counter-cultural understanding of spirituality.

Second, Jason refers explicitly to 'non-violence' on line 24. At this point, links can be made with other non-violent protest movements for instance, Gandhi's protests, as well as the women's protest against nuclear arms at Greenham Common in Britain. In addition, Dorothy Riddle's (1989) work is relevant at this point as she talks about the ways in which a spiritual notion of 'oneness' or 'interconnectedness' implicates a 'respect for all' such that can be translated into non-violent action. In like manner, then, in this extract Jason alludes to direct action and non-violence (lines 21–5). As such, he brings an element of anger together with spirituality as he asserts 'we're angry enough to be passionate and spiritual enough to be non-violent ... ' (line 24–5).

Third, there is a notion of 'oneness', or 'unity' evident in the extract above. Despite the obvious use of the name 'Collective', there are references in the text to 'the most unlonely life' (lines 14), 'communal' (line 17), 'being part of something' (line 20) and 'togetherness' (lines 15, 18 and 21), that work to establish this sense of unity. In addition, Jason asserts that 'everyone (.) anyone who wants to come down here is welcome' (line 27), an inclusive rendering which does not bar anyone on the basis of 'colour, criminal record' (lines 27–28) or differences whether 'sexual (.) spiritual (.) racial' (line 29). In sum, Jason's depiction of the 'Collective' works to construct spirituality as bound up with a counter-cultural discourse and as spiritual 'oneness'. Indeed, such a notion of spirituality is socially embodied within this context, 'lived' by Jason in terms of both non-violent direct action as well as the quality of acceptance that he asserts prevails in the 'Collective's' relationships with one another.

Nevertheless, such a construction of DIY culture and rave as 'oneness' is not unproblematic and the 'politics of difference' is perhaps one obvious line of questioning. At this point we think it of value to go beyond the text and embed this extract within its local context. For this 'collective', the local context is a multicultural town with a high percentage of Asian, African-Caribbean and people from other minority ethnic backgrounds living among white English groupings. Further, it is a town with a history of racial tensions and riots on local authority housing estates. It is within this local context that the people to whom Jason refers locate 'coming together' with a shared aim of bringing about change in their local community. They talk about being fed up with high-rise accommodation on council or local authority housing estates; of unemployment, of 'dead end jobs' and in particular they refer to factory work. Within these local circumstances Jason talks about overcoming differences with others in order to be able to work together to bring about change that will benefit not just themselves but also their local community. Arguably, then, what is being constructed in Jason's account is a way, not of denying, but rather accepting difference. Indeed, out of a historical context of racialised difference and tension, people from diverse ethnic backgrounds can work and party together, producing a culture in which a socially embodied notion of spirituality can actively labour towards social change.

In short, in this chapter we have attempted to question certain transpersonal psychological constructions of spirituality. In particular, we have argued that an individually bounded body works to constitute individualistic and self-contained notions of spirituality. Once open to critical inquiry into the 'politics of self', such self-orientated conceptions of spirituality are viewed as limited in the sense of breaking down intrapersonal boundaries as set within certain parameters. Such a conception simultaneously maintains and substantiates interpersonal divisions between self–other and individual–society through a discourse of divinity. In the latter part of this chapter our aims have been to pose challenges to psychological conceptions by pointing to alternative constructions of spirituality and, by implication, the body. In so doing, we have made reference to the context of rave events and DIY culture in which socially embodied notions of spirituality are located. Within these alternative contexts such as the 'collective' and rave events, a socially embodied notion of spiritual 'oneness' perturbs the boundaries around the individual body, blurs the distinctions between self and other and characterises as unifiable, social differences on the basis of class, 'race', gender and age. Moreover, within the context of the 'collective', spirituality is intricately interlinked with direct action in a manner that provides an active space for an interlinking of politics with spirituality in such a way as to argue for social transformations beyond the distinctly personal.

Finally, we would emphasise that we do not claim the preceding arguments as definitive nor exhaustive of all construals of spirituality extant in the late 1990s in the UK. Accordingly, our aim is to represent neither all those who engage with spirituality nor rave events and DIY culture. In addition, we do not want to espouse rave and DIY culture as ideal formulations of spirituality, as indeed there are many constructions in these domains that invite inquiry. Rather, we offer the contexts of rave culture and DIY culture as posing interesting and in many ways contrastive constructions of spirituality which open up and challenge transpersonal psychological knowledge. Indeed these latter construals of spirituality are rarely visible within the disciplinary boundaries of psychology. While we argue as imperative that a critical psychology engage with understandings of spirituality, it is of equal importance that a critical agenda remains ever sceptical, questioning and in search of ways of bringing a political element to such research.

Note

1. Transcription conventions:
   INT.: interviewer; R.: respondent; ... : omitted text; (.): pauses.

Bibliography

Anthony, D. and Robbins, T. 'Civil Religion and Recent American Religious Ferment', in D. Anthony and T. Robbins (eds), *In Gods We Trust: New Patterns in Religious Pluralism in America* (New Brunswick and London: Transaction Publishers, 1990).

Ballou, M. 'Women and Spirit: Two Nonfits in Psychology', *Women and Therapy*, 16(2–3) (1995) 9–21.

Bayer, B.M. and Malone, K.R. 'Feminism, Psychology and Matters of the Body', *Theory and Psychology*, 6(4) (1996) 667–92.

Bayer, B.M. and Shotter, J. (eds). *Reconstructing the Psychological Subject* (London: Sage, 1998).

Bruce, S. *Religion in Modern Britain* (Oxford University Press, 1995).

Daniels, M. and McNutt, B. 'Questioning the Role of Transpersonal Psychology', *Transpersonal Psychology Review*, 1(4) (1997) 4–9.

Featherstone, M., Hepworth, M. and Turner, B.S. *The Body: Social Process and Cultural Theory* (London: Sage, 1991).

Fontana, D. *Meditation* (Shaftesbury, Dorset: Element Press, 1992).

Frank, A. 'For a Sociology of the Body: An Analytical Review', ch. 2 in M. Featherstone, M. Hepworth and B.S. Turner (eds), *The Body: Social Process and Cultural Theory* (London: Sage, 1991).

Gawain, S. *Living in the Light* (London: Bantam Books, 1993).
Gilbert, J. 'Soundtrack to an Uncivil Society: Rave Culture, the Criminal Justice Act and the Politics of Modernity', *New Formations*, 37 (1997) 5–22.
Heelas, P. 'The New Age in Cultural Context: The Premodern, the Modern and the Postmodern', *Religion*, 23 (1993) 103–16.
Heery, M.H. 'Inner Voice Experiences: An Exploratory Study of Thirty Cases', *Journal of Transpersonal Psychology*, 21(1) (1989) 73–82.
Jones, L.G. 'A Thirst for God or Consumer Spirituality?', in L.G. Jones and J.J. Buckley (eds), *Spirituality and Social Embodiment* (Oxford: Blackwell, 1996).
King, A. S. 'Spirituality: Transformation and Metamorphosis', *Religion*, 26 (1996) 343–51.
Malbon, B. *Clubbing, Dancing, Ecstasy and Vitality* (London: Routledge, 1999).
McKay, G. *Senseless Acts of Beauty* (London: Verso, 1988).
McKay, G. *DIY Culture: Party and Protest in Britain* (London: Verso, 1998).
Monbiot, G., cited in E. Brass and S. P. Koziell, *Gathering Force: DIY Culture – Radical Action for Those Tired of Waiting* (London: The Big Issue Writers, 1994).
Pini, M. 'Women and the Early British Rave Scene', in A. McRobbie (ed.), *Back to Reality* (Manchester University Press, 1997).
Prilleltensky, I. 'Psychology and the Status Quo', *American Psychologist*, 44(5) (1989) 795–802.
Prilleltensky, I. *The Morals and Politics of Psychology: Psychological Discourse and the Status Quo* (Albany: State University of New York Press, 1994).
Return to the Source, P.O. Box 4532, London SW2 2XT. www.rtts.com
Riddle, D. I. 'Politics, Spirituality and Models of Change' in C. Spretnak (ed.), *The Politics of Spirituality* (New York: Doubleday, 1994).
Rose, N. 'Psychology as a Social Science', in I. Parker. and J. Shotter (eds), *Deconstructing Social Psychology* (London: Routledge, 1990).
Sampson, E. E. 'Social Psychology and Social Control', in I. Parker and J. Shotter (eds), *Deconstructing Social Psychology* (London: Routledge, 1990).
Saunders, N. *Ecstasy and the Dance Culture* (BPC: Wheatons, 1995).
Shilling, C. *The Body and Social Theory* (London: Sage, 1993).
Spretnak, C. (ed.) *The Politics of Spirituality* (New York: Doubleday, 1994).
Tagg, P. 'From Refrain to Rave: The Decline of Figure and the Rise of Ground', *Popular Music*, 13(2) (1994) 209–22.
Vitz, P.C. and Modesti, D. 'Social and Psychological Origins of New Age Spirituality, *Journal of Psychology and Christianity*, 12(1) (1993) 47–57.

11

Synchronicity as a Feature of the Synchronic

BENJAMIN SYLVESTER

> In order to decide among the various alternatives, a measurement is required. This measurement is what constitutes an event, as distinguished from the probability, which is a mathematical abstraction. However, the only simple and consistent description physicists were able to assign to a measurement involved an observer's becoming aware of the result. Thus the physical event and the content of the human mind were inseparable. (Morowitz, 1980, p. 38)

Since the time it was claimed by biological science 142 years ago in *On the Origin of Species*, 'modern' psychology has nailed the chronological series to its mast as the mainstay of well-founded explanation. Emphasis on diachronic past → present understanding is not confined to any one domain in academic psychology, for example, study of the brain. The priority given to experimental methods in the subject ensures that, across the board, the search is on for independent variables whose action both precedes and causes almost every phenomenon submitted to psychological investigation. Then → now analysis forms warp and woof of textbook psychology's induction to the discipline in all widely known US varieties. It is also fundamental to theory. Think of assumptions about environmental shaping in behaviourism. Think of the supposed explanatory significance of the Human Genome Project (Lewontin, 2000). Think of the truism that early is deep in developmental psychology. And, after all, isn't all science like that? The aim of this chapter is to establish a different priority for psychological understanding, one that recognises the primacy of the synchronic over the diachronic in unravelling the phenomena of experience.

Note: The author was previously known as B.S. Bradley, and works by him are listed under his former name.

More than one context might be given for this initiative. For example, in wedding itself to the Newtonian physics of a linear 'absolute time' that was dominant in Darwin's era, psychology's assumptions about the physical universe have been rendered increasingly anachronistic by the work of Einstein and his successors. More recently, one might point to Derrida's (1967) arguments against an 'originary thinking' that imagines a source of pure presence for mental and linguistic phenomena, a source that is shorn of any relation to what supplements it and thereby gives it sense. But, in psychology, critique of what has been called the genetic fallacy dates from well before Derrida or even Einstein.

So called genetic fallacies inhere in any kind of idea that the genesis of a proposition or belief or has a bearing on its validity (Lavine, 1962, p. 321). Such ideas are implicit in the assumption that the best way to understand something is to seek for its most primitive form, its roots. To think like this is to conflate the question 'what?' with the question 'how come?' More precisely, in the terms of James (1878, 1890, 1903) and Baldwin (1895), who impugned such a conflation at the dawn of modern psychology,[1] it illegitimately subsumes the primary descriptive questions in psychology, questions of being and of 'essence', under questions of genesis. That these two species of question should never be confused has been argued by empiricists since the day of Locke (1690/1952, p. 261), who wrote that 'the cause of any sensation, and the sensation itself' were 'two ideas so different and distant one from another, that no two can be more so'.

This paper sets out from a reflection on synchronicity: which I will define for the time being as the temporal coincidence of the same or closely related pieces of mental content in two different people. Synchronicity is germane to my purposes because it is impossible to explain from a diachronic 'scientific' perspective, as Evans-Pritchard (1937) argued in his analysis of Azande witchcraft. It is one of those quintessentially psychical phenomena that has been rendered most shadowy and anomalous by the longstanding push to cause–effect thinking in psychology. Hence, in accordance with the tenets of deconstruction, if we can position ourselves to think coherently about synchronicity, we should be well placed to see what is most seriously amiss with the dominant forms of intelligibility in the discipline (see Bradley, 2001; Johnson, 1989).

Elsewhere I have discussed at some length the psychosocial background to the production of synchronicities (or 'synchronisation'; Bradley, 2001), pointing out that social institutions and interpersonal interactions, as a banal matter of course, depend on the continuous reproduction of coincident meanings. My examples for that paper were not extreme forms of synchronicity. Here I want to approach the explanation of some more inexplicable kinds of synchronicity as a means of considering the formal constitution of the domain of the synchronic.

I make four assumptions:

1. Earlier it has been argued that psychology, like any other social science, can be conducted in one of two ways. It can be conducted as a science which uses statistical models, treating its phenomena as living *en masse* and on a different scale from the investigator 'like *Drosophila* in a bottle', phenomena upon which, therefore, the psychologist can look down as from the cold heights of ubiquity and eternity. Or psychology can be conducted as in a science using models where investigator and subject cannot be decoupled (Bradley, 1993; Lévi-Strauss, 1963; Wiener, 1961, p. 189). The first step in my argument here is therefore the decision to study experience non-genetically and in a way which can appreciate that others' realities may differ radically from, but nevertheless connected with, reality as conceived by ourselves (see Bradley and Morss, in press).
2. The reason for taking the step of viewing psychology as a non-genetic form of inquiry is, as implied above, because only thus can we recognise and so address the problem of the differences in meaning between different people's realities (including the reality of the psychologist). But, when we move from the domain of cause to the domain of meaning, we reverse the relative importance of the synchronic and the diachronic for understanding human subjectivity, as argued for psychology's pilot-science linguistics by Saussure (1974; see below).
3. Time functions quite differently in diachronic/statistical understandings and non-genetic/synchronic understandings of human realities. In statistical models, time is Gibbsian: unidirectional, cumulative and irreversible. But in 'mechanical' models time is Bergsonian, that is, non-cumulative and reversible (Ardener, 1971).
4. Finally, in a 'mechanical' model, observer and observed are *on the same scale as each other* and hence cannot be decoupled. The observer A can never have enough knowledge of 'the situation as a whole' to know whether A's perceptions of B are solely due to B's characteristics or are coloured by A's characteristics (see Heisenberg's principle of uncertainty). In our case, this means that, particularly when two phenomena occur in the same time-frame psychological space, their relative temporal order may change, depending on the co-ordinates they are viewed from. This logical possibility has recently been strikingly illustrated in sub-atomic physics by such experiments as Wang *et al.* (2000, p. 277), who have shown that a super-luminal pulse may appear to leave a cell 'even before it enters'.

The chapter is in three sections, devoted respectively to defining synchronicity, to exploring the meaning of the synchronic as developed by Saussure and then returning to synchronicity to see how far the concept of the synchronic can be said to render synchronicity comprehensible.

Defining the Domain of Synchronicity

Diverse forms of psychosocial synchronization – from the theory and observation of intersubjectivity in infancy, Bion's (1961) description of experiences in groups, the repetitiveness of family dynamics and dramas in the workplace – have elsewhere been brought together under the rubric of Althusserian social theory (Bradley, 2001). Any social system, of any size, can survive only if it can reproduce a coordinated membership. Thus a social system, by its very nature, enforces a crude form of 'behavioural' synchronization. This is equivalent to the system's 'redundancy'. Thus it is no surprise if we meet people in some ways 'in the same space' of significance as ourselves – or synchronized with us – when we go to a Bach concert in Sydney or at an academic conference. From here it is but a short step to meeting a long-lost friend at a football match or running into an old colleague in a cake-shop.

So how are we to distinguish these more banal forms of 'synchronicity,' which scarcely give us pause, from those that strike us as uncanny? From the perspective of this chapter, we should at first resist making any such distinction, because the synchronic order underpins both kinds of phenomena. The point of this chapter is to consider how the synchronic order is constituted *per se*, and only then to ask whether and how the most extreme examples of synchronicity might exceed this constitution. Thus the definition for synchronicity given above – the temporal coincidence of the same or closely related pieces of mental content in two different people – potentially covers both banal and extreme examples. The same is true of the definition given in Jung's (1952, p. 25) famous monograph on synchronicity as 'the simultaneous occurrence of a certain psychic state with one or more external events which appear as meaningful parallels to the momentary subjective state'.

Witness, for example, the following three cases of synchronicity. The first may seem only mildly anomalous. The second and third are more extreme:

1. The Sunday afternoon prior to attending the conference at which I first spoke on synchronicity, I drove into Sydney to another meeting. I returned home to work on my paper the next day. One of the e-mail messages I found waiting for me was a reply to a friendly message I had shot off at 16.11pm, minutes before I left for Sydney:

   Sunday, 25 April 1999. 16.58pm. Well, my dear Ben, I turned on the e-mail specifically to write you a brief note and yours is the single new message I received!

   My correspondent, Sean, was a man I had met a year previously at a small week-long 'working conference'. We got on well, quickly discovering that we had overlapped at the same college as undergraduates, and that we shared other points of reference. After the conference we both got involved in a virtual group, a continuation of the conference by e-mail. Over the year, both Sean and I had contributed many messages to the e-group *qua* group – and at least once disagreed fiercely in messages sent to the group as a whole. But prior to this Sunday, I had never sent him a personal e-message 'out of the blue.' Neither had he sent me such a message. Yet, between 4 and 5pm that Sunday afternoon, at a time when I had the need to illustrate synchronicity on my mind, we both had the impulse to send each other private messages.

2. On the night of 23 October 1998, an elderly woman in Durham, England, had a nightmare. She dreamt of two women and a child, *in extremis* as they died on board a burning ship. The scene was backed by tropical palms and the arc of an empty beach. The dream is unusually vivid. Four days later she heard on the radio of a holiday cruise-ship wrecked off northern Brazil in which an eye-witness described two women and a child dying in flames as the ship went down, just as she had dreamt it.[2]

3. In March 2000 a young lawyer was giving a dinner-party at home when she was suddenly filled with dread. In a cold sweat, she stood up and reeled out into the hall. She went into the cloakroom, splashed water in her face, tried to breathe more steadily but returned pale to her guests. 'I just had a most terrible turn,' she told them. Her husband could see how unsettled she was. An hour later the phone rang. She was told that both her parents had just died in a car crash. Later she worked out that she must have been overcome at almost the same time that her parents died.

These examples will serve as reference points for the following discussion.

The Synchronic in Saussure

> The first thing that strikes us when we study the facts of language is that their succession in time does not exist so far as the speaker is concerned. He [*sic*] is confronted with a state. That is why the linguist who wishes to understand a state must discard all knowledge of everything that produced it and ignore diachrony. He [*sic*] can enter the mind of speakers only by completely suppressing the past. (Saussure, 1974, p. 81)

When we are taught the history of psychology, Saussure is unlikely to be mentioned, unless it be as 'the founder of modern linguistics.' Yet Saussure described himself as a psychologist and his work proves relevant to psychology for more than one reason. For instance: Saussure argued that linguistics, in so far as it dealt with language as a system of signs and not as a collection of physical speech acts, had something as its object that, like synchronicity, was at once 'purely social and independent of the individual' and 'exclusively psychological' (1974, p. 18).

Saussure was born in 1857, the year after the psychologist Freud and the year before the sociologist Durkheim. It is a happy simultaneity that places him in this trio, between psychology and sociology, for his *Course in General*

Linguistics is a classic in the methodology of the social sciences as well as a treatise on language, and it is with these two disciplines that its links are strongest. A good way to locate Saussure's work in historical perspective is to treat the founding or renovation of these three disciplines as a single revolutionary move in the development of the social sciences. What Freud, Saussure and Durkheim seem to have recognised is that the social sciences could make little progress until society was considered as a reality in itself. It is as though they had asked, 'What makes individual experience possible? What enables people to perceive not just physical objects but objects with a meaning?' And the answer they postulated rejected historical and causal explanations in favour of the study of interpersonal systems of norms which, assimilated by individuals as the culture within which they live, create the possibility of a wide variety of meaningful activities (see Culler, 1974, pp. xi ff.). Saussure in particular saw linguistics as in the vanguard of the human sciences in general, and psychology in particular, in that what was essential to linguistics was also likely to be essential to other areas of psychological inquiry. In this light, his seminal differentiation of synchronic from diachronic analysis in linguistics was intended as a particularly salient contribution to psychology.

Saussure argued that any science concerned with values, as psychology is, cannot proceed without making a distinction between the system of values *per se* and the same values as they relate to time. He described language as 'a system of pure values which are determined by nothing except the momentary arrangement of its terms' (1974, p. 80). Hence his distinction between two axes of explanation in psychology (see Figure 11.1).

So far as the speaker is concerned, Saussure said, succession in time does not exist. The speaker confronts a single state, a state of simultaneity. The words a speaker utters must be seen as part of a synchronic system that in the first instance must be defined in terms of what the speaker (not the linguist) perceives to be reality. Saussure draws a parallel with chess. In a state of the set of chessmen, the respective value of each piece depends on its position on the chessboard just as each linguistic term derives its value from its opposition to all other terms. Both chess and language are governed by a set of social conventions. And in both chess and language, a single change (for example, insertion of the word 'no' into a sentence; losing your queen) affects the values of all the elements in the system. Hence, each 'diachronic' move separates a synchronic state entirely from its predecessor:

> In a game of chess any particular position has the unique characteristic of being freed from all antecedent positions; the route used in arriving there makes absolutely no difference; one who has followed the entire course of the match has no advantage over the curious party who comes up at a critical moment to inspect the game; to describe this arrangement, it is perfectly useless to recall what had

FIGURE 11.1 *(a) The axis of* simultaneities *(AB), which stands for the relations of coexisting things and from which the intervention of time is excluded; and (b)* the axis of successions *(CD), on which only one thing can be considered at a time but upon which are located all the things on the first axis together with their changes* (Saussure, 1974, p. 80)

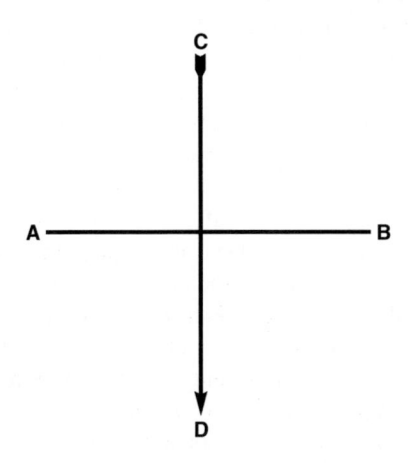

just happened ten seconds previously. All this is equally applicable to language and sharpens the radical distinction between diachrony and synchrony. Speaking operates only on a language-state, and the changes that intervene between states have no place in either state. (Saussure, 1974, p. 89)

Note that when Saussure speaks of synchrony he does not refer literally to events that occur at the same chronological instant. In the same way, so-called synchronicities do not usually occur at exactly the same time. At best, one person does something, phones or e-mails for example, just as the person they were contacting was preparing to do the same thing. The three examples given above show that 'synchronicities' need not occur at exactly the same instant. Indeed, in Jung's (1952) birth charts, decades may separate the relevant events.

Hence, what Saussure means by synchrony has two important qualifications. The first is that, phenomenologically, from the speaker's viewpoint, the 'presence' of the present must be presumed to consist solely in so-called simultaneities. These simultaneities: my mother's wrinkled smile, my father's evergreen absence, a bright winter day, Bach on the radio, the latest carnage in Sierra Leone, my aching head – all constitute my 'here and now'. The second is analytic: 'simultaneities' in both language and experience are to be read in a way to which temporal sequence has no immediate relevance.

It is this second point that Saussure develops with his argument that the relations and differences between linguistic terms in a language state are structured along two contrasting dimensions (see C → D in Figure 11.1). One is made up by the combination of different kinds of term, terms which are both contiguous and (at least) successively present. Saussure calls this form of organisation 'syntagmatic'. Think of the juxtaposition of different kinds of furniture across the floor of a room: bed, chair, dresser, mirror. Or the sequence of a meal: aperitif, entrée, main course, dessert, coffee, liqueur. Or a sentence: subject, verb, qualifier, object. In each case, the terms gain meaning from the order in which they are strung together, spatial or temporal. Thus a word gains some of its significance from its opposition to everything that comes before or after it in dialogue.

At the same time, signs gain value from the place they have in a set of relations and oppositions 'from which the intervention of time is excluded'; that is, 'paradigmatically' (see A—B in Figure 11.1). Here meaning is derived by a process of selection from a single set of semantically related (but different) terms. I select a king-size, four-poster bed, not a single trestle. I choose salad not paté for entrée. A pawn moves in a different way from a knight. I select the verb 'peer' not 'look'. I love Jane, not Robert. Paradigmatic series are tied together by varying degrees of opposition. This is the domain of antonyms and synonyms. It is also the domain of metaphor, and is often personally idiosyncratic, as related terms evoke each other by association (Lemaire, 1977).

Saussure observes that syntagmatic relations occur 'in praesentia' whereas paradigmatic relations occur '*in absentia* in a potential mnemonic series' (1974, p. 123). A synchronic language-state includes both what is present and what might have been present but is absent, being instead actually or potentially 'in the memory'. In James's (1890, p. 573; see below) words, the present 'can never be a fact of our immediate experience'. The present always means more to the individual who experiences it than is ever 'there' in the data available to the senses. Vision, for example, is 'ill-posed' in formal terms: there is never sufficient information in the retinal image uniquely to determine the visual scene. Hence, 'the brain must make certain assumptions about the real world to resolve this ambiguity, and visual illusions can result when these assumptions are invalid' (Bulthoff and Yuille, 1991, p. 286).

Hence, *what I take to be the visible, audible, tangible present is what it is by virtue of events and meanings that are far distant from this 'now' in space and time but, in my idiosyncratic sensibility and experience, can be related to it.* This is where we come close to certain phenomena of synchronicity: where what is observably present (and so, in a crude sense, scientifically 'knowable') is semantically connected to what is empirically absent (that is, 'unknowable'). And, given that synchronically, any thing's meaning depends less on temporal coincidence than on its paradigmatic and syntagmatic differences from other elements in the system of which it forms part – or as Saussure (1974, p. 120) puts it, 'in language there are only differences' – anomaly surrounds a case where two elements in the system are very difficult to differentiate: sameness becomes anomalous. These anomalies are what we call synchronicities. And, in so far as it contains redundancies (see Bradley, 2001), they are just as inevitably a product of the order of the synchronic as non-synchronicitous meanings.

From Saussure we get a picture of psychic reality of which the most prominent dimension is without reference to temporal succession or 'time' as we commonly represent it. For example, our capacities for memory are much better adapted to telling us *that* we have seen something before than *when* we have seen that thing before. Worse, as many studies show, we may not remember that we have experienced something *or* when we have experienced it and yet *still* be affected by the experience.[3] And these 'forgotten' or never-acknowledged experiences may retain as powerful a force as 'remembered' events, sometimes for years after we have undergone them: a fact which gives rise to the concept of repression (Davis, 1987; Davis and Schwartz, 1987). Hence it is no surprise to find that Freud (for example, 1915, p. 191) repeatedly averred that there is no such thing as time in the unconscious. Unconscious processes 'are not ordered temporally, are not [necessarily] altered by the passage of time; they have no reference to time at all'.[4]

But Saussure takes a different step from Freud, holding that the manifold of meanings which any individual's psychic reality coordinates is *collectively produced*. Meaning derives from a collective system of signifiers, '*la langue*', which generate values for individual speakers. As Lacan insisted, this symbolic order pre-exists any individual and it is this order which coordinates one person's meanings with another's and thereby is the indispensable condition affording any possibility of intersubjectivity or shared meaning.

Viewed within an individualistically conceived causal framework, as represented by flow diagrams with arrows pointing from mind A to mind B and back again, intersubjectivity may itself present something of a paradox, a magical correspondence that amounts to 'mind-reading' as one recent title puts it (Whiten, 1991). But in conceiving synchrony and synchronicity, we do not look for causal explanations. The domain of causes and the domain of meanings are complementary but different (Evans-Pritchard, 1937), and we are working here within the domain of meanings. Thus Jung insisted that synchronicity is 'an acausal connecting principle': 'we must conclude that besides the connection between cause and effect there is another factor in nature which expresses itself in the arrangement of events and appears to us as meaning' (Jung, 1952, p. 69). The question therefore is how what we perceive as synchronicities might emerge from the collective order of the synchronic when the psychical order is viewed as acausal and atemporal.

What Remains Anomalous about Synchronicity when Viewed Synchronically?

So far, I have tried to show that synchronicity is less anomalous when viewed as a feature of the synchronic order than when construed diachronically. The possibility that 'the same' thing may occur to different people at more or less the same time is, from a synchronic point of view, quite banal, given the redundancy of the semiotic systems within which human meanings are reproduced. Likewise, the difficulty of finding a causal explanation for synchronicity is the fruit of a conceptual confusion if it is recognised that the synchronic order has to do with meanings not causes. Nevertheless, certain elements of anomaly remain. The three most striking are the non-sequential ordering of synchronicitous events, the specificity of synchronicities, and the occurrence of synchronicity in people separated by great distances. I now want to suggest that each of these features may be understood as corollaries of the super-individual, fieldlike properties of the synchronic.

First, consider the problem of temporal ordering presented by synchronicity. This is most obvious in cases of precognition, as where, for example, King William II of England's priest interpreted his bloody dream to mean that the king should not go hunting the next day (he did go hunting and was killed). Similarly in example (2) above, four days elapsed between the dream and the event. Clearly, within a causal diachronic framework, precognition is inexplicable. However, when viewed as taking place within the same synchronic field, the 'temporal ordering' of two events may be alterable. For the approach from synchrony puts events in the present, the past *and the future* on an equal footing in the ravelling up of sense that produces human subjectivity. Jamesian 'Pragmatism', makes what 'later' becomes of an act decide its meaning (Bradley, 1998). The same is true when decoding a piece of language (the last word may overridingly determine the meaning of all that comes before it – as with verbs in German).

Meanwhile (Wang *et al.*, 2000), we hear that American physicists have discovered a weightless pulse that exceeds the speed of light, 'leaving the accelerator before it enters', and hence reversing temporal ordering in just the way that a causally oriented Victorian physics finds inconceivable:

> For a medium of a length L, it takes a propagation time $L/v_g = n_g L/c$ for a light pulse to traverse it. Compared with the propagation time for light to traverse the same distance in a vacuum, (that is, the vacuum transit time L/c), the light pulse that enters the medium will exit at a moment that is delayed by a time difference $\Delta T = L/v_g - L/c = (n_g - 1)L/c$. When $n_g < 1$, the delay time ΔT is negative, resulting in an advancement. In other words, when incident on a medium with group-velocity index $n_g < 1$, a light pulse can appear on the other side sooner than if it had traversed the same distance in a vacuum. Further more, in contradiction to traditional views that a negative group-velocity of light has no physical

meaning, when the group-velocity index becomes negative, the pulse advancement $-\Delta T = (1 - n_g)L/c$ becomes larger than the vacuum transit time L/c. In other words, it appears as if the pulse is leaving before it enters. This counterintuitive phenomenon is a consequence of the wave nature of light. (Wang et al., 2000, p. 277)

This new discovery of Wang, Kuzmich and Dogariu is an 'order effect', somewhat akin to the effect of line-of-view on the apparent placings of racers in a close finish. The point of principle is that, if events occur close enough together, the point of view of the observer cannot be disengaged from the order of events. Choose one point of view and you see A in front of B. Choose another and you see B before A. Hence, depending on your measuring site, certain points on a light-wave may change order, or at least undo expectation about the uniform passage of time. Of course, quantum mechanics and relativity theory undo a number of traditional assumptions about order and time. For example, it is now theoretically possible for me to take a trip in space and come back younger than my son.[5]

What I would like to suggest here is that synchronicity is of the same logical type as these connected effects, except the field under consideration is microphysical but on a much larger scale (and many times more complex). After all, the world viewed from a synchronic perspective makes a strange thing even of the senses. The senses, seemingly so neatly bundled up as physiological (the eye, for example), themselves become dispersed. Even the way we make sense of the world that is 'physically' present to us is rendered strangely impalpable:[6] 'The knowledge of some other part of the stream, *past or future, near or remote*, is always mixed in with our knowledge of the present thing' (James, 1890, p. 571, my italics).

In this vein Saussure (1974, p. 126) writes that 'a particular word is like the centre of a constellation; it is the point of convergence of an indefinite number of coordinated terms.' What we might loosely call this 'field' of coordinated terms, into which elements from the past and the future, near and remote, are mixed, is the same field, albeit in a less purely linguistic guise, that constitutes synchronicities. Inter-subjectively it is a 'unified field' analogous in type that produces the counterintuitive order effects produced by Wang et al. (2000). And what the phenomena of synchronicity illustrate, when viewed as aspects of the psyche as synchronically conceived, is the inevitability of a certain temporal indeterminacy in the psychic domain.

Two other kinds of anomaly have to do with the specificity of synchronicities and the duplication of mental content at a distance. Regarding specificity, what elevates the kinds of synchronicity illustrated at the start of this chapter above the banal is the fact that they seem too detailed to be simply a product of the redundancies of socio-semiotic reproduction. In Bradley

(2001) I have suggested that synchronicities are most likely to occur when individuals are in a collective state of 'negative capability' (Selby, 1990). Here I would like to add that, even though all mutually intelligible conversation may be said to depend on a sharing of meanings among separate individuals, it is a fact of experience that understandings with some individuals seem far more profound than with others. Thus it can be argued that some people are far more 'in tune' than others:[7] the more specific or accurate your response, the more precise will be my meaning, as well as vice versa and presumably this conformity obtains independently of distance.

Interestingly, reviews of experiments within the Ganzfeld paradigm, where individuals are placed in physically separated rooms and one is asked to choose an item that corresponds to what the other is looking at, show most significant findings for pairs who are related to each other by blood (as compared with spouses, for example; Bem and Honorton, 1994).

So finally, what are we to make of the occurrence of synchronicity at a distance? The findings of the Ganzfeld experiment just mentioned, which do involve physical separation, might be understood by analogy with two accurate clocks, set to the same time, which will keep time with each other just as effectively when separated, even by a great distance, as when in the same room. But this analogy only works for synchronicities that are autonomously generated, as in example (1) at the start of this chapter (an instance of psychosocial redundancy). When external events intervene, however, as in the disasters described in examples (2) and (3) above, the clock analogy fails. Here an additional proposal is required: that there is some basis for a real coordination between the 'psychical' and the 'physical' dimensions of the cosmos. Thus, the semantic connectedness in the synchronic between the observably present and related but absent events would, in at least some cases, have a material dimension such that, when the car accident occurred and the lawyer's parents died, the world would change in concert independently of what was, prior to Einstein, known as absolute space.

The idea that the physical and the mental are but aspects of the same flux is of course fundamental to philosophical monism (for example, Davidson, 1980; James, 1904; Spinoza, 1677/1977) as well as many contemporary approaches to brain science. Thus this proposition is not new or controversial in itself. What is new is that the 'material mind' is not individualised but collective. Once again, this is not new or controversial, as widely held theories assuming super-individual coordination of meanings show, including not only Saussurean approaches but theories of intersubjectivity and intermentality (for example, Bion, 1961; Trevarthen, 1993; Vygotsky, 1978). Put the two propositions together, however, and at once we enter a domain most often trodden by the theorists of modern physics, attempting to succeed where Einstein failed – by producing a 'unified field' theory. See, for example, Bohm's (1980) theory of 'implicate order', Capra (1974), Davies (1984) on 'superforce', and Sheldrake's (1995) stock-piling of evidence for 'formative causation' leading to a trans-global 'morphic resonance.'

Conclusions

The focal point of this chapter is to establish the plausibility of that neglected garden of psychology: the synchronic. It argues that psychology has, since the heyday of Victorian science, been dominated by diachronic thinking. Just to pause and acknowledge the (possible) existence of the synchronic is to move into a logical domain far better suited to the explanation of synchronicities than is a then → now causal logic. The separation of ontological from genetic questions fundamental to the birth of empiricism seems to have been lost in the rush to supposedly scientific explanation in psychology, a rush the descriptive implications of which have long been deplored by writers such as Saussure, James and Freud.

Once one acknowledges the existence of the synchronic, the anomalies surrounding synchronicity no longer fall beyond the pale of psychological understanding. I refer to the difficulties of explaining synchronicity 'causally' and anomalies of the temporal ordering, specificity and physical separation of synchronicitous events. The synchronic order constitutes a super-individual collectivised organisation of meaning that lies orthogonal to the diachronic order. Hence, within this purview, synchronicity is an acausal phenomenon, inimical to causal construction. Furthermore, the synchronic is atemporal or 'timeless,' a field in which temporal ordering is therefore (paradoxically) reversible, as has analogously been demonstrated within microphysical fields of superluminal wave mechanics for example. Finally, the synchronic field, as in language, is materially based. What is needed to explain the most inexplicable instances of synchronicity (for example (2) above) is a monistic account of our collective physicality. It is here that the work of those who puzzle over 'morphic resonance' makes its invitation to the debate on synchronicity.

Acknowledgements

My thanks are due to L.J. Wang, Katrina Schlunke, Mike Smithson, Terry Bossomaier and as ever to Jane and Peter Selby.

Notes

1. James is typically represented as a disciple of Darwin in contemporary histories of psychology. No-one seems to have read enough James to know of his

repeated attacks on evolutionary thinking as a basis for psychology. See James 1878, 1890 ch.VI, 1903, *passim*.
2. I do not deal in this chapter with why we find synchronicity so shocking and/or intriguing, or with what features intrigue us most – except in so far as I imply that the synchronic itself is counterintuitive to an intelligence habituated to diachronic understanding.
3. It might even be said that, so far as meaning is concerned, we can be affected by the fact that we have not experienced an event; that is, reality would be different to us if we had experienced it.
4. 'A humiliation that was experienced thirty years ago acts exactly like a fresh one throughout the thirty years, as soon as it has gained access to the unconscious sources of emotion' (Freud, 1900, p. 734).
5. For a set of other even more fascinating examples, e.g. 'entanglement', see Cho, 2002.
6. 'Let anyone try, I will not say to arrest, but to notice or attend to, the *present* moment of time. One of the most baffling experiences occurs. Where is it, this present? It has melted in our grasp, fled ere we could touch it, gone in the instant of becoming. As a poet, quoted by Mr. Hodgson, says, "Le moment où je parle est déjà loin de moi." – and it is only as entering into the living and moving organization of a much wider tract of time that the strict present is apprehended at all ... Reflection leads us to the conclusion that it must exist, but that it does exist can never be a fact of our immediate experience.' (James, 1890, p. 573)
7. Indeed, following Gergen (1994), we may argue that what 'I think/mean,' when viewed relationally, as within a synchronic field, is a consequence of how you respond to me.

Bibliography

Ardener, E. 'Social anthropology and the historicity of historical liguistics', in E. Ardener (ed.), *Social Anthropology and Language*, A.S.A. Monographs, vol. 10 (London: Tavistock, 1971).

Baldwin, J.M. *Mental Development in the Child and the Race: Methods and Processes* (New York: Macmillan – now Palgrave, 1895).

Bion, W.R. *Experiences in Groups* (London: Tavistock, 1961).

Bohm, D. *Wholeness and the Implicate Order* (London: Routledge & Kegan Paul, 1980).

Bradley, B.S. 'A serpent's guide to children's "theories of mind"', *Theory and Psychology* 3 (1993) 497–521.

Bradley, B.S. 'Two ways to talk about change', in B. Bayer and J. Shotter (eds), *Reconstructing the Psychological Subject: Bodies, Practices and Technologies* (London: Sage, 1998).

Bradley, B.S. 'The role of values in psychology: Implications for a reformed curriculum', in M. Leicester, C. Modgil and S. Modgil (eds), *Education, Culture and Values, Vol. 3. Classroom Issues: Practice, Pedagogy and Curriculum* (London: Falmer Press, 2000).

Bradley, B.S. 'An approach to synchronicity: From synchrony to synchronization', *International Journal of Critical Psychology* 1 (2001) 119–44.

Bradley, B.S. and Morss, J.M. 'Social construction in a world at risk: Towards a psychology of experience', *Theory and Psychology* (in press).

Bulthoff, H.H. and Yuille, A.L. 'Bayesian Models for seeing shapes and depth', *Theoretical Biology* 2 (1991) 283–314.
Capra, F. *The Tao of Physics* (London: Wildwood, 1974).
Cho, A. 'Multiple choice', *New Scientist* 2324 (2002) 12–15.
Culler, J. Introduction, in F. de Saussure (1974), *Course in General Linguistics*. (Harmondsworth: Penguin, 1974).
Davidson, D. 'The Material Mind', in *Essays on Actions and Events* (Oxford: Clarendon, 1980).
Davies, P.C.W. *Superforce* (London: Heinemann, 1984).
Davis, P.J. 'Repression and the inaccessibility of affective memories', *Journal of Personality and Social Psychology* 53 (1987) 585–93.
Davis, P.J. and Schwarz, G.E. 'Repression and the inaccessibility of affective memories', *Journal of Personality and Social Psychology* 53 (1987) 155–62.
Derrida, J. *Of Grammatology* tr. G. Spivak (Baltimore: Johns Hopkins University Press [1967] 1976).
Evans-Pritchard, E.E. *Witchcraft, Oracles and Magic Among the Azande* (abridged edition) (Oxford: Clarendon Press, [1937] 1976).
Forster, E.M. *Aspects of the Novel* (Harmondsworth: Penguin [1927] 1976).
Freud, S. 'The unconscious', in J. Strachey (ed.) *The Standard Edition of the Complete Psychological Works of Sigmund Freud, Vol. 14* (London: Hogarth [1915] 1953–57).
James, W. 'Remarks on Spencer's definition of mind as correspondence', in *Essays in Philosophy* (Cambridge: MA: Harvard University Press [1878] 1978).
James, W. *The Principles of Psychology* (Cambridge, Massachusetts: Harvard University Press [1890] 1981).
James, W. *The Varieties of Religious Experience* (Harmondsworth: Penguin Books [1903] 1982).
James, W. 'Does consciousness exist?', in *Essays in Radical Empiricism*. (London: Longman & Gree [1904] 1912).
Johnson, B. *A World of Difference* (Baltimore: Johns Hopkins University Press, 1989).
Jung, C.G. *Synchronicity: An Acausal Connecting Principle* (Princeton University Press [1952] 1973).
Lavine, T.Z. 'Some reflections on the genetic fallacy', *Social Research* 29 (1962) 321–36.
Lemaire, A. *Jacques Lacan* (London: Routledge & Kegan Paul, 1977).
Lévi-Strauss, C. *Structural Anthropology* (New York: Basic Books [1963] 1976).
Lewontin, R. *It Ain't Necessarily So: The Dream of the Human Genome and Other Illusions* (London: Granta Books, 2000).
Locke, J. *An Essay Concerning Human Understanding* (Chicago: Encyclopaedia [1960] 1952).
Morowitz, H.J. 'Rediscovering the mind', in D.R. Hofstadter and D.C. Dennett (eds), *The Mind's I: Fantasies and Reflections on Self and Soul* (Harmondsworth: Penguin Books, [1980] 1981).
Saussure, F. de *Course in General Linguistics* (Harmondsworth: Penguin Books [1917] 1974).
Selby, J.M. 'Uncertainty in counselling and psychology', in *Proceedings of the Third National Conference of the Alcohol and Drug Foundation* (Brisbane: Drug and Alcohol Foundation, 1990).
Sheldrake, R. *The Presence of the Past: Morphic Resonance and the Habits of Nature* (Rochester, VT: Park Street Press, 1995).

Spinoza, B. *Ethics* (New York: Dover [1677] 1977).
Trevarthen, C.B. 'The self born in intersubjectivity: The psychology of an infant communicating', in U. Neisser (ed.), *The Perceived Self: Ecological and Interpersonal Sources of Self-Knowledge* (Cambridge University Press, 1993).
Vygotsky, L. *Mind in Society: the Development of Higher Psychological Processes* (Cambridge, Massachusetts: Harvard University Press, 1978).
Wang, L.J., Kuzmich, A. and Dogariu, A. 'Gain-assisted superluminal light propagation', *Nature* 406 (2000) 277–79.
Whiten, A. (ed.) *Natural Theories of Mind: Evolution, Development and Simulation of Everyday Mindreading* (Oxford: Blackwell, 1991).
Wiener, N. *Cybernetics, or Control and Communication in the Animal and the Machine* (New York: Wiley (2nd edn) 1961).

12

Refiguring the Sacred: Re-enchantment and the Postmodern World

KATHLEEN McPHILLIPS

The emergence of critical psychology as a discourse of knowledge signifies I believe a shift not only in collective understandings of the meaning of self and subjectivity, but also in the ways in which selfhood is culturally formed and historically bounded. Critical psychology makes possible a broad contextualisation of how we understand who we are and the conditions in which we struggle for integrity and meaning, both as a personal and as a collective journey. The broader context also makes possible the linking of psychology to other cultural domains, and of specific importance to this essay, things religious and spiritual. It could be argued that spirituality and religion have, in past histories of the west, been the central domain of understanding and managing individual psychology. However, this connection was severed with the increasing dominance of rational forms of secularism, which scientific psychology embraced and promoted. The emergence of post-structuralist accounts of the self has provided a much needed untying of the relationship between secularism and rationality, and the possibility of reimagining the realms of the sacred with regard to new understandings of selfhood.

In this chapter I want to explore the politics of a continuing engagement with the idea that postmodernity somehow represents or holds as possible the re-enchantment of the world.[1] I am particularly keen to explore the connections between the cultural desire for re-enchantment with the emergence of new forms of religious imagination in the postmodern west: forms which might possibly support new notions of subjectivity, new figurations of embodiment, and a resituating of spirit and soul. In particular, I want to concentrate on reading the phenomenon of enchantment – in numerous guises – as a possible signification of a cultural shift in constructions of the sacred. Given that modernity has been characterised in various theoretical discourses as representing a disenchantment of the world, it may be the case that one of the singular features of postmodernity is the desire for a re-enchanted world, where the relationships between self, body and community are configured through new notions of the sacred.[2]

This chapter responds not only to the development of these ideas in theoretical discourse, but also to the pursuit of the spiritual as a worthy quest of the postmodern (embodied) subject – exemplified in the increasing popularity of practices such as meditation, Buddhism, reiki, massage and tai-chi to give some examples. In such practices, it could be argued that what is imperative to practitioners is a reordering of ethics around the relationship between body and spirit in such a way that the body becomes a potential site of spiritual revelation and redemption – as opposed to the denigrated – even repressed – body Other in traditional religious discourse. On the one hand these practices recognise not only the interconnectedness of body and spirit but also the autonomy and intelligence of the body, independently of mind and soul. And on the other hand, these practices emerge from and are contextualised by a cultural climate where consumption and production are the driving forces of social meaning and cultural location and where the body is positioned as a project to be worked on and subject to dominant disciplining regimes. Such contradictions are at the heart of late modernity and signal social and cultural change – such at least is Anthony Giddens's argument in his book *Modernity and Self Identity* (1991). However it may be that new forms of the spiritual self emerge from late western modernity, it could also be the case that modernity does not – or cannot – contain these subjectivities and practices, and this in itself raises questions regarding spiritual transformation and the generation of hope for a new ethical social order, where value and fact can exist harmoniously together.

In addressing these questions, enchantment – in the sense that one is literally taken over by a sense of the magical or uncanny, and which cannot be readily explained by the dominant logics of scientific rationality – is one site of analysis that bears closer inspection and certainly some description. Not in the sense that it offers redemption from the ravages of modern life, but discursively, as a mode of analysis which might render insight into the mechanisms by which enchantment behaves. In exploring such an area, I am immediately confronted by a strong sense of unease and discomfort. I take this as a sign that my own subjectivity is constructed within the logics of modern rationalism which asks us to be sceptical of anything that is metaphysical or engaged with questions of faith and belief. As Giddens (1991, pp. 2–3) argues, modernity as a post-traditional order is characterised by the institutionalisation and embodiment of *radical doubt*. However, it is precisely this condition which brings us to the brink of disbelief and creates the desire for an experience of self and world which is not bound so completely by the desire for rational control. I begin by examining the nature of rationality in modernity before turning to enchantment and its contemporary forms.

Instrumental Rationality and the Crisis of Meaning

In his analysis of western modernity the German sociologist Max Weber characterised the modern world as dominated by a particular form of cultural and economic rationality – instrumental rationality – which led to the inexorable disenchantment of the world (Gerth and Mills, 1970, p. 299). Weber's thesis on rationality is particularly important for two reasons. First, he deliberated carefully on the location of religion and the sacred in modernity and the ways in which instrumental rationality in both its material and ideological forms impacted on religious imagination and practice. Second, Weber's thesis on modernity put together the loss of religion with the progressive disenchantment of the world. Hence, the loss of religion is also the loss of meaning-making systems which act to enchant the world around us. The notion of religiosity as a sacred canopy[3] which acts as the overarching fabric of meaning and faith is fundamentally lost in the modern west.[4]

Weber argued that instrumental rationality – exemplified in scientific discourse – was one of the forces responsible for the revolutionary changes that moved Europe from premodern, communal, kinship-based economies to highly urbanised, industrialised and capitalist economies. Unlike Marx who contextualised modern society as a class-based economic system premised on gross exploitation and ever increasing structural contradictions which would eventually be resolved by complete social and economic transformation, Weber was much more sceptical of the possibility for real change in capitalist culture. The reason for this was connected to the way in which he understood the processes by which collective meaning – and therefore social transformation – was generated. In short, Weber argued that it was the institutions of religion and religious imagination which produced and managed meaning-making. The loss of religion propelled the world into a crisis whereby the structures that had sustained the generation of meaning were marginalised by new institutions that were much more concerned with managing a self and community that was secularised and focused on individual need rather than broader community concerns.

Instrumental rationality is the child of modern scientific inquiry, which sees materiality, proof, order and evidence as pre-eminent forms of knowledge and goes hand in hand with an ethos that generated a relationship of utilitarianism to the natural world. Science lifted the premodern veils of magic and enchantment by developing methods and ways of knowing which exposed the engines driving the way things worked and made sense of them in terms of universal laws governing the natural and human worlds. Linked into this, instrumental rationality relied on an ethos of goal-oriented behaviour and work ethics which above all were to be productive in a capitalist sense – that is, tied into the management and expansion of the market and the generation of wealth in the form of profit. Such logics replaced the enchanted, mystical sciences of the middle ages, and paved the way for knowledge systems which were premised on the separation of subject and object, the notion of universal truths and the denigration of the body to the mind. Science and by extension society could be rational, goal-oriented, calculating, formalistic, detached and objective, as opposed to the magical and naturalistic, where the body was an extension of the natural world and God at the centre of reason.

Modernity produced not only certain forms of knowledge and community; it also produced a certain kind of self, largely premised on the ideology of competitive individualism where the needs of self came before Other, resulting in self-interest, and where one's social identity was premised – not on kinship location and obligation – but on one's economic location in the work place. Autonomy, formality and impersonality were the central motifs for modern existence. For Weber the outcome of this was that modern capitalist culture led inexorably to a crisis in the production of cultural and individual meaning because it generated a universe which suppressed and devalued the social necessity of kinship, community and religious systems, as the basis for generating value systems and through that a moral universe by which the existential conditions of life could be articulated and appreciated. In the modern west, sites such as religion and the family[5] are not only privatised: their value is determined by their relationship to logics of productivity and consumerism. They are sites of potential markets, moments to reinforce work ethics, as well as structures of contradiction in a highly rationalised world.

Weber argued that this kind of society can bring certain benefits. One of them was freedom from the entrapment of kinship and obligation, which could often be difficult and dangerous and which in European feudalism had been based on oppressive forms of patriarchalism.[6] The modern city, with its emphasis on impersonality and the individual, could provide a freedom and anonymity that had never been expressed before. And the objectivity that instrumental rationality was premised on has been the foundation of dealing with social relationships which have been discriminatory. An example of this would be the gains made over the last 120 years by the feminist movement, which has been able to utilise logics of freedom and equity to argue that there is no sustainable reason why women should be discriminated against or mitigated to particular spheres of work and non-work.

In terms of religion and the sacred, the impact of modernity generated two forces. The first is secularism, which operates from a logic that rejects religion as a sphere of social necessity and replaces the adoration of a transcendental Other with humanity itself as the subject of history. The second is privatisation and individualism, which means that belief, and in particular religious belief, becomes a matter of individual choice, as opposed to the glue that binds the community together.[7] The sorts of religious principles and styles that are valued in a disenchanted modern world are those which in themselves have been rationalised, routinised and stripped of magic. For Weber (1991), Protestantism, with its ordered and logical theologies, demagicalised text-based liturgical practices and work ethics that bind the accumulation of wealth and hard work with salvation, is the exemplar of religion in the modern west.[8]

Modern society is, for Weber, locked in an iron cage and grappling with the conundrum that while the forces of modernity could promise freedom they simultaneously strip the world of meaning. This leads to some immense and overwhelming cultural anxieties and contradictions between the ideas of choice and constriction, freedom and entrapment, and the deep sense of loss of community and self-identity that the forces of globalisation and economic rationalisation have generated. Evidence of this social dislocation is found not only in the ongoing crises of contemporary major institutions, such as the family, marriage and the workplace but also in increased suicide rates, drug-related problems and what is sometimes called 'twentieth-century sadness'.

Late Modernity and Meaning

It is clear that Weber had a particularly pessimistic outlook on modern life. And although I agree in large part with his thesis on religion and rationality, I do not think that the disenchantment of the world is by any means complete. It is possible to argue that the immense and overwhelming contradictions of self and community produced by late twentieth-century modernity have encouraged the emergence of enchantment as a cultural desire for the sacred, together with new forms of spirituality which are embedded in different logic systems whose aim is to generate discourses of meaning. This may be an indicator of the presence of not only a postmodern, post-traditional world, but also of new ways of culturalising the sacred and freeing up religious imagination. This is an argument not for a return to a premodern romantic sentiment or the literalisation of a supernatural realm, but for a particular reading of certain contemporary cultural practices as forms of resistance against the dominance of instrumental rationality.

Since Weber, numerous social theorists have responded to the positioning of the sacred in western modernity, and the understanding of cultural rationality. Habermas (1981) reworked the Weberian problematic of rationality in terms of a theory of language that was the basis from which new forms of democratic citizenship could generate ethical communities of care, and which included an incorporation of the sacred as axiomatic to communicative rationality. Giddens (1991) takes a slightly different tack, and argues that one of the outstanding features of western modernity is its generation of post-traditionalism. Where religious traditions in particular generated the spheres in which the moral questions of community and self were expressed, modernity destroys such a sphere, which creates a great deal of personal and cultural angst and leads to certain substitutive behaviours such as risk-taking, which has at its heart the desire for deeper understandings of the moral issues which modern life raises.

In the modern world, the self-as-project replaces the community as the site where ethics and responsibility are generated. For Weber, this was clearly inadequate for dealing with the massive contradictions that rationality and capitalist organisation brought with it. This was largely because religion had been the terrain in which not only meaning was made but also ethics were generated, and the loss of religion generated an ethical crisis in the sense that without these forces at play society could not generate the deeper understandings that were required to provide a sustaining moral web of meaning and hope. Rather, what modern capitalist life required was the *repression* of these questions of ethics and existentialism, which in turn generates personal and collective anxieties. Giddens (1991, p. 8) argues that collective and individual anxiety emerges from a type of institutional repression required to manage the complexity of modern life. If modern institutions are understood as the controlling mechanisms of modern life, what needs to be repressed are the very questions of existence and morality which not only raise issues about modern life but also allow questions of politics to surface which aim to find sustaining answers to the conundrums of modern life and where passion is not bled out of social action.

Unlike Weber, Giddens (1991, p. 9) argues that the repression of meaning processes is not complete. The contradictions that life in late modernity raises, through either the huge inequities of globalisation or the issues that lifestyle choices engage, mean that political questions cannot be put aside. While radical forms of doubt are the heritage of the scientific revolution, religious imagination has not died away as predicted but continues to be a place in which collective anxieties and moral concerns are addressed (1991, p. 207).

Yet while religiosity remains a central concern of late modernity the question is: how should we read both the desire for enchantment and the emergence of new spiritual practices? Are they merely the offspring of – or coopted by – dominant and aggressive forms of economic consumerism and globalisation, or is there evidence that they might constitute a transgressive and resistive space in a highly rationalised west, and thus signify a politics of hope by generating new rationalities and meanings around important questions of ethics, embodiment and divinity? I want to suggest that a discussion of enchantment might be particularly useful in exploring cultural events that bleed across the boundaries of secularised forms of social analysis.

Some Enchanting Moments

In a general sense, enchantment can be defined as the sensation with which one experiences events or circumstances that are at complete odds to our usual experience of the world, and which produce a sense of the mysterious, the weird and the uncanny.[9] Such experiences can be said to be at odds with the dominant forces of cultural rationalisation which relegate religious imagination and the life of the soul to the edges of cultural importance. Sociologist Mark Schneider (1993, p. 5) suggests that we

> become enchanted when we are confronted by circumstances or occurrences so peculiar and so beyond our present understandings as to leave us convinced that, were they to be understood, our image of how the world operates would be radically transformed. To be enchanted is thus different from being deeply delighted or charmed – since we are faced with something both real and at the same time uncanny, weird, mysterious or awesome ... How deeply enchanted we become quite likely depends upon how fundamentally our understanding of the world is challenged. To be confronted in this way is exciting and perhaps even thrilling, though the uncanny might well cause a sense of unease. The excitement comes from being lifted out of our mundane existence and situated on the verge of a new understanding of our world, while the unease derives from the assault upon our prior sense of how that world works – and thus upon our practical competence in dealing with it. Should we be unable to recapture this, the world around us may never again acquire the solid and predictable form that allows us to rest comfortably within it.

It is no doubt fairly clear that a dominant institution in the production of enchanted texts is the media, and in particular the genres of popular culture and film. Film in particular traffics in the production of enchantment to such an extent that the process of filmgoing could be said to be akin to a religious experience of transcendence into the presence of otherness. However, I am more interested in exploring social and symbolic spaces where enchantment has long-lasting effects, in much the same way as Geertz (Christ, 1982, p. 71) describes the function of religion: 'Religion is a system of symbols which act to produce powerful, pervasive, and long lasting moods and motivations in the people of a given culture.'

Carol Christ (1982, p. 71) goes on to say that

> A 'mood' for Geertz is a psychological attitude, such as awe, trust, and respect, while a 'motivation' is the social and political trajectory created by a mood that transforms mythos into ethos, symbol system into social and political reality.

It is possible to conceive of a relationship between enchantment and religion where enchantment provides the initial force of imaginative space and religion then acts to socialise the original phenomenon. As well as religion undertaking this function, it could be argued that other institutions come into play, and particularly that a culture can encourage enchantment as a mode of being:

> We can think of a culture as enchanted when it customarily traffics in the odd and unexplained ... Enchantment in other words, can be something of a commodity, and we can investigate its production and consumption. There are two modes of response to enchantment. The first is that which goes about seeking explanations for it and might be characteristic of science in a quest for explanation and which brings with it an inevitable sense of 'disenchantment', and a return to intelligibility and practical competence. Scientific explanation domesticates the uncanny by revealing the logics behind it. The second response to enchantment is to seek to preserve or renew the circumstances that evoked it ... that a particular field [of human inquiry] is enchanted seems to be a function of both of its subject matter and of the way inquiry is organized (Schneider, 1993, p. 3).

Schneider's argument suggests that just as instrumental rationalities are enmeshed in and observable through beliefs, notions of power, institutions and practices of the self, so a cultural logics of enchantment may also be observable. Using Schneider's definition I can pinpoint at least three sites of modern-day enchantment, as follows.

1. Enchantment as Alternative Cultural Logic

Enchantment as an alternative cultural logic might be best explained as moments and events of inexplicability such as the global mourning that the death of Diana evoked. It was highly disruptive in the sense that many people were caught up in a wave of emotional response and pathos, often despite how close one felt to her life and story. The Diana that most of us were familiar with was the Diana constructed through the media, but also here was a real person living out a driving myth of western culture: the marriage of the young woman to a rich and handsome prince. Fairy tale and reality collided and produced: a modern-day enchantment. Somehow many of us had to negotiate this story, and we were under its spell in some way or another.[10] The evidence of this is that the world was overwhelmed by the events surrounding her death and the mourning that resulted was in many ways beyond rational explanation. The barrage of analysis that followed her death could be read as both the quest for rational explanation and the need to find intelligible reasons for the depth of such mourning; and also as a desire to preserve the inexplicability of it, and by doing so traffic in it. It also heightens the contradictions of contemporary culture and it is no wonder that it has produced so much cynicism, when one considers how much profit media empires have made from her life and death (indeed were even implicated in the cause of her death), and how we are somehow implicated in this scenario by the very processes by which we consumed the details of her very public life.

The forces of disenchantment and enchantment lie very close together here in very unresolved ways, but the potential that Diana's death provides is a moment of collective insight that neither of these spheres can properly contain and which takes us to the brink of rational explanation. It could also be argued that the continuing media obsession with the post-Diana royals, focused particularly around Edward and Sophie, continues to fuel enchantment as a necessary function of media consumption.

2. Enchantment as Conscious Resistance

The second argument is whether enchantment takes up the space that the disenchantment with humanism brought.[11] If modernity signified the loss of religion as the place where ethics was generated, then humanism took up these questions, producing grand narratives such as Marxism and liberalism. But they too are crumbling, and what of politics now and the place of ideologies of social transformation? It is possible that the environment movement signals a profound resistance to instrumental rationality and encourages new kinds of political values: values which Weber argued were unable to be generated by the dominant discourses of the public domain. The evidence for this lies in the fact that the environment movement has emerged from a deep disenchantment with industrialisation as the mode in which creative human potential can be reached. It wants to refigure the relationship between culture and nature and in particular to invest in nature a respect and autonomy – even subjectivity[12] – based not on exploitation but on mutuality, intelligence and healing. It challenges not only the dominant paradigms between the built and natural worlds but also those between animal and human, and plant and human worlds. In analysing prevailing attitudes to the natural and animal worlds, moments of reflection on how humanity itself is defined are opened up, and new possible configurations of the human–natural dialectic are made possible which resist the notion of the necessity of dominance and submission as integral to any relationship.

There are two contradictions at the heart of this struggle. The first is that on the one hand while the answers to contamination and toxic waste are being sought in scientific and rational discourse, nevertheless the motivating force behind environmental activism is often a profound sense of awe and respect for the beauty and magnificence of the natural world, indeed even as a repository for the sacred.[13] There has also over the last twenty-five years been a growing interest in earth-based spiritual practices which link into a politics of the environment and which are specifically concerned with a quest for re-enchantment – here I am thinking of paganism, Wicca and goddess spiritualities. Again, these are figured into a politics of privatisation and consumerism, but are also strongly connected to environmental politics.[14]

The second contradiction concerns the foundational narratives that environmental politics are based on, at least in the west. Images of wildness, wilderness and uninhabited and unspoiled ecosystems clash resoundingly with indigenous histories, issues of land ownership, continuous occupation and dreaming stories which bring into being highly sophisticated social systems. Indigenous rationalities are profoundly different from the romantic, European-based colonial narratives that environmentalism has emerged from, and only recently have there been attempts to bridge the gap. The development of a postcolonial politics in which indigenous land claims are seen as a necessary part of environmental politics has been the focus of the struggle of the Mirrar people in Kakadu, Northern Territory, Australia, against government-supported mining operations in Jabiluka. The Australian Conservation Foundation (ACF) joined forces with local and regional indigenous groups to ensure that the Mirrar culture and lands are protected from the destruction of land that mining will cause. This relationship has generated significant tensions between authorising narratives and political action but it is a beginning point for reconciliation. More research needs to be done here about how a postcolonial, reconciliation-style politics will change the ways in which the struggle for environmental justice is conceived and fought for. In a real sense what we are witnesses to here is the refiguring or re-enchantment of Enlightenment values into new relationships between land, people and society with resistance to economic and instrumental rationalities at the heart of such a politics.

3. Enchantment as Sacred Space

The third argument is that if modernity inhibits sacred space then it is possible to see the desire for enchantment as an attempt to recapture some of this space. I think the current fascination with angels and other (dis)embodied, metaphysical beings is relevant here. Angels as messengers of an invisible divine (God) have a long history in western Christianity and have more recently become the subject of New Age philosophies and practices.[15] Reading the presence and reality of the angel as metaphorical is probably much more satisfying and soulful than insisting on the rational existence of such a force. But even such an insistence that angels actually do exist is understandable given the power of scientific rationality to order reality around the logics of materiality. Could the desire to believe in aliens and angels be in part a desire for the divine other, outside formalised religions and notions of the sacred?

A final example of enchantment as sacred space is the idea of the miracle which speaks of a profoundly inexplicable happening. The disenchantment of formal religion means that the power and authority of the miracle is certainly diminished, but even with the modern-day canonisations of Mary MacKillop and Mother Theresa we are witnesses to miracles – mostly bodily healings from cancer, itself an unexplainable, medically uncontrollable disease – that must accompany such processes. Like environmental politics, the process of canonisation is highly rationalised and bureaucratic: each miracle must be interrogated by a Vatican committee that includes ethicists, medical doctors and theologians whose job it is to approve and substantiate the truth of the happening. The moment of recognising a miracle is also the moment where inexplicability steps in and rationalist discourse meets its limits of explanation.

The contradiction – or perhaps danger – is that in the effort to analyse expressions of cultural enchantment we use the very techniques which cause disenchantment. As well, the sites of enchantment erupt into the midst of consumerist formations and so we see new markets opening up around New Age philosophies on the body, the spirit, human relationships and healing paradigms. Given the contradictions and anxieties that such an analysis produces, what can be said here about what is possible, for ourselves and the planet, about optimism and most of all, about hope?

Emergent Spiritualities and the Question of Hope

The spiritual practices that characterise late modernity share some characteristics. They are not as tied to institutions, traditions and doctrines as more organised religions tend to be, and where there are obvious traditions and doctrines, as in say Theravada or Mahayana Buddhism, their entry from the east has been into a largely secularised and pluralistic western terrain. In this sense postmodernity is definitely post-traditional. This terrain is already appropriated in large part by the logics and ideologies of consumerism, which means that we can effectively shop around for the sort of spiritual practice that best suits us. But I would not want to argue that consumerism is capable of completely containing the spiritual arena. It may in large part appropriate it, and in this regard 'New Age' could be read as a product of consumerist logic, but I also think that there is some evidence to indicate that there is an authentic and conscious search for new ways of being, new understandings of self that bring together body, spirit and mind without the need for replicating either the repression of one for the sake of the others or a union with consumerism. And in the contradictions that are generated between competing discourses of body and spirit, optimism is born in the sense that we might know otherwise about the rationalisation of self and body that we are so constantly forced up against – that we do want to resist the cynicism that rationalisation produces.

It occurs to me that the deep cultural search for meaning – itself born from but not contained by modernity – most often cements around notions of connection, between body, mind emotion and spirit: connections in which people want to recognise the autonomy and intelligibility of each facet of self but which when considered together seem to produce a totality that is more than the parts put together. An example of this is the realm of the inexplicable: that there are clearly moments where words fail to explain what is being experienced, and where there are no new words or logics that offer explanation. This points to new rationalities and new ways of configuring hope: hope not as an eternal romantic value which stands outside time, but born out of the struggle for meaning, where it is possible to, first, glimpse different modes of rationality which are not explainable by the logics of modernity and, second, create spaces for the refiguring of self and spirit which might support these 'postmodern' rationalities.

Lastly, I would point to current moments of enchantment which hold within them possibilities of meaning beyond the aggressive rationalisation of the inexplicable. In this, my feeling is that the developing politics of reconciliation, and the contradictions and potential which it raises, is a site in which deep collective meaning is being produced and which involve a re-evaluation not only of the colonial imagination of nationhood but also of the significant and embedded connections between self–body–Other.

Notes

1. Various texts and disciplinary terrains have engaged with notions of enchantment. For example, archetypal psychology or post-Jungian discourse develops a

notion of *anima mundi*, or soul of the world, which is based on the necessity of enchantment for the health of humanity. See, for example, the work of James Hillman and other post-Jungians. And directly on enchantment see Thomas Moore (1996). In sociology Peter Berger (1967) has written on the notion that meaning derives from the sacred, a theme which the founding fathers of sociology and anthropology wrote of extensively (see below).
2. Despite the continuing effects of secularisation on self and world, I would argue that notions of the sacred and religious imagination have been significant concerns of cultural and social discourse, which indicates among other things that the sacred is a site of ongoing theoretical and practical work. A popular theoretical representation of the sacred is as a dualistic opposite to the realm of the profane, as classically articulated by the anthropologist Emile Durkheim (1915). One of the problems with this representation is that it has become reified in social theory, where it operates as a prescriptive category, rather than as a deductive process. For a analysis of the sacred/profane category and its usage in social theory, see Penelope Magee (1995, pp. 101–20).
3. This is Peter Berger's term from his influential text (1967).
4. The notion of modernity as generating a crisis in the production of meaning is a general theme of sociology. For a recent text see John Carroll (1998).
5. Weber and his contemporaries argued that cities in particular are places where we don't need to know people in order to live. This does not mean we cannot live our lives well. We know some people but we can negotiate our daily lives, from going to the bank, to the supermarket, to enrolling at university without needing to *know* in any deep sense who we are talking to. We only need to know each other's institutional location: the shopkeeper, the bank teller, the public servant, the consumer. The family, which could be a site of resistance to impersonality, is itself vulnerable to practices of autonomy and formality through the constant incursion of the state and the market into family life and structure. The best example of this would be the argument that the ability of the family to generate security and safety is largely a question of economic location. This contradiction is often referred to as the division between *gemeinschaft* (community) and *gesellschaft* (society). See Tönnies (1955).
6. This argument is developed in the work of Weber by Thomas (1985).
7. This refers to Durkheim's (1915) definition of religion which posits it as the primary force of social cohesion in traditional culture.
8. We could consider Anzac Day as one such public occasion that produces social and spiritual meaning. Recent analysis (SMH Arena) indicates that Anzac Day attendances are on the increase, which might indicate that the tradition is being successfully handed over to younger generations mindful of the importance of certain cultural histories and their contribution to images of the nation. The problem with Anzac Day is that although premised on the generation of collective values, the values are at the expense of certain groups in the community, which would have as their aim the generation of meaningful community relationships. I am thinking in particular of women, whose voice, role and abuse in war is constantly repressed and allowed into the public arena in highly selective modes (basically as aides to the war machinery). The violent histories of white Europeans against Indigenous communities in Australia is also repressed in the public narrative surrounding Anzac Day.
9. Particular texts which have long deliberations on the social nature of modern-day enchantment include those by Mark Schneider (1993) and Morris Berman (1988).

10. A more detailed development of this argument can be found in Kathleen McPhillips (1997).
11. See Keith Thomas (1971) for a more sustained development of this argument.
12. See Anne Elvey, 'Leaf Litter': for an argument that the earth can be read as subject.
13. Texts such as David Suzuki (1997) link the politics of environmentalism with a sense of the natural world as sacred.
14. See in particular the work of Charlene Spretnak who has written on the necessity of Goddess-based spiritualities connecting to environmental activism.
15. For example, see the work of Matthew Fox and Rupert Sheldrake (1996), which attempts to address the relationship between science and spirit.

Bibliography

Berger, P. *The Sacred Canopy. Elements of a Sociology of Religion* (New York: Doubleday, 1967).
Berman, M. *The Re-Enchantment of the World* (Bantam Books, 1988).
Carroll, J. *Ego and Soul: The Modern West in Search of Meaning* (Melbourne: HarperCollins, 1998).
Christ, C. 'Why Women Need the Goddess: Phenomenological, Psychological and Political Reflections', in C. Spretnak (ed.) *The Politics of Women's Spirituality* (New York: Anchor Press/Doubleday, 1982) 72.
Durkheim, E. [1915] *The Elementary Forms of the Religious Life* (London: Allen & Unwin, 1976).
Elvey, A. 'Leaf litter: Thinking the Divine from the perspective of Earth', in K. McPhilips (ed.) *What's God Got to Do With It?* (University of Western Sydney: School of Humanities, 2000) 59–68.
Fox, M. and Sheldrake, R. *The Physics of Angels* (San Francisco: Harper, 1996).
Gerth, H. & Mills, C.W. (eds) *From Max Weber, Essays in Sociology* (London: Routledge & Kegan Paul, 1970).
Giddens, A. *Modernity and Self-Identity: Self and Society in the Late Modern Age* (Cambridge: Polity Press, 1991).
Habermas, J. *The Theory of Communicative Action, Volume One* (Cambridge: Polity Press, 1981).
McPhillips, K. 'Postmodern Canonisation', in *Planet Diana: Cultural Studies and Global Mourning* (ed.) (Research Centre in Intercommunal Studies, University of Western Sydney, Nepean: Re:Public, 1997) 87–92.
Magee, P. 'Disputing the Sacred: Some Theoretical Approaches to Gender and Religion', in U. King (ed.) *Religion and Gender* (Oxford: Blackwell Press, 1995).
Moore, T. *The Re-Enchantment of Everyday Life* (Sydney: Hodder & Stoughton, 1996).
Schneider, M. *Culture and Enchantment* (University of Chicago Press, 1993)
Spretnak, C. and Capra, F. *Green Politics: The Global Promise* (New York: Dutton, 1984).
Suzuki, D. *The Sacred Balance* (Sydney: Allen & Unwin, 1997).
Thomas, J. 'Rationalisation and the Status of gender Divisions', in *Sociology*, vol. 19. No. 3 August (1985) 409–20.
Thomas, K. *Religion and the Decline of Magic* (London: Penguin, 1971).
Tönnies, F. *Community and Association (Gemeinschaft und Gesellschaft)* (London: Routledge & Kegan Paul, 1955).
Weber, M. [1930] *The Protestant Ethic and the Spirit of Capitalism* (London: HarperCollins, 1991).

Index

Ackroyd, S. 26, 29, 30, 31
Adorno, T.W. 20, 86
aesthetics 65, 66
affect 66
alienation 28
altered states of consciousness 135, 139, 142
alterity 55–60
　see also Other
Altounian, J. 81
Ambedkar, B.R. 116, 117
ambivalent position 91, 94–9
Améry, J. 45, 49
ancestors 61–2
angels 187
Anthony, D. 154
Apfelbaum, E. 79, 83
apprenticeship 58–9
Arendt, H. 78–9, 84, 86
Arthur, C.J. 28
Asian boys 103–4
Auschwitz 41–2
Australian Conservation Foundation (ACF) 186

Ballou, M. 151
Baczko, B. 84, 85, 86
Baldwin, J.M. 162
Baudrillard, J. 21
Bauman, Z. 14, 16, 46, 47–8
Bayer, B.M. 151
Beck, U. 7, 17–18
becoming 33–4, 35
being 55–6
Benjamin, J. 15, 55
Bhabha, H. 55
bhakti movement 116–20
　revolt 118–20
　unity of multiple identities 117–18
Bhawlakar, T. 120
biographical time 60, 61
Bion, W.R. 21–2, 164

black boys 76, 101–3
Black Skin, White Masks (Fanon) 60–3
Blackman, L. 134, 137, 145
body
　feminist corporeal theory and worker subjectivity 8, 32–6
　imaginary body 34–5
　and mind 32, 33, 141, 145
　non-rationalist philosophy 135
　temporality 59–60, 61–2
　'vehicular' 150–1, 153
　see also embodiment
Bohm, D. 173
Bollas, C. 15
Bordo, S. 26
Borowski, T. 48
boys 76, 101–10
Braverman, H. 25, 28
Broszat, M. 41–2
Brown, N. 107
Bulthoff, H.H. 168
Burawoy, M. 25
burn patients 111–12
Butler, J. 53, 54, 110

Cambodia 82
capitalism 179–80
　anti-black racism and 106–8
Capra, F. 173
Carpenter, E. 139
Cash, J.D. 90
caste 115–16, 119
Castoriadis, C. 15
catastrophic change 21–2
Chamisso, A. 86
change
　catastrophic 21–2
　political in Northern Ireland 75–6, 88–100
　self-help practices 136–9, 145–6
　social change 158
　subjective 9–10, 60–7

191

Index

children of uprooted families 81–2
choreography 55, 57
Christ, C. 184
Christian ethics 40
Christians, persecution of 122
class 25–6
Clement, C. 135
cognition 39, 43, 46–7
collective mind 173
'Collective of people' 155–8
collective public chronicle 80
complex forms of insanity 143–4
concentration camp syndrome 45
conflict 75–6, 88–100
connectedness 153–9
connections 188
conscious resistance 185–6
consciousness 28, 34
   altered states 135, 139, 142
consumerism 188
control 25–6, 29, 30
corporate economism 2, 19–20
corporeal theory 8, 32–6
counter-culture 157
counter-stereotypes 123–4
Criminal Justice Act 1994 154
critical psychology 2, 24
Culler, J. 166
culture 57–8, 183–4
   enchantment as alternative
      cultural logic 184–5

Dandekar, S.V. 117, 118
Davies, P.C.W. 173
debt 64
dehumanising position 91, 95–9
Delcroix, C. 81
Deleuze, G. 135
Democratic Unionist Party (DUP) 95
deregulation 11–12, 17, 19
Derrida, J. 31, 55, 63–4, 162
Descartes, R. 145
devolution 89
dharma 115–16, 117
Dhere, R.C. 120
diachronicity 161, 166–7
Diana, Princess of Wales 132, 184–5
difference 158
discontent 13–14
discursive psychologies 133, 134–5

discursive relations 138–9
disidentification 61–2
disruptive events 66
distance 172–3
distorted communication 96–8
diversity 113–14
DIY culture 153–9
Dnyaneshwar 117–18, 119
Donnelly, M. 139
dream state 142
Drumcree 95
Durkheim, E. 166

economic rationalism 2, 19–20
Einstein, A. 162
Elias, N. 79
Elliott, A. 15
embodied knowledge 151–3
embodiment 34, 59–60
   psychological phenomena 134, 136–46
   social 153–9
   of the spirit 130–1, 149–60
   see also body
emergent spiritualities 146, 178, 187–8
emotional immunisation 8, 41–3
emotionality 8–9, 39–50
enchantment 131–2, 177–90
environment movement 185–6
Epicurean ethics 39–40
Ertel, R. 84
Esquirol, J.E. 143–4
ethic of expansion 145–6
ethical reading 31
ethics of work 35–6
European politics 1
European Union 96
Evans-Pritchard, E.E. 162, 170
exclusion 104
exclusivist position 75–6, 91–4, 95–9
expectant attention 141
expectation 58
experience 57–8
extermination camps 9, 41–9
Ezzy, D. 25

false consciousness 28
Fanon, F. 60–3
fantasies of omnipotence 7, 18–22

fascism 8–9, 39–50, 84
Feldman, S. 26, 31
feminism 83, 180–1
  corporeal theory 8, 32–6
  women's movement in India 123
Fernandez, B. 123
Fire 122
Fontana, D. 150, 153
Foucault, M. 1, 30, 39, 44, 56, 58–9
  discourse analysis 137, 138
  religion and madness 140
  silence 80
fragility of identity 108–10
fragmentation 12, 14–16
Frank, A. 151
free parties 154, 155
  see also rave culture
Freud, S. 131, 166
  pleasure in discontent 13–14
  self-control and morality 40–1
  time and the unconscious 169
Friedrich, J. 43
Fuss, D. 134

Gandhi, M. 121, 157
Ganzfeld experiment 172
Gatens, M. 32, 33, 34, 35
Gawain, S. 151–2
Geertz, C. 184
Geeta 118
genealogical continuity 81–2
genetic fallacy 162
genocide 82, 86
Gerth, H. 179
Giddens, A. 13, 178, 182
Gilbert, J. 155
Gilroy, P. 54

globalisation 2
  plural identities 122–3
  risk 16–18
Good Friday Agreement 89
Greenham Common protest movement 157
Grosz, E. 32, 33, 34, 35
group identity 82–4
Guattari, F. 135
guilt 43–4
Gujarat 122

Habermas, J. 17, 182
habit 141, 142
Halbwachs, M. 78, 80, 82
Haley, A. 83
Hall, S. 53–4
hallucination 130, 133–48
hauntology 63–4
hearing voices 130, 133–48
Hearing Voices Network (HVN) 130, 134, 136–8
Heery, M.H. 151
Hegel, G.W.F. 26–8
hegemony, battle for 98
Heidegger, M. 52, 59
heteronomous 'I' 55–60
Hilberg, R. 41
Himmler, H. 41
Hinduism 113–24
  'Hindu mind' 116–17
  identity 115–16
  law 113–14
Hindu extremists 114, 122, 124
historical time 60, 61
history
  group identity 82–4
  refiguring subjectivity 9–10, 51–71
  see also legacy
Hoffman, E. 81, 84
hope 141–2
  emergent spiritualities 187–8
Höss, R. 41–2
humanism 185
Husserl, E. 52
hypnosis 140, 142

identity-building 12–14
identity politics 7, 11–22
  individualisation 16–18
  modern and postmodern strategies of identity 12–16
ideologies 90–9
imaginary body 34–5
imagination 15–16, 66
  history of voice hearing 139–46
implicate order 173
inclusivist position 75–6, 91, 94–9
India 76–7, 111–26
indigenous land claims 186
individual 153

194 Index

individualisation 181
  fascism 44–5
  morality 47–8
  privatisation 12, 16–18
  workplace 24–5
insanity, moral 139–45
instrumental rationality 179–81
intensity 144–5
interaction of plural identities 122–3
interior, discourses of the 134–5
intersubjective (historical) time 60, 61
intragroup conflict 93
Ireland, Republic of 96
Irigaray, L. 33, 57

'Jamaica' 103
James, W. 131, 135, 162, 168, 171
Jews 42, 84
  see also extermination camps
Jones, L.G. 154
Jung, C.G. 164, 167, 170
justice 64

Kakar, S. 115–16
kaleidoscopic vision 123–4
Kershaw, I. 46
Kertész, I. 44, 45–6
King, A.S. 154
Klein, M. 91
Knights, D. 29, 35
knowledge, embodied 151–3
Kovel, J. 106–8
Kren, G. 86
Kristeva, J. 15, 20–1
Kulturträger 41

labour process theory 25–6
  post-structuralist theory and 28–32
Lacan, J. 34, 36, 52, 67, 169
  conflict between discourses 88
  psychoanalysis 13–14
Lalitha, K. 120
language 65, 182
  linguistic dispossession 84
  synchronicity 166–8
Lasch, C. 14–15
Lavine, T.Z. 162
leadership 99
legacy 75, 78–87
Lemaire, A. 168

lesbian relationships 122
Levi, P. 43–4, 45, 80–1, 86
Lewontin, R. 161
linguistics 165–6
Littler, C. 25, 28
local community 158
Locke, J. 139, 162
loss of identity 75, 78–87
Lyotard, J.-F. 14, 59, 64

MacKillop, M. 187
Maharashtra 117
Malbon, B. 154
Malone, K.R. 151
management agency 30
managerial control 25–6, 29, 30
Maras, S. 33
market 11–12
Marx, K. 179
  post-structuralist theory 28–32
  worker subjectivity 26–8
masculinity 114–15
Maudsley, H. 139, 143
McKay, G. 154, 155
McRobbie, A. 136
meaning
  hope and search for 188
  instrumental rationality and crisis of 179–81
  late modernity and 181–3
  synchronicity and 169–70
'mechanical' inquiry 163
meditation 150–1, 153
memorisation 64
memory 75, 78–87
memory time 60, 61
mental illness 116
  moral insanity 139–45
Merleau-Ponty, M. 59, 60, 135
meta-morality 48
Millennium World Conference in Critical Psychology 1, 2
Mills, C.W. 179
mind
  and body 32, 33, 141, 145
  see also mental illness
minimal self 15
miracles 187
Mirrar people 186
Mitchell, G. 89

modernity
  crisis of meaning   179–81
  identity strategies   12–14
  late modernity and meaning   181–3
  refiguring subjectivity   9–10, 51–71
  tradition and in India   120–1
Mommsen, G.   25
Monbiot, G.   154
monism   173, 174
monomania   144
moral therapy   134, 139–46
morality   8–9, 39–50
Morowitz, H.J.   161
morphic resonance   173, 174
Morrison, T.   66
Mueller, M.   117, 118
multiple identities   76–7, 111–26
Muslims   122
mystics   151

narrative   9–10, 51–71
nationalism   104–5
  India   114, 115
nationalist movements   84
nationality   113–14
Nazism   8–9, 39–50, 84
Newton, T.   25
Nietzsche, F.   111
Nightingale, D.   133
non-genetic inquiry   163
non-violence   121, 157
normality   43
Northern Ireland   75–6, 88–100
Northern Ireland Assembly   89, 94–5, 96
Northern Ireland Executive   89, 97
Norway   83
nuclear tests   114

object   26–7
occult phenomena   129
omnipotence, fantasies of   7, 18–22
oneness   153–9
Orange Order   94, 95
order effects   170–2
organisational theory, corporeal   35–6
origins   82–4
Other   31, 55, 65, 67, 105
  becoming Otherwise   60–5
  heteronomous 'I'   55–60
  racism and psychoanalytic Other   76, 101–10

Paisley, I.   75, 92–3, 95
Papon, M.   82
paradigmatic relations   168
Pauley, M.   92
Peitsch, H.   43
persecutory position   91–4, 95–9
phenomenology   52
physical separation   172–3
physics   129, 162, 173
  superluminal pulse   131, 163, 171
Pini, M.   155
Pinochet, General   80, 82
pleasure in discontent   13–14
PLUR (peace, love, unity and respect)   155
plural identities   76–7, 111–26
Poland   84
political change   75–6, 88–100
Porter, R.   139
postcolonial politics   186
postmodernity
  identity strategies   12, 14–16
  re-enchantment   131–2, 177–90
post-structuralist theory   28–32
post-traditionalism   182
posture   150–1
power   29, 30, 53–5
  emotionality, morality and   8–9, 39–50
power-to-act   54–5
prayer   141–2
present   168–9
Prilleltensky, I.   153
primacy of the social   57
privatisation   181
  and identity politics   7, 11–22
  of risk   18–22
project, self as   12–14, 182
projection   105–10
protest movements   157
Protestantism   181
psychoanalysis   76, 101–10
psychology   166
  critical psychology   2, 24
  discursive   133, 134–5
  mechanical models and statistical models   163

psychology – *continued*
  morality and fascism 46–9
  transpersonal psychology 149–50, 150, 152–3
psycho-physical principles 140–5

racism 61–2
  and psychoanalytic Other 76, 101–10
Rappoport, L. 86
rational economism 2, 19–20
rationality 179–81
rave culture 153–9
reappropriation 120
recognition 63
reconciliation commissions 82
re-enchantment 131–2, 177–90
referendum of 1998 89, 92–3, 95, 99
refigured subjectivity 9–10, 51–71
reflexive scanning of imagination 15–16
reification 28
religion 179, 181, 184
  spiritual church 138
  see also sacred; spirituality
rememorisation 64
replying-elsewhere 32–6
repressed strangeness 20–1
repression 182
resistance
  control-resistance model of worker subjectivity 25–6, 29, 30
  enchantment as conscious resistance 185–6
  reclaiming a past legacy 84
responsibility 64
  denying responsibility for fascism 42–3
Return to the Source 154
revolt 118–20
Ricoeur, P. 54–5, 57, 59, 64, 67
Riddle, D.I. 154, 157
Riley, D. 133
risk 16–18
  privatisation of 18–22
Rizzo, T. 33
Robbins, T. 154
Roots (Haley) 83
Rose, N. 24, 25, 58, 62, 136, 145, 153
Ross, A. 146
Rustin, M. 105–6

sacred 131–2, 177–90
sacred space 187
Sampson, E.E. 153
Sangari, K. 115
Sangh Parivar (Hindu extremists) 114, 122, 124
Saussure, F. de 131, 163, 171–2
  the synchronic in 165–70
Saunders, N. 154
Savitri 120
Scarry, E. 44, 49
Schneider, M. 183, 184
science 179–80
  see also physics
secularism 177, 181
self-control 39–41
self-distrust 49
self-help practices 136–9, 145–6
self-management 62–3
separation, physical 172–3
shame 43–4, 80–1
Sheldrake, R. 173
Shiv Sena 122
Shukla, S. 120–1
silenced cultures 75, 78–87
simple forms of insanity 143–4
simultaneities 166–8
Sinn Fein 97
sitting meditation 150–1, 153
slavery 83, 107
'social' anxiety 40
social change 158
social constructionism 62–3, 133–4
social embodiment 153–9
social systems 164
sociology 166
Solidarnosc (Solidarity) 84
Solomon, R.C. 39
Sonderkommandos 42, 45
space, sacred 187
speaking-otherwise-within 32
speaking-with 32
specificity 172
spiritual church 138
spirituality 129
  emergent spiritualities 146, 178, 187–8
  politics of psychology and 130–1, 149–60
  see also sacred

Steiner, G. 86
stigmata 141
Stoics 40
strangeness 20–1
strategies of identity 12–16
stream of consciousness 135
subject-in-process 21
sublime 59
successions 166–8
super-ego 40–1
superforce 173
superiority 103–4
superluminal pulse 131, 163, 171
survivors of trauma 75, 78–87
suspension of the will 139, 142
sympathy 141, 142, 145
synchronicity 131, 161–76
　defining domain of 164–5
　remaining elements of anomaly 170–3
　synchronic in Saussure 165–70
syntagmatic relations 168

Tagg, P. 155
Tanner, J. 26
Taylor, C. 27
Taylor, J. 94
telepathy 138
Thackeray, B. 114
Tharu, S. 115, 120
Theresa, Mother 187
Thompson, P. 25, 26, 29–31, 35–6
time
　synchronicity and 163, 169;
　　temporal ordering problem 170–2
　temporal disjunctures 55–60, 61, 63–5
Todorov, T. 48
tradition 122
　and modernity 120–1
transcendence 151
transfiguration 65–7
transformation, subjective 9–10, 60–5
transpersonal psychology 149–50, 150, 152–3
trauma 65
　morality, emotionality and fascism 8–9, 39–50

uprooted communities and silenced cultures 75, 78–87
trials 82
tribal groups 113–14
Trimble, D. 75, 93, 95, 95–6, 97
Tukaram 117, 118–20
Tuke, D.H. 140–5

Ulster Unionist Party (UUP) 94–5, 97
uniformity, imposition of 114–15
unionism 92–6
United Kingdom 96
United States 96
unity
　multiple identities in *bhakti* movement 117–18
　oneness in rave and DIY culture 153–9
universal social 27
Upadhya, C. 122
uprooted communities 75, 78–87

values 166–8
Vargas, L. 80
varkari movement 117
Vasquez, A. 79
'vehicular' body 150–1, 153
Venn, C. 51, 52, 55
violence 65, 106
　India 114–15, 121–2
　see also fascism
voice-hearing 130, 133–48

Walsh, M. 31, 32, 34
Wang, L.J. 163, 171, 172
Wardell, M. 29
Warhurst, C. 26, 30
Weber, M. 131, 179, 180–1
weightless pulse 131, 163, 171
Weir, A. 27
Whiten, A. 169
will 139
　insanity as problem of 140–2
　suspension of 139, 142
Willmott, H. 29, 30, 31, 35
women 76–7, 111–26
women's movement 123
work, ethics of 35–6
working through 64

workplace subjectivities 7–8, 23–38
  feminist corporeal theory 8, 32–6
  labour process theory 25–6
  post-structuralist theory 28–32
World War II 86
  fascism 8–9, 39–50, 84

Yiddish 84
York Retreat 130, 134, 139–45
Yuille, A.L. 168

Zizek, S. 27